A History of Europe

VOLUME II

HENRI PIRENNE was born in Belgium in 1862. He lectured at the University of Liége, and in 1886 became a professor of medieval and Belgian history at the University of Ghent. During World War I, while teaching at the University of Ghent, he was arrested and deported to Germany as one of the leaders of Belgium's passive resistance. In 1922 he was invited to deliver a series of lectures in America. *Medieval Cities*, which appears in the Anchor series, grew from these lectures. At the time of his death in 1935 Pirenne was professor emeritus at the University of Ghent.

His works include: *History of Belgium*, 7 volumes; *Belgium Democracy: Its Early History; An Economic and Social History of Medieval Europe;* and *Mohammed and Charlemagne.*

A History of Europe

VOLUME II

*From the Thirteenth Century
to the Renaissance and
Reformation*

Henri Pirenne

DOUBLEDAY ANCHOR BOOKS
DOUBLEDAY & COMPANY, INC.
GARDEN CITY, NEW YORK
1958

Translated by Bernard Miall

The painting used on the cover is "The Banker and His Wife" by Quentin Matsys, 1466–1530, Flemish School. Cover design by Leonard Baskin. Typography by Edward Gorey.

CONTENTS

BOOK THREE

The Renaissance and the Reformation

BOOK ONE

The Hegemony of the Papacy
and of France in the
Thirteenth Century

CHAPTER I

The Papacy and the Church

1. The Situation of the Papacy in the 13th Century

Between the battle of Bouvines at the beginning of the century and the conflict between Philip the Fair and Boniface VIII at its close, the 13th century stands out as an epoch characterized by the double hegemony of the Papacy and of France. Whether separately or by common agreement, they determined the course of policy, while both exerted a profound influence over intellectual, moral and social life: the one through the Church which it directed, and the other through the superiority of her civilization. Fatal as the triumph of the Papacy over the Empire was to Germany, it was equally favourable to France, whom circumstances had associated with it.

It must be repeated that the motive which for two and a half centuries had determined the hostility of the Emperors to the Papacy was by no means their eagerness to defend the temporal power against the encroachments of the Church. To envisage the question thus is to transport into the heart of the Middle Ages ideas and problems which belong only to our modern times. Neither the humiliation of Henry IV at Canossa, nor that of Frederick Barbarossa at Venice, nor that of Otto IV at Bouvines, was the humiliation of the civil power before priestly arrogance. In reality, the conflict was not a conflict between State and Church: it was an intestine struggle within the Church itself. What

the Emperors wanted was to compel the Popes to recognize
them as governing the universal Church, a right which they
claimed was theirs from the time of the Carolingian Empire,
as the Ottos and Henrys had done, or from the time of the
Roman Empire, as the Hohenstaufens had done. Their pretensions thus imperilled, in every country, that temporal independence of which, by the strangest of confusions, they
had been regarded as the defenders. The cause of the Pope
was the cause of the nation, and with the liberty of the
Church was bound up the liberty of the European States;
to such an extent that the victory of Philip Augustus at
Bouvines was the triumph of both causes.

But the collapse of Otto IV did not mean the end of the
Empire. It continued to exist until the threshold of our
modern age. Napoleon I, who shattered so many things in
Europe, abolished this venerable relic in 1806 by the creation of the confederation of the Rhine (July 1806). Yet we
may say that from the beginning of the 13th century the
historic rôle of the Empire was finished. It ceased to exist
as a universal power, as a European authority. While the
Emperors continued to entitle themselves "ever-august Roman Emperors," while they retained the terrestrial globe
among their emblems, and while, down to Charles V, they
continued to go to Rome for their coronation, they were actually merely the sovereigns, or to speak more exactly, the
suzerains, of the medley of principalities and municipal republics constituted by the Germany of the late Middle Ages
and the modern epoch, and which from the 14th century
onwards was known as the "Holy Roman Empire of the
Germanic nations."

After the fall of the Empire only one universal power was
left in Europe: that of the Pope, and its isolation made it
seem greater than ever. The whole government of the
Church depended on the Pope: this government was a
monarchy, a truly universal monarchy, and it was steadily
becoming more completely centralized. All the bishops
now swore fealty to the Pope; no religious order could be
founded without his authorization; the Court of Rome
heard appeals from all Christendom, and in every country
his legates watched over the execution of his orders and the

maintenance of discipline. To govern such a body, and to direct its activities, two things were indispensable: a code of law, and finances. The canon law, whose most ancient monument, the Decree of Gratian, was proclaimed in Rome in 1150, was rapidly enlarged under those great jurists, Innocent III and Innocent IV. By the end of the 13th century it was complete, and suffered hardly any subsequent modifications. As for the pontifical finances, which must be carefully distinguished from the finances of the Pope as sovereign of Rome, they were furnished by "St. Peter's Pence," levied upon England and Aragon, and by the more and more numerous taxes imposed upon the dignitaries of the Church: annates, reservations, dues of the Pallium, of indult, etc. It was these taxes that constituted the treasury of the Holy See, and enabled it to play the universal rôle which was allotted to it: to subsidize the Crusades, to maintain the missions, and to add to its spiritual influence the purely worldly influence of gold. It is impossible to realize the immense ascendancy of such a pontiff as Innocent III if we fail to regard him as a financial power. On the other hand, it must be noted that this financial power, which was nourished and maintained by the Catholic hierarchy in every part of Europe, was made possible only by the economic progress due to the revival of trade. So long as the West had remained in the stage of agricultural civilization the Pope had not and could not have had other resources than those of the domains of St. Peter's patrimony. Hence the Pope's efforts to increase his power in Italy, and secure the possessions of the Countess Matilda in Tuscany, and his original resistance to the expansion of the Norman State. But when the circulation of money was an accomplished fact, when it was replacing, more and more completely, the system of revenues in kind, the fiscal system of the pontiff was free to develop within the extreme limits of the pontifical authority. It was then that this innovation appeared: the pontifical taxes. Before this they would have been impossible. In the history of ecclesiastical organization they are the consequence of the economic transformation which was at the same time beginning to render possible a regular system of taxation in the various States. And it is interesting to see how the Pope took advantage, as regards their collection, of the capitalist organization which was beginning to evolve in the great Italian communes. The men whom he entrusted with the collection and transmission of his revenues were merchants, the bankers of Siena, and afterwards those of Florence. The Popes, even earlier than the lay sovereigns, were in intimate relations with the financiers, and the fact that the latter had to collect their revenues in all parts of Europe, convert them by exchange into Italian or international money, and place them at the Pope's disposal, without the necessity of transporting them, at the cost of great expense and danger, across the mountains, contributed in no small degree to the origin of the first banking operations and the first letters of credit, the remote ancestors of our bills of exchange. Compared with their predecessors of the 11th century—a Gregory VII, an Innocent II, and even with the contemporaries of St. Bernard—the great Popes of the 13th century undoubtedly seem more worldly characters. One might say that they had dragged God and the heavens down into the Church. They gave the Church an incomparable power and majesty, but on considering this power and majesty one is too conscious of the human effort. It was an admirable attempt to constitute a perfect society on earth. One is put in mind of a Gothic cathedral; it shoots up into the heavens, yet it does not contain them, however lofty its vaulted roofs, nor does it contain all humanity, however numerous its sculptures, where men and kings are represented beside God and the saints and demons. Like ecclesiastical law, theology was essentially an achievement of the 13th century. The scholastic philosophy of the previous centuries finds its climax in the *Summa* of St. Thomas (1274), in which Christian morality and the Christian dogmas are expounded in accordance with the Aristotelian method.

The point of departure, of course, was revelation. Faith provided the unshakable foundation of a rational theological construction which comprised the whole of society and the whole of life. Its aim, of course, remained what it had always been: eternal salvation. But men no longer sought to attain salvation through mysticism, through immediate contact with God. Everywhere the Church interposed. A St. Bernard would have been inconceivable in the 13th century, as the counsellor of Popes who regarded St. Francis of Assisi with suspicion. What men were now seeking to achieve was the government of their souls by the Church, itself governed by the Vicar of Jesus Christ. And these souls were accepted in the bodies which they animated; which is to say, that society was accepted; heroism was not required of it, nor were men expected to desert the world. They had only to obey the Church, and allow it to lead them to salvation. Every human being, every profession was subject to the Church, and therefore to the Roman pontiff. There were political sins (unjust wars) and commercial sins (undercutting) which ecclesiastical law defined and punished. Thus the whole of life was placed under the perpetual control of the Church, the secular life no less than the religious. The ecclesiastical tribunals, in their *forum mixtum*, were the ordinary instance, not only for churchmen, but for a host of purely secular questions: testaments, civil status, marriages, usury. All those who had received baptism belonged to the Church, and had to bow to its teaching, under penalty of penitence, or excommunication, or, in case of need, of taking part in a Crusade. Here was a majestic unity, a complete doctrine, which imposed itself upon a world of believers, all of whom accepted it; a doctrine so complete that it gave rise to the one truly universal poem in European literature: the Divine Comedy of Dante, completely steeped in the spirit of St. Thomas. In the same way, of course, the whole of intellectual life was subjected to the authority of the Church. All the scholars of the period were theologians or jurists. Philosophy, *ancilla theologiae*, and the universities, all modelled on that of Paris, were placed under the direct authority of the Pope. All their teachers were clergy from the monasteries and the cathedral schools; it was there that learning was now to be found. And learning was completely impregnated with the dialectical spirit that inspired the new knowledge. It broke the last ties that bound it to antiquity, if we make an exception of Aristotle, and what had been learned of Plato through the Jews and the Arabs. A new Latin was in course of formation, the true Latin of the Middle Ages, which was to survive until the Renaissance: lucid and analytical, everywhere the same, the language of the jurists and theologians. The *belles lettres* of the Latin language disappeared. The new tongue was what one might describe as Gothic Latin, for although, like Gothic architecture, it had its origin in antiquity, it had become as independent of the literature of antiquity as Gothic architecture had become of its art.

At the moment when the Church, having vanquished the Empire, had arrived at this summit of power, which gave it the hegemony of the Occidental world, a new adversary rose up against it: heresy. Since the Arian heresy, which the Goths had brought from the East in the 4th century, the Latin Catholic world, for many centuries, had unanimously professed the same faith, and acknowledged the same dogmas, presenting a notable contrast, in the permanence of its orthodoxy, to the religious disputes which, down to the 10th century, had never ceased to trouble the Greek Church. This tranquillity may be readily explained. In the West, as contrasted with the Byzantine Empire, there was no philosophical tradition, no learning outside the ranks of the clergy; there were no contacts with civilizations professing different religions, no social conditions liable to direct men's minds toward dangerous innovations. How could faith have been disputed, in a society living in isolation, accustomed by its purely agricultural civilization to respect tradition and authority, and in which the Church, the only literate body in the midst of universal ignorance, knew no other literature than the Latin—that is, a completely orthodox literature? The 11th century, which saw the revival of commerce, the development of navigation, and the rise of the first cities, was also to see the first symptoms of restlessness appear in religious life. By unknown ways, but probably by the trade routes, the Manichaean doctrines were trickling in from the East—into Lombardy, and from Lombardy into France and Rhenish Germany. Few at first, their adepts became more numerous in the course of the 12th century, and for reasons of which we know little they were concentrated more especially in the County of Toulouse and the region of Albi, whence their name of Albigenses. Even more mystical and ascetic than their orthodox contemporaries, they went so far as to reject in the name of the Spirit, the sole principle of life and truth, not only society, but the Church itself, corrupted as it was by wealth and power. In order to attain to Christ, whose only disciples they declared themselves to be, a man must divest himself of his whole terrestrial nature, arriving at a state of perfect purity. Hence their name of Cathars (καθαροί), as greatly dreaded and abhorred in the 12th century as the name of Anabaptist was in the 16th, and from which is derived the word that denotes the heretic in the Germanic languages (*Ketzer, Ketter*). Like the Anabaptists, moreover, these visionaries menaced both the social and the religious order. They preached both the community of goods and the annihilation of the Church, and we cannot be surprised that the French barons responded with enthusiasm to the appeal of Innocent III when he preached the crusade against the Cathars. Between 1208 and 1235 they were hunted down and exterminated in every part of Languedoc, amidst such circumstances of horror as were not to be seen again until the outbreak of the religious wars of the 16th century. However, the Catholics did not succeed in slaying them all; and as always, persecution, though it killed the body, did not destroy the spirit, and in this respect their doctrine was justified. Until the appearance of Wycliffe nearly all the heretical sects—Apostolics, Brothers of the Free Spirit, Begards, etc.—the Waldenses alone excepted—seem to have had some fundamental relation with the Cathar mysticism. And for this very reason none of them was really very dangerous. The radicalism of their aspirations could never be realized in practice, and everywhere it excited the hostility of the social authorities. It was among the proletariat of the cities that they recruited most of their adherents; and this explains both the naïvety of their communistic dreams and—except for certain moments of crisis—their somewhat restricted diffusion. Save in a few of the great industrial cities, the proletarian workers constituted only a very small minority of the bourgeoisie. The great majority of the bourgeois consisted of small employers, master craftsmen; in short, that middle class which is as hostile to capitalism as it is to communism.

Moreover, from the end of the 12th century the Church employed every means of persecuting and opposing heresy. It tolerated the Jews because they were outside the Church; but it could not tolerate the heretics, in whom it saw, so to speak, traitors guilty of spiritual *lèse-majesté*. If they refused to abjure their doctrines it cut them off from its communion; then, having passed its capital sentence on the soul, it delivered them to the secular power, which undertook to destroy the body. This division of labour corresponded perfectly to the conception that allied the Church to the State, while reserving to each its own domain—the souls to the former, the bodies to the latter. Before the 12th century we find, here and there, in the upper ranks of the clergy, the expression of doubts as to the legitimacy of inflicting the sentence of death on heretics. But no such doubts recurred after Innocent III had ascended the Papal throne, and the Church had achieved its majestic and powerful unity. Here again we see a manifestation of the juridical and governmental spirit with which the ecclesiastical constitution was impregnated. Orthodoxy, having become a body of doctrine which was imposed on all men and on all their activities, could no longer tolerate dissidence, and every individual opinion, every deviation from the norm, became a crime. The Order of the Dominicans, founded in 1216, devoted itself especially to the examination and prosecution of heretics. Side by side with the ancient episcopal Inquisition there now appeared the pontifical Inquisition created by Gregory IX in 1233, a kind of universal police whose function it was to watch over the safety of dogma. And the secular authority eagerly collaborated with it. In accordance with the principle of the State religion, anyone who placed himself outside the Church was regarded as a criminal. Did not the kings hold their power from God, and were they not the protectors of the Church? In the cities, perhaps, the civic sentiment may unconsciously have disapproved, not of the faith, but of the consequences involved by its abandonment. There, and there only, we see feeble manifestations of the first symptoms of the independence of secular society in respect of religious society.

2. The Papal Policy

It is often said that the 13th century was a theocracy. But we must define the term. If by theocracy we mean a state of affairs in which the Church enjoys an incomparable prestige and in which no one can escape from its moral ascendancy, the 13th century was undoubtedly a theocracy. But it was not a theocracy if theocracy consists in confiding to the Church itself the guidance and government of political interests.[1]

It was only when a sovereign was the open enemy of the pontiff—as Frederick II had been—that the Pope deprived him of the sovereign power. But this case must be regarded merely as an ultimate consequence of the relations between the Papacy and the Empire, and the vassal status of Sicily. Elsewhere, although the kings were obedient sons of the Church, they took good care to prevent it from intervening in their private affairs. Of course, there were few political events between the end of the 12th century and the beginning of the 14th in which the Popes did not intervene. But they did not intervene as masters; whether as allies or opponents, they acted as an individual power, in so far as intervention forwarded their own policies. They had, it is true, a terrible weapon: excommunication, but it was blunted by abuse.

For the Popes had their own policy, both as the heads of the Catholic world and as Italian sovereigns. The two policies were often confounded; but they were really quite separate.

The true Papal policy was the policy of the Church, as

[1] Theoretically the Popes aimed at theocracy, although they never actually achieved it, but it was acknowledged that they possessed—and in any case they claimed for themselves—a rudimentary power of supreme arbitration, which, however, often excited opposition, though not open conflict.

derived from the universal mission of the Church. It was
summed up in a twofold activity: the Crusade, and union
with the Greek Church; the two motives being so often
confounded that it is not always easy to separate them.
Even Urban II had hoped to put an end to the schism by
means of the First Crusade. Actually, however, the Crusade
merely rendered the schism more tenacious, owing to the
antipathy which it excited between the Latins and the
Greeks. Moreover, the position of the Latins in the East was
so precarious that a Second Crusade was necessary in 1143.
This, preached by St. Bernard, provoked a wave of mysticism comparable to that which had inspired the First. However, although it had been inspired by the Pope, it was not
so completely subject to his guidance as the wholly feudal
expedition of 1098. The King of France, Louis VII, and the
King of Germany, Conrad III, both took part in it, and although their collaboration had no important results, it
showed that Rome would henceforth have to reckon with
the political powers of the West. For the rest, the object
of the Crusade was not achieved. The settlements of the
Crusaders in Syria were not saved from the perils that
threatened them. A few years later Saladin captured Jerusalem, and once more the West had to be summoned to
deliver the tomb of Christ. The Third Crusade brought the
rulers of three States upon the scene: Frederick Barbarossa,
Philip Augustus, and Richard Cœur-de-Lion. Frederick
died without having succeeded, as he had hoped, in restoring the prestige of the Empire; Philip and Richard
thwarted each other and parted full of rancour, without
achieving anything. The experience was conclusive. It was
evident that thenceforth the Holy Land would not be reconquered, and that worldly ambitions were playing a
greater and greater and always more disastrous part in the
"Holy War." Henry VI, during his short reign in Sicily, had
conceived the notion of what one may call a purely temporal crusade, from which he expected nothing but the
extension of his power in the Mediterranean. Innocent III,
however, still inspired by Christian idealism, made preparations for a new expedition with the intention of attacking
Egypt, the base of the Fatimid power. This time, however,

the kings had had their fill of crusading. Their affairs kept
them at home. The princes of the Low Countries, Champagne, and Blois, set out on the Crusade; but the Venetians,
the owners of the fleet, who had not been paid in full for
their services (these expeditions were becoming more
costly, and the nobles were ruined), persuaded the Crusaders to attack Zara, a Christian city which incommoded their
trade in the Adriatic. The Pope excommunicated them, but
in vain. At Zara, Alexius Angelus, the brother-in-law of
Philip of Swabia, an enemy of the Pope, and the son of
Isaac Angelus, who had just been blinded and dethroned
by his brother Alexius III, implored them to attack Constantinople, promising them, as reward, the union of the
Greek with the Roman Church. The Pope was opposed to
this change of plan, for he could not trust a kinsman of the
Hohenstaufens. However, his opposition was ignored: they
were no longer to be ruled by Rome. On the June 23rd,
1203, the fleet appeared before Constantinople, and Isaac
was restored to the throne. But the hatred of the Greeks
for the Crusaders who had restored the Emperor to the
throne provoked a revolt. The people chose the valiant
Alexius Ducas Murtzuphlos as their Emperor. He broke
with the Latins, who thereupon seized the city (April 12th,
1204). On May 16th Baldwin, who had the largest number
of soldiers, was elected Emperor and crowned by a Papal
legate. Innocent III had suddenly reversed his policy. His
confidential agent, the Venetian Tomaso Morosini, was
created Patriarch of Constantinople. However, it was not
really the Church that profited by this expedition, but
mainly Venice, who founded a magnificent colonial empire
in the ancient Byzantine provinces.

As for the Latin Empire, an improvised creation, born of
the commercial ambitions of Venice, the dynastic quarrels
of the Byzantines, and the impetuosity of the Western
knights, to what future could it look forward? When we
think of the consequences, then, and even now, of the
capture of Constantinople by the Turks two hundred and
fifty years later, one can but conjecture the prospects of a
Latin Constantinople at the beginning of the 13th century.
But in history nothing is improvised, and here once more

we can see how untrue it is that little causes lead to great results. Here the events were on a small scale, and so were their results. The Westerners could enter Constantinople by assault, but they could not keep it. To retain and govern such a city, against the will of its people, would have called for such resources in men and money as were not then to be found in Europe. It would have been necessary to occupy and hold Thrace and Asia Minor. What State was capable of such an effort? It would have needed standing armies, and a constant influx of reinforcements. Constantinople could be taken and kept only by a warlike and barbarous people like the Turks, still in the phase of the invasions, or by a civilization which from the military and administrative point of view was the equal of the great States of our own age. As it was, the capture of Constantinople in 1204 was no more than a skirmish. We have only to read Villehardouin to realize that the conquerors had no suspicion of the stupendous consequences that might have followed from the capture of Constantinople. They did what they could: they created an Emperor, and on the sea-coast they constituted fiefs, principalities, and colonies —and that was all. In 1205 Baldwin fell into the hands of the Bulgars. His brother Henry (1206–1216) had, on the whole, a glorious reign, despite enormous difficulties: it is true that just then the Greeks of Nicaea were having much trouble with the Seldjuks and various Greek rivals. After this the condition of the Latin Empire was pitiable: Pierre de Courtenay (1217–1219) sold his possessions in France in order to maintain himself in power. Robert, his son, failing to repulse the Greeks, was reduced to the possession of the city. Baldwin II went to Europe to beg for money, sold the Crown of Thorns to St. Louis, and pawned his County of Namur. It was useless; the Greek State of Nicaea was now confident of victory. In 1261 Michael Palaeologus, with the help of the Genoese, who were jealous of the Venetians, recaptured Constantinople and restored the Empire. Of the union of the Greek and Roman Churches not a trace was left. The only result had been to increase the colonial empire of Venice at the expense of Byzantium, unable to recapture the islands or the settlements in Greece. The

Empire was weaker than it had been, less capable of resisting the Turks. This was the practical result of the Crusade!

Yet the Papacy still had its illusions. Urban IV and Clement IV negotiated with Michael Palaeologus for the union of the Churches, and in 1274 the Council of Lyons proclaimed that union. But it soon had to admit the reality, which was that Michael, in negotiating for the union of the Churches, was merely sounding the possibility of obtaining military assistance. Martin IV proclaimed the rupture of the union and favoured Charles of Anjou's designs upon Constantinople.

The Crusades were rapidly degenerating. The Fifth (1218), enthusiastically supported by Honorius III (1218–1221), was merely an expedition led by the titular king of Jerusalem, Jean de Brienne, against Damietta, with troops recruited from Hungary, the North of Europe, France, and Europe. It failed, because, in defiance of common sense, it was directed by the Papal legate, and because Frederick II, who had promised his assistance at the time of his coronation in 1220, did not keep his word.

The last three Crusades, of which more will be said later, had little of the Crusade about them but the name.

What was the reason of this *decrescendo* in the achievements of the Crusades, which had been so pompously inaugurated? It is readily explained. The Crusade in itself, as the Pope had originally intended it, was quite unrelated to any temporal aim, and in this lay both its greatness and its weakness. Europe had no need of Syria and Jerusalem. She took them in a fit of enthusiasm and had not the strength to retain them. Their retention would have involved a permanent crusade, and the transformation of all Europe into a military Order. This was impossible. Moreover, the agricultural civilization which had made the levy *en masse* possible was gradually disappearing, so that each successive Crusade was recruited with greater difficulty. The urban populations, and the rural populations who maintained them, could no longer be uprooted. The knights were ruining themselves, and they had to be paid. But it was long before the crusading spirit was quite extinct among them.

In the maritime cities, on the other hand, which had profited only too well by the Crusades ever since the sea route had been followed, it very soon disappeared. And lastly, there were political reasons for its decline. There was the policy of the kings of Northern Europe, who could no longer fling themselves into such purposeless adventures, and there was the Sicilian policy of Frederick II and Charles of Anjou, which had conquests in view. Faith had not declined, but the Crusades were no longer possible. The Pope alone remained faithful to the old ideal. It was his constant preoccupation. It outlasted everything: the transplantation of the Teutonic Knights to Prussia and the punishment of the Templars. The Knights of St. John of Jerusalem were at last the only reminder of the original spirit. In the Christian sense of the word, in the sense understood and intended by the Popes, the Crusade had failed, and with it, the pontifical policy. It was shattered against the realities of a Europe whose conditions of political and social life had evolved while the Papacy had remained faithful to its ideals. It was wrecked because it sought the impossible. Taking it all in all, the universal policy had been as unsuccessful in the spiritual sphere, with the Popes, as with the Emperors in the temporal sphere.[2]

[2] Nevertheless, the spirit of the Crusade continued to survive in Spain, because there it was associated with the necessity of self-preservation. Elsewhere, contact with Islam resulted in a greater commercial activity; in Spain it continued to give rise to war.

CHAPTER II

The Papacy, Italy, and Germany

1. *Italy*

Compared with the rest of Occidental Europe, Italy, from the 11th century, was notable as the land of cities. In no other part of the Continent were these so numerous and so active, and nowhere else did they play so preponderant a part. To the north of the Alps, even in the regions where they were most fully developed, as in Flanders and the Low Countries, they were far from governing the entire social life of the country: the nobility and the rural classes existed independently beside them, and had different interests. In Italy everything was subject to their influence, or contributed to it. The rural population was subject only to the cities, and laboured only for them; and in the cities the nobles had their crenellated "palaces" and towers, as different in their aspect from the castles of the Northern barons, which were scattered about the countryside, as was the life of their inmates from that of the Northern chivalry. This social concentration upon the cities must doubtless be attributed to the persistence of the ancient tradition. The municipal organization of the Roman Empire had impressed itself upon Italy so profoundly, and had packed the population so densely around the cities, that when the latter woke to life again under the stimulus of commerce it was inevitable that they should reassume their dominant situation. Municipal life became as preponderant in Lombardy and Tuscany as it had been in antiquity, but while its material conditions were almost unchanged, its spirit was different. The Roman municipality had enjoyed only a local autonomy, subordinated to the formidable power of the State. The Italian city of the Middle Ages—at least, in the north and the centre of the peninsula—was a republic.[1]

From the 11th century onwards the mercantile and industrial class which was in process of formation took advantage, as we have seen, of the conflict between the Pope and the Emperor to rebel against the bishops, and to wrest from them the administration of the cities. The first Italian communes were sworn by the "Patarenes"[2] in the midst of the turmoil of the War of Investitures: a time of mystical exaltation. Their origin was purely revolutionary, and from the time of their birth they contracted a habit of violence that was to characterize them to the end. By force or by agreement, the commune imposed itself, in each city, on the mass of the population, and its elective consuls, like the aldermen of the Belgian cities, exercised both the judicial and the administrative power. But as the bourgeoisie developed the social contrasts in its ranks were accentuated, and parties were formed in support of various conflicting interests. The names by which they were known are sufficiently eloquent of their nature. The party of the *grandi* was composed of the urban nobility, with whom were associated a good many enriched merchants; the party of the *piccoli* comprised the corporations or guilds of artisans of every kind, whose numbers multiplied as prosperity increased. The absence of a princely power, above the parties and capable of moderating their quarrels, gave the conflicts between the two groups, arising from questions of taxation and the organization of municipal power, a bitterness and severity unequalled elsewhere. From the middle of the 12th century civil war became a chronic epidemic. The *grandi* had the best of it; the *piccoli* were pitilessly massacred; if they surrendered they were driven out of the city; their houses or palaces were destroyed, and while waiting for the

[1] Except in the kingdom of Sicily, of which more later.
[2] The name of Patarius seems to be a mere corruption of Catharus.

moment when they could avenge themselves they lived on the adjacent countryside, pillaging and harassing their compatriots.

As a general thing these exiles found protection and allies in a neighbouring city. For while there was permanent warfare in the heart of the bourgeoisies, the mutual relations of the cities were also generally warlike. Constituting as they did so many independent economic centres, each of them thought only of itself, doing its utmost to force the peasants and population of the surrounding countryside to furnish its food supply, striving to compel the traffic of the surrounding region to centre upon it, to exclude its rivals from its market, and, if possible, to deprive them of their trade outlets. Thus the clash of interests was as violent outside the city as within it. Trade and industry were developed by means of battles. In all these little closed and immured worlds, watching one another from the height of their towers, human energy was expended with equal vigour in production and in destruction. Each city imagined that its prosperity depended on the ruin of its rivals. The progress of urban economy was accompanied by an ever narrower and more ferocious policy of municipal particularism. There was no truce to mutual hatred save under the pressure of a common peril. It took the threats and brutalities of Frederick Barbarossa to unite the Lombard League against him and to bring about the victory of Tagliacozzo.

Although the Hohenstaufens did not succeed in imposing their Caesarism on the Italian bourgeoisies, it did furnish them with a new element of discord. Having ceased to be dangerous after Tagliacozzo, the Emperor was able to act as auxiliary in the civil conflicts if one of the parties appealed to him for assistance. Those who did so appeal were usually the *grandi*. The names of Guelf and Ghibelline found their way from Germany into Italy, and became so well acclimatized there that they remained in use until the end of the 15th century, the name of Guelf being given to the adversaries and that of Ghibelline to the allies of the Imperial intervention, even when the Emperor was no longer a member of the House of Hohenstaufen. Neither of the two parties flying at each other's throats had any notion of the origin of the names which they had adopted, and which, transported into the midst of these urban quarrels, no longer had any correspondence with their primitive application. The Guelfs and the Ghibellines were both republican; the only difference between them was that the Ghibellines looked to the Emperor to help them against their adversaries, while the Guelfs, in order to maintain themselves in power, naturally endeavoured to ally themselves with the enemies of the Emperor.

The ferocity with which the parties sought to destroy each other did not prevent them from devising means of strengthening the municipal government. From the second half of the 12th century attempts were made to render it independent of civil conflicts by confiding it to a podestà. The podestà was, so to speak, a temporary prince elected by the commune, and in order to guarantee his impartiality and his independence of the parties it usually chose him from an alien commune. However, the institution did not yield the results which had been expected of it. Almost always the podestàs were obliged, in order to make their power respected, to rely on the support of one of the hostile factions. In certain cities they succeeded, as early as the 13th century, in possessing themselves, either by cunning or by violence, and thanks to the general lassitude, of the supreme authority, and in founding the first of those tyrannies which were to play so considerable a part during the epoch of the Renaissance. I need only mention the Scaligers of Verona and the Visconti of Milan.

The political and social ferment of the Italian cities naturally influenced their religious life. There were simultaneous outbreaks of mysticism and heresy, which provided fresh food for the fever that consumed them. St. Francis of Assisi was the son of a merchant, and the Order of Franciscans found its true field of action in the bourgeoisies. Moreover, there were swarms of Cathars, Brothers of the Free Spirit, and Waldenses. In 1245 the Dominicans provoked a revolt against the podestà of Florence, whom they accused of favouring the heretics. The atrocious laws against heretics promulgated by Frederick II prove that their numbers must have been considerable—at all events, in the larger cities—but it is unfortunately impossible to determine with any exactitude the importance of their activities.

It can hardly be doubted that they would have recruited the majority of their adherents among the workers engaged in production for export. As in Flanders, this trade was already highly developed in the Italy of the 13th century, and as in Flanders, it resulted in the formation of a veritable working-class proletariat. The weavers of Florence, the great cloth-producing centre of Southern Europe, differed as widely as the weavers of Ghent, Ypres or Douai from the usual type of urban artisan. Far from working on their own account, they were mere wage-earners, employed by the merchants. The nascent capitalism of the age subjected them to its influence, and its power, like its influence, increased in proportion as the merchants developed the export trade. By the first half of the 13th century the Florentine cloths were exported to all parts of the Orient, and the merchants of the city were importing their wool from England. Such an active manufacture naturally presupposes a considerable degree of capitalistic development. The fortunes accumulated by the trade in merchandise were still further increased by financial transactions. In the course of the 13th century the money-changers (bankers) of Siena and Florence found their way into all parts of Western Europe, where they were known as Lombards, and in England, to this day, the expression "Lombard Street" is a synonym for the money-market. We have already seen what services they rendered to the Papacy as financial agents. But in England, the Low Countries, and France they advanced larger and larger sums to the cities, princes, and kings, and were employed as collectors, treasurers, and guardians of money. Under Philip the Fair the Sienese Mouche (Musciatto) and Biche (Albizo) Guidi played the twofold part of bankers and financial ministers to the Crown, and were also employed by the Pope and the King of Sicily, while they were interested in the affairs of various commercial companies, like that of the Peruzzi. The Sienese company of the Bonsignori was still more important. A document relating to its bankruptcy in 1298 informs us that it was the most celebrated company in the world, which had rendered services innumerable to popes, emperors, kings, cities and merchants. That very year it had already paid two hundred thousand golden florins to its creditors, and it was given time to pay the rest, part of its capital being engaged in loans made in various parts of the world, which could not be realized immediately. On the disappearance of this company Florence became the chief money-market and banking centre of Europe, and so remained until the 15th century. The relations between the city and the Orient must at an early date have drawn the attention of its men of affairs to the trade in metals. The low prices of gold in the Levant enabled them readily to acquire great quantities of the precious metal, which they disposed of at considerable profit. We know that it was in the form of Florentine florins, minted from 1252 onwards,[3] and presently imitated by Venice (ducats), and then in France, that gold coins, abandoned since the Merovingian epoch, once more made their appearance in international trade, providing the instrument of exchange which had become indispensable to its progress. The cessation of commerce had given Europe its silver money; its revival gave it its golden coinage.

The social position of the Italian bankers and merchants brought them so closely into touch with the nobility that they were often confounded with it. This process took place all the more rapidly, inasmuch as the Italian nobility, instead of residing in the country, like the nobility of Northern Europe, had its dwelling-houses in the city. By the end of the 12th century the nobles were already beginning to interest themselves in commercial operations, while the merchants, on the other hand, were often ennobled. In short, under the influence of capital the line of demarcation between the juridical classes, which elsewhere remained so clearly drawn, in Italy grew fainter, almost to the point of disappearance, during the course of the 13th century. An aristocracy was formed for which social position was of

[3] Frederick II, in 1231, had already caused golden Augustales to be struck in Sicily, but their circulation seems to have been somewhat restricted.

greater importance than blood, while individual worth overcame the prejudice of birth. Social life was more varied, political life more individual; the ambitious man saw no limit to his prospects; there were fewer conventions, fewer castes, more humanity; there was also more passion. Here again Florence took precedence of all the other cities. Florence, to the undying honour of her people, produced and shaped the genius to whom the world owes what was, with the Gothic cathedrals of France, the greatest achievement of the Middle Ages: the Divine Comedy.

Neither in their wealth, nor in their political, social or intellectual activity could the Papal States bear comparison with Lombardy or Tuscany. They presented, from the beginning, and retained until the end, the artificial character of a purely political creation, intended to assure Rome of the independence of the Holy See. Spreading across Italy between the kingdoms of Sicily and Tuscany, cut in two by the Apennines, and without good ports, either on the Mediterranean or the Adriatic, their situation could hardly have been more unfavourable. Moreover, the Pope's government was never able to make itself respected. The families of the great nobles, even when they had ceased to fight for the tiara, still retained considerable power, both in Rome and in the surrounding countryside, and their private wars were unending. To this must be added the state of insecurity to which the country was condemned by the Imperial claims, and the difficulty, in Rome itself, of governing a vain, arrogant and idle people, always ready to follow the tribunes who flattered them by recalling their ancient greatness. It is a characteristic fact that the greatest of the Popes—those who, like Innocent III or Innocent IV, had the power to depose or excommunicate kings—were never at peace in their capital, and were exposed without defence to the insurrections of the mob. Although the Roman people lived, so to speak, by the Papacy, it might almost be said that the Papacy was encamped in its midst. Rome was the centre of the universal Church, the headquarters of ecclesiastical policy, but the life of the Church was not centred within its walls. It contained no great educational establishment, and none of the learned doctors of

the period, no Albertus Magnus, no Thomas Aquinas, ever
lived there. The artistic life of the city was as insignificant
as its intellectual life. No new religious movement ever had
its source in Rome. St. Francis came from Assisi, St.
Dominic from Spain. One might say that in the climate in
which the government of the Church had evolved, neither
art nor faith nor science was able to prosper.

The kingdom of Sicily, in the south of the peninsula,
was another world. While it was as wealthy as Northern
Italy, and while its life was feverish and exuberant, it was
politically apathetic. The Byzantine and Arab administrations had trained the people to accept the discipline of the
State. It knew nothing of autonomy; it had no communes;
its great cities were governed by the administration; the
people were trained to pay their taxes and obey the
authorities; these authorities were salaried and permanent
officials, and the sovereign was all powerful: this was the
spectacle presented by the country whose agricultural development was far in advance of all the rest of Europe.
It was more densely populated than any other part of
Europe. In the 13th century (1275) it was estimated that
the inhabitants numbered 1,200,000, a population greater
than that of England. Henry VI, and after him Frederick
II, had developed the administration in the direction of a
pure despotism. There was an administration of the State
domains, monopolies, and magazines, a fiscal organization
which knew nothing of privilege, and which was not unlike
a sort of proto-mercantilism, while the creation of the University of Naples and the toleration extended to the Musulmans are suggestive of an enlightened despotism. There is
more than one point of similarity between the Frederick II
of the 13th century and the Frederick II of the 18th century, and this is easily explained, if we reflect that they
could both do anything they liked with the peoples whom
they governed. The constitutions promulgated by Frederick
II in 1231 completed the Norman institutions, in the sense
that they equipped them with what might be called a
bureaucracy. In the Europe of the 13th century the kingdom of Sicily was something unique, with its expert and
despotic constitution, borrowed from the Byzantine and

Musulman worlds which had shared the country between them until the Normans made their appearance. Not until the modern era did the European States achieve so complete an administrative system. But here we have the proof that a constitution which does not originate with the people is unable to influence its civilization, and that organization is not everything. In point of government, this Prussianized Sicily was greatly superior to all the rest of Europe. But it did not produce a Dante, nor a Gothic art, and it played no part, later on, in the flowering of the Renaissance.

2. Frederick II

The destiny of the Hohenstaufens had made it increasingly necessary that they should make Italy their political base. From Conrad III to Frederick Barbarossa, and from Frederick to Henry VI, they became less and less German in character, and with Frederick II their evolution was completed. Born of a Sicilian mother and reared in Sicily, he was himself a pure Sicilian. His fair hair, like the fair hair of that pure Spaniard Philip II, if we insist upon always regarding it as a sign of Germanic "race," merely proves that race is without influence upon moral tendencies and mental characteristics.

Gregory IX and Innocent IV accused Frederick not only of heresy, but of blasphemy, and his enemies declared that he was the author of a celebrated pamphlet in which Moses, Jesus and Mohammed were alike treated as impostors. He did not believe in God (*fidem Dei non habuit*), according to Salimbeni, who knew him personally, and by this, of course, we must understand that he did not believe in the Church. His more than semi-Oriental morals, his harem of Moslem women, and the incredulity of his son-in-law Ezzelino da Romano, who refused the sacraments when dying (1259), justify us in believing that he was actually a "libertine" in the matter of faith. However, he always denied the imputation. What is more, he promulgated, against heretics, laws whose cruelty was never equalled until the reign of Charles V. He did so because he thought his policy would benefit, and because for him, as for the Italian tyrants of the 15th century, to whom he bore a striking resemblance, all means were good that achieved their end. Lying, cruelty and perjury were his favourite weapons; in a later age they were to be the favourite weapons of a Sforza or a Visconti, and to make the analogy more complete, he had their love of art and their respect for learning. He has been called the first modern man to ascend the throne, but this is not true unless we understand by a modern man "the pure despot who will stop for nothing in the search for power."

This Frederick, whom the Popes were later to describe as the Beast of the Apocalypse, the servant of Satan, the prophet of the Antichrist, began his career under the auspices of Innocent III, and as an instrument of the Church. We have seen already how Rome incited him to oppose Otto of Brunswick, and how the battle of Bouvines won him the throne of Germany. It now only remained to make sure of the Imperial crown, and in order to obtain this from the Pope he lavished his promises with a liberality that was all the greater inasmuch as he was resolved to honour none of them. He renounced all control over the episcopal elections and all claim to the territories of the Holy See, acknowledged the kingdom of Sicily to be a fief of the Papacy, pledged himself never to unite it with the Empire, and took an oath to set out on a Crusade in the following year. How could the pacific Honorius III, who had just succeeded Innocent III, hold out against so much goodwill? Frederick was crowned in Rome on November 22nd, 1220.

Thenceforth his long reign was passed almost entirely in Italy. Of Germany he asked only one thing: that it would not give him any trouble. In 1232, by the famous statute *in favorem principium* he renounced the shadow of power that the monarchy had still retained in Germany, granting the princes complete independence under the nominal rule of his sons—Henry, followed by Conrad. This realistic policy shows that he was very well aware that this was the only means of solving the problem. The truth was that Germany had become ungovernable. Any attempt to restore the royal prestige in that country would have meant to condemn himself to an interminable and sterile war against the princes, to revive the conflict of the Guelfs and the Ghibellines, to provoke fresh intervention on the part of France and England, and once more to become subject to the arbitrage of the Pope. The simplest course was to make an end once and for all of an impossible situation, and to throw to the princes the remnants of a power which actually was not worth the trouble of defending. For that matter, what did Germany mean to Frederick? He did not even know the German language. For him it was merely the path which he must follow in order to obtain the Empire. The basis of his strength was in Sicily. There, thanks to absolutism, he had the financial and military resources necessary for the accomplishment of his designs.

It is always difficult to determine exactly the aims of a policy which has failed. Frederick's first intention would seem to have been to subject the whole of Italy to the despotic administration of Sicily; then, this end having been attained, to seek in his turn, as his father and his grandfather had sought, to restore the Roman Empire. However, as he could not accomplish even the first part of this programme, he barely made a beginning with the second part. His policy was exclusively Italian; it was hardly in any sense Imperial.

Yet it was destined, even more than the policy of his predecessors, to bring him into conflict with the Papacy. The Papacy regarded him as its most constant and most dangerous enemy, and there are historians who see in the conflict between Frederick and Gregory IX and Innocent IV a clash of principles, which won him the honour of having, for the first time, upheld the independence of the temporal power against the pretensions of the Church. But the question is not so simple as it appears at first sight. Personally, if you will, Frederick was a freethinker, but he was the opposite of an anti-clerical. He had no political theories but those of his contemporaries. With them he acknowledged, at all events in words, the divinity of the ecclesiastical institution, the duty of princes to defend it and to persecute heretics, and the obligation which was incumbent upon them of professing the Catholic dogmas. His treatment of the Church was inspired, not by a principle, but solely by his personal interests. Provided the Church did not hinder the realization of his policy he was ready to make it every concession. But this policy was directly contrary to that of the Holy See. In reality, the Popes made war against him for temporal rather than religious reasons. The quarrel between Frederick and the Popes reveals itself, in its essentials, as a quarrel between two Italian powers. It was only towards the end that it became something more comprehensive, impelling Frederick, excommunicated and deposed by Innocent IV, to represent himself as the champion of the cause of the kings as against the pretensions of the Church.

But from the very beginning his position in respect of the Church was extremely unfortunate. In order to justify his claims upon Italy he had to become Emperor, and in order to become Emperor he had to tie his own hands. The promises which he made at his coronation gave the Papacy an advantage over him. By acknowledging that Sicily was a fief of the Holy See he had placed himself in the falsest position. The suzerainty of the Pope over the kingdom of Sicily was incompatible with the absolute power which he himself exercised in that kingdom. He therefore made up his mind that he would simply ignore his engagements. The patience of Honorius III prevented the immediate outbreak of the conflict. But Gregory IX had hardly ascended the throne of St. Peter (1227) when Frederick was called upon to fulfil his obligations, and, first and foremost, to set out on a Crusade. He tried to gain time; he embarked, and then returned. He was immediately excommunicated. He tried to put matters right by complying with the Papal requirements. In July 1228 he set sail for the Holy Land, and concluded a treaty with the Sultan which enabled him to enter Jerusalem without striking a blow, and to stipulate that Christians should be free to visit the tomb of Christ. The Pope remained inexorable. The Papal interdict was placed on all the towns through which he passed, and the prayer which he offered up at the Holy Sepulchre was made to seem a profanation. Not a priest could be found who would consent to crown him King of

Jerusalem, and he was reduced to placing the crown on his own head.

However, Gregory IX renewed the alliance between the Papacy and the Lombard cities, and invaded Sicily. Frederick returned to Italy to fight him. Peace was at last concluded on August 28th, 1230. Once more the Emperor accepted the conditions dictated by the Papacy, and guaranteed the completest liberty of the Sicilian Church, which he had subjected to taxation and to the jurisdiction of the State, and at this price he was absolved from the excommunication which had been pronounced upon him three years earlier.

Reconciled with Rome, he directed all his efforts against the Lombards. The struggle was long and violent. Not until 1238 did fortune at last smile upon Frederick; and he then thought the moment had come to extend the Sicilian administration to Northern Italy, stifling by his despotism the autonomy and the republican spirit of its cities. Puffed up by his success, he believed himself henceforth the master of Italy; he appointed his "vicars" and "captains" throughout the country, made the heiress of Sardinia marry his bastard Enzio, and gave the latter the title of king. Of his promises to the Papacy nothing remained. He had forgotten that Sardinia, like Sicily, was a fief of Rome, and the Sicilian Church was subjected more completely than ever to the secular power. Moreover, as the States of St. Peter were henceforth enclosed between the Imperial possessions in the north and the south, there was a danger that they would become dependent upon the latter. This time Gregory IX acted both as a sovereign and as the head of the Church. Once more excommunication was launched against Frederick (1239), and at the same time his subjects were absolved from their duty of obedience to him. A furious war of pamphlets broke out, the Emperor reproaching the Pope with his perfidy and ingratitude, the Pope accusing the Emperor of perjury and heresy. Frederick appealed to the judgement of the Council, and when the Pope took him at his word and summoned the bishops to Rome, Frederick sent out vassals to attack the ships which were carrying them Romewards, seized them, and kept the prelates in captivity. Death prevented Gregory IX (1241) from taking his revenge, and the long vacancy of the Holy See gave Frederick some respite. But Innocent IV, almost immediately after his election (1243), assembled the Council at Lyons, and having subjected the Emperor's case for examination before the Assembly, he solemnly deposed him and excommunicated his followers.

Of old, the Emperors excommunicated by the Popes used to have the Pope deposed by a German Synod and replaced by an Antipope. But those days were gone and would not return. Now the entire Church was obedient to Rome. Already, in Germany, the Archbishops of Mayence and Cologne had proclaimed the Landgrave of Thuringia king (May 1246). This king, Henry Raspe, who died a few months later, was succeeded by a second anti-king, who, like him, was a mere instrument of Innocent IV: Count William of Holland (October 1247). All that Frederick could do was to endeavour to persuade the other kings that their cause was one with his. He did his best; while resuming the struggle against the Lombard cities, which had again risen against him, he exhorted the sovereigns to support him, and to refuse, in their own interest, to allow the Pope to dispose at will of the temporal power. His protests aroused no echo; and they could not have been echoed. Whatever he might say, there was nothing in common between his cause and that of the national and hereditary monarchs who were reigning in France and England. These were well aware that the Pope had no hold upon their crowns, and that their dynastic right was not in any way involved in the Hohenstaufen's quarrel. Frederick forgot that the Pope had a twofold advantage over him. As King of Sicily, was he not the vassal of the Holy See? as Emperor, had he not received the crown from the Holy See? It was idle to compare the ceremony of the coronation with that of the anointing of the kings; no one could accept the comparison. For the ceremony of anointing did not make the king, while his coronation did create the Emperor. In short, this Empire, which had fought so long against the Papacy, revealed itself, at the decisive moment, in all its weakness, and incapable of defending the independence of the temporal power whose champion it professed to be. Its religious origin condemned it to remain attached to the Papacy. In claiming autonomy it gave the lie to history and deprived itself of its foundation. The problem could only be solved by a king upon whose crown the Pope could formulate no sort of claim. The man who was destined to solve the problem was not the Emperor but the King of France, and where Frederick II failed, Philip the Fair, fifty years later, succeeded.

The reign of Frederick was a sort of epilogue to the tragedy which began with Gregory VII and ended at Bouvines. Since the reign of Otto of Brunswick the Empire had existed only in name. Frederick's attempt to restore it by means of his Sicilian kingdom could only end in catastrophe. He wore himself out, fighting against all hope, waging war against Lombardy and wasting his troops and finances on a lost cause. On December 13th, 1250, he died, shortly after suffering a bloody defeat by the forces of Parma. His death made no impression in Germany, but it caused a tremendous sensation in Italy. Prophecies relating to the coming of the Antichrist were accepted as referring to Frederick, and more than once it was rumoured that he had returned to earth. It was the echo of these Italian rumours that gave birth, in Germany, to the legend of the Emperor who was sleeping in the mountain of Kyffhäuser, a legend which the popular imagination, deceived by the similarity of the names, was presently to accept as relating to Frederick Barbarossa.

As for the kingdom of Sicily, the Pope hastened to retrieve it for ever from that "generation of vipers," the Hohenstaufens. He decided to give it to France.

3. Germany

The Empire was not only fatal to Germany because it imposed upon its kings a universal policy, forcing them to sacrifice the nation to the Church, and finally compelling them to leave their quarry and chase its shadow; it had the further result of allowing the Pope to intervene directly in German affairs. Since the King of Germany, or to speak more exactly, the King of the Romans, was the Emperor designate, Rome, directly she was strong enough to do so, claimed that her approval was indispensable to his election. The Hohenstaufens had clearly recognized this danger, and in order to guard against it they had endeavoured to make their dynasty hereditary. But heredity, the indispensable condition of all monarchical power, of all power based upon the State, since in the Middle Ages the monarchy was the only possible form of the State—heredity, which constituted the strength of the King of England or the King of France, had become impossible in Germany from the beginning of the 12th century. The country was merely an agglomeration of ecclesiastical and secular principalities, incapable of common action, and still more incapable of enduring the government of a central authority. To explain this situation by the accepted fable of Germanic individualism is futile. For there were no territorial principalities among the Scandinavians, nor among the Anglo-Saxons, though these were both Germanic peoples, but they did exist among the French, a Latin people. To the right as to the left of the Rhine, they had their origin in the dissolution of the Carolingian Empire at a time when its economic system was dominated by the great estates; they resulted from the seizure of the royal prerogatives by officials who had become autonomous, thanks to their domainal power. But in France the king also possessed his own domain; like his great vassals, he was rooted in the soil, and from the 10th century onwards he patiently awaited the moment when he should be able to claim from them the prerogatives which were his by virtue of the crown. This moment came in the 12th century, which made him the natural head of the resistance to England, brought him the support of the bourgeoisies, and led him to choose the "capital" city as his residence. And toward this city gravitated the whole activity of the nation, excited and increased by the great economic and social transformation inaugurated by the revival of trade and the ever-increasing circulation of men and of goods. In Germany, on the other hand, the kings were nowhere at home. They remained faithful to the Carolingian custom of wandering about the country. They had their palaces, but no fixed residence. There was nothing in Germany like the Île de France; still less was there anything resembling Paris. And yet, until the end of the 11th century, the personal power of the kings was very great. The gradualness with which the feudal system had developed on the right bank of the Rhine enabled them to dispose of a quantity of estates and counties which in France would have been appropriated long before by the seigneurs. But the economic system did not allow them—why, we have already seen[4]—to retain these reserves and appropriate the profits to their own use. It was still too early to dream of an administrative organization of the monarchy. On the whole, they adopted the best solution possible, by transferring the rights and the domains at their disposal to bishops appointed by them and attached to their service. Henceforth their power was of necessity bound up with the maintenance of this Imperial Church; and after the War of Investitures, when this support was withdrawn, their power collapsed. It was then too late to re-establish it on a new basis. The Hohenstaufens have been blamed for not relying on the support of the cities. But those who blame them forget that except along the Rhine the German cities were then only beginning to develop.[5] This is why the cities, in order to escape from the control of the princes, constituted themselves, as in Italy, free republics. Nominally they were dependent on the Emperor; in reality they were so far independent of him that he could not draw upon their resources. He had to choose between them and the princes, and Frederick Barbarossa, like his successor, could not hesitate to choose the princes. Thus, at the moment when in France the king was beginning to impose his power upon his great vassals, in Germany he was becoming subordinate to them. In order to maintain himself on the throne he had to constitute a party among the princes. But as he had to pay for their services by means of all sorts of privileges and concessions, he could keep in power only by exhausting his resources,

---

[4] See *A History of Europe*, Vol. I (Anchor ed.), p. 174 et seq.
[5] I do not include the cities of the Baltic, which hardly belonged to them.

and even in Barbarossa's time the king was reduced to what was really a policy of expedients. The war between Philip of Swabia and Otto IV finally demolished, if not the authority of the royal power, at least what prestige remained to it. Frederick II, in 1232, merely recognized in law what already existed in fact, in ceding to the princes the last nominal prerogatives of the Crown, by recognizing them officially as the lords of their estates (*domini terrae*), and by renouncing the right to build fortresses on their domains or to appoint judges, or to mint money, or to regulate trade and circulation. Henceforth Germany was merely a federation of individual sovereigns whom the Emperor left to their own devices. It is true that he had left in his place his son Henry, a child who was elected King of the Romans in 1222, and who, having grown up under the tutelage of Archbishop Engelbert of Cologne, rebelled against his father, who left him to die in prison; and after him his other son, Conrad IV, who was nine years of age when in 1237 the princes accorded him the royal title! But neither the Emperor nor the princes could or did believe that such regents could exert any real influence. Moreover, after the excommunication and deposition of Frederick, Innocent IV, resolved to make a clean sweep of the Hohenstaufen dynasty, ordered a new election. No one, apart from a few cities in Swabia, supported Conrad's interests, and the crown, as we have already seen, was given first to Henry Raspe, Landgrave of Thuringia, and then to Count William of Holland. As a matter of fact, the princes took little interest in these elections, which were essentially the work of the Archbishops of Cologne. Henry and William merely served to confirm the victory of the Pope. Henry died a few months after his election: William, as a Dutchman almost a foreigner to the Germans, hardly showed himself except in the valley of the Rhine. His County of Holland meant more to him than his kingdom, and almost the only profit that he derived from his title, which he owed to the protection of Rome, was to assert, to the detriment of the Counts of Flanders, the claim of his house to Zeeland. It was again his Dutch policy that induced him to undertake an expedition against the Frisians, in the course of

which he was killed, on January 28th, 1258, in the battle
of Hoogwoude. When he was dead, Alfonso X, King of
Castile, whose mother Beatrice was the daughter of Philip
of Swabia, made this Hohenstaufen connection a pretext
for claiming the crown of Germany, through which he
hoped to obtain that of Sicily. But Sicily excited the covet-
ousness of the King of England also, the old ally of the
Guelfs, who had hopes of obtaining the crown for his son
Edmund. In order to obtain support for him, he incited his
brother, Richard Earl of Cornwall, to obtain the succession
to Count William of Holland. In order to obtain it, the two
rivals relied only on their treasury, and like Charles V and
Francis I three hundred years later, they bid against each
other for the dignity of the King of the Romans. The national ideal was so completely alien to the German princes,
and the monarchy seemed to them of such secondary importance, that their one thought was to sell it on the most
favourable terms. Some allowed themselves to be bought by
Alfonso of Castile, others by Richard of Cornwall, and in
1257 both princes received the crown, as though it had
been a parcel of merchandise. Seven princes had taken part
in this double election. This was the origin of the College
of Electors, which henceforth exercised the right of electing
the king of the Romans!

The bargain concluded by Alfonso and Richard could not
hold good unless the Pope interested himself in the matter.
But it was enough for Rome that she had extirpated the
Hohenstaufens; she allowed the two rivals to overwhelm her
with their solicitations without intervening on either side.
Under these conditions, it seemed to Alfonso that he might
as well stay where he was, and Germany never saw him.
Richard spent some time on the banks of the Rhine, had
himself crowned at Aix-la-Chapelle, signed a few State doc-
uments, and was then recalled to England by the disturbances which occurred during the reign of Henry III; he
never went back to Germany, and in 1272 he died. The
electors were in no hurry to replace him. For that matter,
Alfonso was still living. But the Pope would not hear of his
claim, as he had no wish to quarrel with the new King of

Sicily, Charles of Anjou.[6] On the other hand, he made haste to dispose of Charles's intervention in favour of the candidature of his nephew, the King of France, Philip the Bold, whose nomination would have reconstituted the Empire of Charlemagne for the benefit of the Capetian dynasty. He gave the electors to understand that they had better make haste if they did not wish him to create a new king himself. They complied, and in 1273 they gave the crown to Rudolph of Habsburg, whose talents, as mediocre as his fortune, were not such as to cause them any disquietude. The period of the "great interregnum" which had begun with the nomination of Henry Raspe was at last ended.

Engrossed in their duel with England, the kings of France did not attempt to take advantage of the increasing weakness of Germany in order to reopen the Lotharingian question which had so preoccupied their Carolingian predecessors in the 10th century. Philip Augustus, Louis VIII, and St. Louis actually maintained the most cordial relations with the Hohenstaufens, who naturally inclined, in consequence of the Guelf alliance with England, to take the side of France. However, it was impossible that the decline of the German monarchy should leave the question of the western frontier unaffected. Drawn by the Treaty of Verdun, in an age of purely agricultural civilization, it had divided the territories affected as one divides a domain, the chief object of the division being to assure each of the sons of Louis the Pious of an equal share, without any regard for the populations or the geographical situation. In the Europe of the 13th century, awakened to new life by the circulation of trade and the new social relations which were the consequence of that trade, the old frontier was merely an archaism, which the respect for the status quo could not preserve indefinitely. The cities which had sprung up in the basins of the Meuse and the Scheldt were naturally looking westwards, attracted by those two great economic centres, the fairs of Champagne and the ports of Flanders. Under their influence, those populations whose language was Romanic—the populations of Lorraine, Luxemburg, Liége

[6] See p. 54 et seq.

and Hainaut, as well as the Germanic populations of Holland and Brabant—were insensibly detaching themselves from Germany, which, being more and more subdivided, did nothing and could do nothing to retain them. The feudal tie which bound the princes of the frontier to the Empire was growing weaker and weaker. Towards the end of the 13th century the Dukes of Lorraine and Brabant, and the Counts of Luxemburg, Hainaut, and Holland, had become almost completely alienated from the Empire. Even under Frederick Barbarossa, the Hohenstaufens' agent in the Low Countries, Count Baldwin V of Hainaut, had regarded himself as independent, and considered that he had acquitted himself of his duty to the Emperor by declaring himself neutral in respect of France and Germany. The kingdom of Burgundy, acquired by Conrad II, in 1033, detached itself still more rapidly from the Imperial bloc. Stretched out along the Saône and the Rhone, and inhabited by a people who spoke a Romanic language, everything attracted it toward the Mediterranean, or toward France. The kings of Germany, to whom its last possessor had bequeathed it at a period when it was regarded merely as so much territory, had never been other than foreigners in Burgundy, and had never made any attempt to strike root there. Marseilles and Lyons had never felt that they belonged to the Empire, nor did the Counts of Provence, Dauphiné and Franche Comté ever trouble their heads about the nominal suzerainty which it exercised over them. Thus, the old frontier, drawn on the map at a period of economic stagnation, was erased, so to speak, by the friction of a more intensive civilization and more complex interests. No one attempted to rectify it, people were content simply to ignore it, and as the Imperial power declined the outlines of the Empire became more vague and undefined.

The kings of France could not and did not fail to take advantage of a situation which they had not created, but which increasingly demanded their attention. As the princes of the frontier forgot the Emperor they turned toward the kings of France, seeking to obtain their support or appealing to their arbitrage. Many of them received fiefs or pensions from the Crown. In the Low Countries, where the territorial constitutions were robust, and the principalities compact, the influence of France was purely political. But it was otherwise along the border of Lorraine and in the valley of the Rhone. Here the dovetailing of territories, the confusion of rights and prerogatives, and the great number of seigneurs who possessed land both in France and in the Empire, gave rise to incessant disputes, of which the kings took advantage by extending the influence of their bailiffs on the other side of the frontier. With the consent of the interested parties they thus increased their own influence, by successive advances, by gradual and almost imperceptible efforts, over this intermediate zone, so that presently their power had actually replaced that of the Emperor.

While in the West, Germany was gradually crumbling under the influence of a civilization superior to her own, in the East she was expanding largely at the cost of the Barbarians. The conquest of the Slav regions on the banks of the Elbe, which had been begun by Otto I, but was abandoned after his death, was resumed, and had made rapid strides since the middle of the 12th century. It seems at first sight strange that German colonization should have made such progress, advancing further and further as the power of the Emperors declined in the interior of the country. The fact is that this great effort of expansion, which was afterwards to exert so essential an influence over the destinies of the German people, owed nothing to the Emperors. It was accomplished without their participation, and without the manifestation of the slightest interest on their part. While Frederick Barbarossa was uselessly wasting his strength in Italy, the princes on the banks of the Lower Elbe, and above all Henry the Lion, and the Margrave of Brandenburg, Albert the Bear (1170), energetically furthered the Germanization of the Wendish lands along the Baltic shore. There was no question here of a purely political conquest, but rather of a veritable work of colonization, thanks to which, by a refluent movement, the Germans took the place of the Slavs in the countries which they had abandoned at the time of the great invasions of the 4th century. Its success would have been impossible without the economic transformations which we have already indicated:

the increase of the population in the course of the 12th century, the abandonment of the domainal system, the appearance of a class of free peasants, and lastly, the formation of the bourgeoisies. Thanks to these changes the physical and moral conditions indispensable to the peopling of the new country were both present: a surplus population and the spirit of enterprise. As the raids of the Duke of Saxony's and the Margrave of Brandenburg's knights drove back the Slavs and massacred them, the colonists, under the direction of contractors (*locatores*), took possession of the regions thus cleared. They came from Franconia, Thuringia, Saxony, the banks of the Rhine, and even Flanders and Holland, the Dutch being especially useful on account of their skill and experience in the operations of draining and embanking. Each colonist received, on the payment of a modest quit-rent, sufficient land for a single holding (*Hufe*), and he could easily recruit the necessary workers from among the Slavs who had escaped massacre. Cistercian monks founded their monasteries among the new villages and furnished the clergy for the parish churches. Before the end of the 12th century the wave of colonization had already reached the banks of the Oder. Along the rivers the cities were founded which furnished the peasants with the necessary supplies and served as markets for the surrounding countryside: Brandenburg, Stendal, Spandau, Tangermunde, Berlin, and Frankfort-on-the-Oder.

The Slav States to the east and the south—Poland and Bohemia—sought before long to attract these Germans, who brought from beyond the Elbe the methods of Western agriculture and the knowledge of various urban trades. The Polish dukes of Silesia (Piastes) did their utmost to induce the Germans to settle in and around Breslau. The King of Bohemia, Wenceslas I (1230–1253), and his successor Ottocar II offered these pioneers still more favourable conditions. German villages were scattered amidst the Czech villages, and German towns—Kuttenberg, Deutchbrod, Iglau —were called into being by the mining or weaving industries: burgesses and peasants retaining intact their language, their customs, and their law, in the midst of the native population, thereby bequeathing formidable problems to the future. The Germanic colonists even made their way into Hungary, where they settled in Transylvania under the protection of the king, who in 1224 conferred important privileges on them.

This expansion makes one think involuntarily of the invasions of the Roman Empire in the 5th century. In each case there was the same surging forward of a people seeking fresh means of subsistence outside their own country. But while the Germans of the 5th century were rapidly absorbed by the Romanic population, whose customs and language they adopted, those of the 12th century imposed their own nationality by violence on the Slavs, or retained it where they settled in their midst. To explain this contrast, it is not enough to invoke the inferiority of the Germanic civilization in the 5th century as compared with the Romanic civilization, and its superiority in the 12th century as compared with the Slav civilization. The Normans who invaded England in the 11th century were far more civilized than the Anglo-Saxons, yet in the long run they became intimately mingled with them, and the mixture constituted a new people. It was the same with the Swedes who in the 9th century seized the government of Russia. Nothing of the sort was observed beyond the Elbe. Even to this day the difference between the descendants of the emigrants of the 12th century and the Slav populations in whose lands they settled is as great and as clearly marked as it was at the time of the invasion. It would be puerile to suggest that this phenomenon is explained by "race," since it is a matter of everyday experience that the Germans very readily become denationalized in an alien environment. The explanation of their persistence in Bohemia, Poland, and Hungary must be sought, first of all, in the fact that they settled in compact groups, unlike the Normans in England, who were dispersed amidst the Anglo-Saxon population; but undoubtedly the principal explanation is the fact that among the Slavs they were the initiators, and for long centuries *par excellence* the representatives of the urban life. The Germans introduced the bourgeoisie into the midst of these agricultural populations, and the contrast between them was, perhaps, from the very first, that of social classes rather than national groups. Thanks to the Germanic peasants of the surrounding districts, the German towns were always able to recruit their populations by an influx of compatriots, while the influence which they brought to bear upon these peasants prevented their absorption by the Slav population.

While the Germanic expansion in Slav countries was explained, in the first place, by economic factors, it was not long before religious motives played their part in this expansion, and very notably accelerated its progress. The paganism which had disappeared before the advance of the German colonists between the Elbe and the Oder still persisted throughout the plain that extends from the shores of the Baltic between the Elbe and the Niemen. Its inhabitants, the Prussians, a people of Slavic origin, resisted the attempts at their conversion made at the end of the 10th century by St. Adalbert, Bishop of Prague, and later by the Cistercian monks of Poland. At the beginning of the 13th century the Polish Duke of Mazovia summoned the knights of the Teutonic Order to undertake the conversion of these obstinate heathen. Founded at Saint-Jean d'Acre in 1198 among the Friars Hospitallers of German nationality, this order had been invited, twenty years earlier, by King Andrew II of Hungary, to fight the hordes of pagan Kumans who were invading his eastern frontiers. But before long disputes arose between the Hungarians and the knights, and the appeal of the Polish Duke of Mazovia offered them an opportunity of displaying their zeal for the faith in a more favourable field of action. The poor Prussians, with their bows and their wicker shields, could not resist the heavily-armed knights who came to conquer with the sword a new land for Catholicism, but not a new people. For there was no question of converting the Prussians. They were treated as the enemies of Christ and the Pope, though they knew nothing of either. Since the Crusades evangelization had been replaced by the Holy War. And this Holy War was a war of extermination. It ended only in 1283, when there were no more pagans to massacre. As the Teutonic knights advanced they organized the country. Fortresses, of which a curious specimen may be seen at Marienburg, not far from Danzig, marked the stages of the conquest. German colonists came to occupy the surrounding country, and there too, as between the Elbe and the Oder, Germanization was the consequence of war. Nothing was left of the Prussians but the name, which was now borne by the invaders. The knights retained the lordship of the country, which they received as a fief from Pope Gregory IX in 1234.

While the Germans were thus colonizing the great plain to the south of the Baltic, they were also swarming along the shores of this sea, which had hitherto been navigated only by the Scandinavians. Here the movement started from Lübeck, a Slav village destroyed by Henry the Lion, and then repeopled by emigrants from the adjacent German districts. The new settlement was admirably situated. The proximity of Hamburg destined it to become the intermediary between the trade of the North Sea and that of the Baltic, and its development was surprisingly rapid. From 1163 Visby, on the island of Gothland, became a sort of factory, in constant communication with Lübeck, and from this point the German ships very soon began to sail for the eastern shores of the Baltic. The mouth of the Duna, which offered an excellent means of communication with the Russian regions of the interior, was constantly frequented by the German ships. And here trade cleared the way for Christianity. In 1201 a bishopric was established at Riga, and there Bishop Albert of Bienne created the Order of the Brothers of the Sword, whose mission was to fight the pagans of Livonia and Esthonia. A few years later the German merchants were trading with Novgorod. However, in the north, Dorpat, captured from the Russians by the Brothers of the Sword, became, like Riga, the seat of a bishopric.

The German preponderance in the Baltic was first menaced by the kings of Denmark. The War of Investitures had enabled the latter to shake off the yoke to which they had been subjected since the reign of Otto I. In 1104 the Pope had detached their country from the diocese of Bremen, and Lund had been created the religious metropolis of the Northern kingdoms. When war broke out between the Hohenstaufens and the Guelfs the Danes naturally sided with the latter. Waldemar, under whose reign a beginning was made with the development of the port of Copenhagen, was the ally of Henry the Lion, whose daughter married his son Canute VI (1182–1202). He took part in Henry's expeditions against the Wends, and conquered the island of Rügen. Canute refused to swear the oath of fealty to Frederick Barbarossa, and imposed his rule upon Pomerania, Mecklenburg, and even Lübeck and Hamburg. Waldemar II (1202–1241) increased his brother's conquests by the addition of Schwerin, and subjected Norway to tribute. Presently his fleet appeared in the Eastern Baltic. In 1219 he landed in Esthonia, and after a great victory over the Esthonians (the victory mentioned in the legend of the Danebrog), he founded the city of Reval. About the same time he seized the island of Oesel (1221) and threatened Riga. But this expansion was purely political, and it included territories which were already largely colonized by the Germans. When Waldemar fell unexpectedly into the hands of the Count of Schwerin (1223), a general revolt broke out against him. Four years later he made a vain attempt to recover his position. The defeat which he suffered at Bornhöved (July 22nd, 1227) decided the future, and made the Germans for a long time the masters of the Baltic.

The trade of the Baltic, a sea surrounded by new and sparsely populated countries, could be developed only by the export of corn from the North of Germany and Russian furs to the Western countries, in return for wines, spices, and costly fabrics. Bruges, which was the terminus of the great trade route between Flanders and Italy, had long been the objective of the German navigators of the North Sea. The navigators of the Baltic made for the same destination, and the community of their interests resulted in an immediate rapprochement. These economic relations were the origin of the Hansa: that is to say, the confederation not of the merchants alone, but of the cities of which they were burgesses, from Riga to Cologne. In the end it even included a few inland cities, such as Breslau and Münster. Lübeck, in the middle of the long stretch of coast extending from the Scheldt to the Duna, became the headquarters of the Hansa as early as the middle of the 13th century. The commercial interest of all the members of the League were sufficiently homogeneous to ensure the maintenance of a good understanding between them, apart from local and ephemeral differences. Thanks to the Hansa, German navigation retained its preponderance in the two northern seas until the middle of the 15th century.

The gist of these last few pages may be expressed by saying that since the close of the 12th century Germany had been playing a more and more insignificant part in European politics, and had been occupying a larger and larger area on the map of Europe. Assisted by a number of enterprises aiming at conquest and religious propaganda, the Germanic colonization extended from the Lower Elbe to the Niemen, and interposed itself between the sea and the Slav States of the interior, Poland and Russia, thus preparing the way for the conflicts and the wars which, from the 14th century onwards, did not cease periodically to disturb the peace of Eastern Europe. The absence of natural frontiers in these regions, where only the difference of language divided people from people, predestined them to become the theatre of a struggle which was bound of necessity to assume the character of a national conflict, in the most brutal —that is to say, the ethnographical—sense of the word. Where the contours of the soil divide the States into distinct areas, and where Nature herself, so to speak, has traced the frontiers of the different countries, wars are purely political, and conquest does not involve the enslavement of the vanquished. The various foreign governments to which the Italian people was subjected from the 10th to the 19th century did not in any way change its essential nature. But it was otherwise in these vaguely delimited plains where there was nothing to protect a people against the aggression of its neighbours. In these regions, consequently, war assumed the character of a war of extermination. The conqueror did not feel that he was safe until he had dismembered the enemy State, extirpated its institutions, and destroyed its language and religion, in order to replace them by his own. Such was the treatment which the German colonists of the 12th century meted out to the Slavs of Pomerania and Prussia; it was thus that the Hohenzollerns treated Poland at a later date, and Russia the Germans of the Baltic provinces. Under such conditions of life men became hard and callous; energy and the spirit of discipline and of organization were predominant because they were indispensable; might appeared the supreme right and the only basis of the law. And such conditions existed from the first in the new Germany which extended eastward from the Elbe. In respect of intellectual culture these colonial regions were far in arrears of the Germany of the West and the South. It is hardly possible to cite the name of a single scholar or poet or artist previous to the 18th century. They had no energy to spare for anything but work and warfare. In the Margraves of Brandenburg and the Teutonic Knights of the 13th century, in the petty nobles who employed the knights and fought for them, were emerging the first characteristics of what was one day to be known as the Prussian spirit.

CHAPTER III

France

1. *France and European Politics*

By defeating at Bouvines the coalition which had been
formed against it the French monarchy had given proof of
its military strength, and with that it won its place at the
head of the European powers. From Germany, where its
victory had given the crown to Frederick II, it had nothing
more to fear. It profited by the situation and proceeded to
attack England. The circumstances could not have been
more favourable. The English barons, in rebellion against
John Lackland, called upon the son of Philip Augustus to
defend the Great Charter and offered him the crown. For
a moment the future King of France was King of England.
But the death of John (1216), which, fortunately for his
son, Henry III, aroused the sentiment of nationalism and the
spirit of feudal loyalty, disposed of the possibility of a dynastic union which certainly could not have lasted. Louis
returned to France, and seven years later, in 1223, he succeeded his father as Louis VIII.

Philip Augustus, on ascending the throne, was still the
immediate ruler only of the ancient royal domain, a little
enlarged by Louis VI and Louis VII, but still without outlets to the sea, and threatened on the west and the north
by the alliance of the Count of Flanders and the King of
England. On his death he left his son in possession of
Poitou and Normandy and assured of the obedience of

the Count of Flanders, who was reduced to the rôle of a protégé of the Crown. There was no longer any prince in the kingdom who was in a position to oppose him successfully. However, the Midi was still independent of the monarchical power. In respect of the County of Toulouse, Louis VIII was in almost the same situation as Clovis had been, eight hundred years earlier, in respect of the kingdom of the Visigoths. As with Clovis, it was a religious motive that furnished him with the opportunity of intervening. Clovis in the 5th century attacked the Visigoths on the pretext that they were Arians; Louis VIII was impelled to annex the County of Toulouse on account of the heresy of the Albigenses. In both cases the religious motive merely served to hasten what was inevitable. In the interests of the geographical unity of France its political unity was indispensable. The North and the South were not opposed to each other; on the contrary, each was merged into the other. Add to this the attraction of the Mediterranean, the highway *par excellence* of maritime trade, the sea-road to the East. It had been this under Clovis; and had become it again at the beginning of the 13th century. From Paris, the kings of France were bound to make for it, as the kings of the Franks had done. Moreover, their suzerainty extended to the Pyrenees. At the beginning of the 13th century there was perhaps no region in Europe so radiant with life as Languedoc. Thanks to the Mediterranean trade, its cities were numerous and prosperous. Like Genoa and Pisa, Marseilles and Montpellier despatched their vessels to the ports of Egypt and Syria. Like Siena and Florence, Cahors was engaged in the silver trade, and the fame of her bankers extended even to the Low Countries. The importance of Toulouse, in the plain of the Garonne, was analogous to that of Milan in Lombardy. However, the French cities of the Midi, unlike the Italian, were not autonomous republics. As in the North, they acknowledged the overlordship of the territorial principalities which had been constituted since the dismemberment of the Carolingian Empire, the most important of which was the County of Toulouse. The situation of the Counts of Toulouse, in the south of the kingdom, was very like that of the Counts of Flanders at the opposite extremity. Rich and powerful like the latter, they took advantage, like them, of their eccentric position, behaving, as far as the king was concerned, with almost absolute independence. Lastly, just as a certain proportion of the subjects of the Counts of Flanders spoke "Thiois," the subjects of the Counts of Toulouse spoke Provençal, and this linguistic individuality helped to emphasize the political individuality which distinguished the County of Toulouse from the rest of France; the more so as the Provençal literature of the 12th century was greatly superior to that of the north of France. Its songs of love and war (*sirventes*) were greatly appreciated by the nobles of the Midi, and they made their way into Italy, and even into the north of France, thanks to an infatuation analogous to that which in the 16th and 17th centuries set all the *beaux esprits* reading the Italian, and then the Spanish writers. Richard Cœur-de-Lion, Frederick II, and Henry II, Duke of Brabant, composed poems in the Provençal language, whose literary development was in advance of that of all the other Romanic languages. This alone is enough to show that the intellectual activity of the Midi was in no way inferior to its economic activity. Indeed, this intellectual activity was so potent that while it inspired the poets it also provoked a formidable religious crisis.

At the end of the 12th century Languedoc was swarming with those mystics who aspired to lead the Church and the age back to apostolic simplicity, condemning both the religious hierarchy and the social order[1] as manifestations of the love of evil—that is, of the flesh—for which they wished to substitute the reign of the spirit. These "Cathars" were especially numerous in the County of Albi, dependent on that of Toulouse, whence their name of Albigenses. Their propaganda had won them adherents not only among the people of the cities, but also among the wealthy merchants, and even in the ranks of the nobility. Despite the objurgations of the clergy and the remonstrances of the Pope, Raymond VI, Count of Toulouse, who was the great-grandson of the hero of the First Crusade, treated the heretics with a tolerance that drew suspicion upon himself. In 1208 In-

[1] See p. 8 et seq.

nocent III had him excommunicated by a legate, Pierre de
Castelnau, when a knight in the Count's service, beside himself with fury, felled the prelate with a blow of his lance.
This was too much for the Pope; he banished from the communion of the faithful a prince and a country guilty of
outraging the majesty of Rome and the Catholic faith.
From the north of France, under the leadership of Simon
de Montfort, companies of knights hastened southwards,
equally inspired by their hatred of the heretics and their
hope of booty. The war was merciless and atrocious. Bé-
ziers and Carcassonne were sacked. King Pedro II of Aragon, having come to the aid of Raymond VI, his kinsman,
fell in battle, as did Simon de Montfort in 1218. Simon bequeathed to his son Amaury the territory which he had
conquered from the Count of Toulouse. However, Raymond VI was succeeded by his son Raymond VII, and
Amaury appealed for assistance to the King of France.
Louis VIII, who as prince royal had taken part in the crusade against the Albigenses, now appeared in Languedoc
as sovereign arbiter, at the head of an army. Amaury ceded
his rights to him; Raymond VII did not dare to resist. The
Midi in its turn submitted to the Crown. However, Louis
VIII had no time to complete the process of absorption:
on November 8th, 1226, in the course of the campaign,
death unexpectedly closed his career.

A child of eleven succeeded to the throne. A long regency
was in prospect. The deceased king had appointed as regent
Queen Blanche of Castile, who thus assumed a rôle that
no Queen of France would play again before the advent
of Catherine de Medicis.

It was natural that the great vassals should take advantage of this opportunity and seek to recover the ground
which they had lost since the advent of Philip Augustus.
But nothing is more eloquent of the consolidation of the
monarchical power than the suppression of their rebellion,
despite the support of the King of England, Henry III. The
social order had been transformed. At the time of the dissolution of the Carolingian Empire, when the civilization
was still agricultural, and the revival of trade was a thing
of the future, it had favoured the princes, and had procured

for them the acquiescence of the population, since the princes alone were capable of preserving the public order, which the kings could no longer maintain. Now, in a society liberated from the domainal system, traversed by the merchants, and transformed by the novel needs of the bourgeoisies, the small local parties naturally tended to group themselves under the powerful tutelage of the Crown, and to detach themselves from the princes, whose pretensions no longer corresponded with the needs of the age. However, the opposition of the princes was neither general nor very vigorous. Like that of all the reactionary parties, it was lacking in enthusiasm and confidence, because it was inspired only by personal interests. It quieted down as soon as the princes realized that success was impossible. Raymond of Toulouse, who naturally took part in the revolt, lost the half of his territory that still remained to him, and was obliged to betroth his heiress to the brother of the king, Alphonse de Poitiers, who in 1249, on the death of his father-in-law, inherited the county.

The reign of St. Louis (Louis IX, 1226–1270) began, like that of Louis XIV, amidst the turmoil of a tumultuous regency. It also resembled the latter reign in respect of the glory that it won for France—but in no other particular. For the rest, the contrast between the two policies was as striking as that between the characters of the two princes, each of whom has remained, for posterity, the very incarnation of his epoch. The absolute State of the 17th century found its classic representative in Louis XIV, just as the Christian State of the Middle Ages found its representative in St. Louis. Religious minds will always prefer this gentle figure, so simple and pious that he almost makes one think of a crowned St. Francis of Assisi—and yet he was a great king —to the great and domineering Popes of his time. The Christian ideal of peace, justice and charity was far more completely realized during the reign of St. Louis than during the pontificate of Innocent III or Innocent IV. But we must realize that this flower of mediaeval royalty could not have unfolded its full beauty save for a fortunate conjunction of circumstances. It was a piece of good fortune for St. Louis that he did not ascend the throne until after the Crusade

of the Albigenses, so that he never had to soil his hands
with the massacres of this bloody enterprise, into which the
ardour of his faith would doubtless have drawn him. It was
another and even greater piece of good fortune that he had
inherited from his father and his grandfather a kingdom
which was both powerful and respected. Imagine if he had
been born in the 12th century, and had been obliged to
fight his vassals, and to wage a difficult war on the frontier
of Normandy against the King of England! History might
have remembered him as a Louis the Pious, but nothing
more, for he was neither a great politician nor a great war-
rior. He was merely a good man, and the virtues which he
could not have displayed if he had been forced to fight for
power were able to unfold themselves at ease, thanks to his
possession of the power which made possible the accomplishment of his ideal. He had the good fortune to reign
over a kingdom which contained no heretics and no enemies, and it was reserved for him to ennoble and consolidate
and complete in peace what his predecessors had achieved
with the sword.

In the interior of the country the royal authority made
itself felt without difficulty, and there were no obstacles to
its growth, because each step in advance was accompanied
by a benefit to the country. Hitherto the monarchical administration had served, more than anything else, to safeguard the rights of the Crown, to favour its jurisdiction,
and to develop and systematize its finances. Under the new
reign it was employed to safeguard public order and to improve the condition of the people. The practical Christianity
which inspires the ordinances of St. Louis reminds us of the
capitularies of Charlemagne. Even the institution of the
missi dominici had its counterpart in that of the royal com-
missioners whose duty it was to check the activities of the
bailiffs and to see that they did not oppress the persons under their jurisdiction. Charlemagne, as we have seen, could
realize his intentions only very imperfectly, as the executive
means were lacking. St. Louis, on the contrary, possessed
in the Parlement and the functionaries created by Philip
Augustus the necessary personnel for the accomplishment
of his designs. Private wars were abolished, personal serf-

dom was suppressed on the royal domains, the judicial system was completed by providing for the right of appeal, and taxation was rendered more equitable. The Parlement exercised its control over the provincial courts of law, and its activities contributed to the unification of the law and the suppression of such superannuated usages as trial by battle and the ordeal. A Chamber of Accounts, by systematizing the finances, helped to make things easier for the taxpayers. For the first time the people felt that the government was not merely a machine designed to oppress them, an instrument of exaction; for the first time the official seemed not a master but a protector; for the first time the people realized that the power of the Crown was allied with justice, that the king watched over them from afar and had compassion on their misfortunes. The monarchy was becoming popular; it was striking root in the provinces, rallying public opinion, and showing itself to be necessary, indispensable, because beneficent. It really seems that the form of national sentiment which finds expression in the cult of the monarchy dates, in France, from St. Louis. The kingdom became a mother-country, whose inhabitants were bound together by their common love of the king. This love was to find its incomparable expression, two hundred years later, in Joan of Arc. But it was St. Louis who first inspired this love in the French, an affection so indelible that it was transferred to all his successors.

The peace and justice that he wished to prevail among his subjects were also the constant criteria of his foreign policy. He might have attempted, with the greatest possibility of success, to wrest from the King of England the last remnant of his continental possessions, or he could have deprived the King of Aragon of the fiefs which he held in Languedoc. Despite the advice of his counsellors, he offered to make friendly arrangements with both princes. By the Treaty of Abbeville (1259) he agreed to acknowledge Henry III's rights in Perigord and Limousin, provided he abandoned his claim to Normandy, Anjou, Touraine, Maine and Poitou, which had been added to the Crown by Philip Augustus. By the Treaty of Corbeil he obtained from Jaime II of Aragon his Languedocien territories in return for the cession of the French suzerainty over Catalonia (1258).[2] During the furious conflict between the Pope and Frederick II he never departed from his attitude of neutrality, and this, in so obedient a son of the Church, may be taken as a discreet condemnation of the violence of Innocent IV. The confidence inspired by his equitable behaviour won for him, in the outer world, a political prestige which was all the more substantial in that he had not sought it. In the Low Countries the d'Avesnes and the Dampierres appealed to him as arbiter in their long quarrel, while in England Henry III and the rebellious barons submitted their differences to him.

But for him, as for the great scholastic philosophers of his time, while a war between Christians was always a misfortune and often a crime, war against the infidel was an obligation. His faith was so ardent and his sincerity so complete that he was bound to regard the reconquest of the Holy Sepulchre as the foremost of his duties. The calculating and interested spirit which was withdrawing more and more of his contemporaries from the Crusade had no meaning for this idealist. For him, as for the Popes, the Crusade still constituted the honour and the essential business of Christendom. In vain did those about him remind him of the dangers of the enterprise, its cost, its uselessness, and its almost certain failure; their arguments were powerless to convince a king who valued his crown mainly because of the obligations toward God—that is, toward the Church —which it imposed upon him. The more prosperous and peaceful his kingdom, the more ardently he longed to depart. The enthusiasm of the first Crusaders was born again in this prince, who wrote the final chapter of the history of the Crusades. But were the two expeditions which he undertook against Islam—the first in 1248, the second in 1270 —really Crusades? Yes, if we consider their aim, but not if we consider their composition. Christendom as a whole paid absolutely no attention to them. They were both purely French undertakings, in which the chivalry of France followed the king rather in a spirit of personal devotion and

2 On the north of the Pyrenees, Aragon retained only the County of Roussillon and Montpellier.

loyalty and love of adventure than in a spirit of religious
enthusiasm. Both expeditions were complete failures. It was
only after six years of effort (1248–1254), after a long and
persistent siege of Damietta, after falling into the hands of
the Turks, after seeing his best beloved companions die, and
sorrowfully enduring the reproaches of the others, that the
king at last resigned himself to returning to France. He
would doubtless have shown the same constancy in the second expedition (1270), but he had hardly disembarked at
Tunis when sickness procured for him the death of which
he had always dreamed: he died, as he had wished, while
battling for the Faith. His death put an end to an under-
taking upon which no one but himself had entered in sincerity of spirit. It was for the sake of his brother, the new
King of Sicily, Charles of Anjou, who laid claim to the suzerainty of Tunis, that St. Louis had made for this city before
setting sail for Egypt. Without suspecting it, the pious monarch had been a tool of the realistic and predatory policy
which his reign had for a time interrupted.

The problem of Sicily, which was at the bottom of the
war between the Pope and Frederick II, had not been
solved by the death of the Emperor. After the premature
death of his son Conrad IV his bastard Manfred, instead of
administering the country in the name of Conrad's heir
(known to history by the name of Conradino, which the
Italians gave him), seized the crown for himself (1258).
Alexander IV, who had just succeeded to Innocent IV, had
first of all acceded to the proposals of the King of England,
and had bestowed the kingdom of Sicily upon the king's
son, Edmund, a child who could and did accomplish nothing. It was necessary to solve the problem once and for all,
and to choose some powerful prince, upon whom Rome
could rely, to restore Sicily once and for all to her proper
place under the suzerainty of the Holy See. France alone
could provide such a prince. St. Louis having refused the
crown on behalf of his younger son, Urban II entered into
negotiations with the king's youngest brother, Charles of
Anjou, whose marriage in 1246 had made him Count of
Provence. Charles, who was ambitious, had long paid close
attention to Italian affairs, and the Guelfs of Italy regarded

him as their protector and their future leader. In 1266 he received the crown of Sicily, in Rome, from the hands of Clement IV, and set out to take possession of his kingdom, at the head of a numerous and brilliant retinue of knights, excited by the lure of Sicilian wealth. The French arms brilliantly justified the reputation which they had acquired since the battle of Bouvines. The battle of Benevento (February 1266) destroyed Manfred's army, and Manfred himself was slain. Thirty months later (August 1268) the army which Conradino had brought from Germany was likewise destroyed at Tagliacozzo. The young prince contrived to escape, was recaptured, delivered to the conqueror, sentenced to death for the crime of *lèse-majesté*, and executed. The Hohenstaufen dynasty, that "generation of vipers," as Innocent IV had called it, was annihilated. The Pope would not allow Conradino, whom he had excommunicated, to be buried in consecrated ground. Some time later the Archbishop of Cosenza had the body of Manfred removed from the tomb which the French knights had raised above it in homage to his courage, and ordered that it should be buried by the banks of the Verde. His wife died in prison. This rancour on the part of the victorious Curia is enough to explain poor Conradino's fate. The romantics of the 19th century deplored his death, regarding him as a victim of France, the hereditary enemy of Germany, and their indignation was naturally utilized for the purpose of nourishing the national hatred which the adroit politician so skilfully exploits. Nothing could be more completely misleading than these retrospective hatreds. The Franco-German hostility which has been so carefully cherished in our own time is of quite recent date, and it would be impossible to discover any trace of it in the 13th century. Conradino was sacrificed merely for reasons of State, and the person responsible for his death, after the Pope and Charles of Anjou, was Frederick II himself. For Frederick II was the first to pursue to its final consequences and to apply without mercy to his adversaries the principle that no law can be superior to the interests of the prince. Did not Roman law justify this theory, which harmonized so admirably with his own unscrupulous nature? Conradino's judges were merely his disciples; there would be others later—the Italian tyrants.

Charles of Anjou's policy might be defined by describing it as that of the last Hohenstaufen's, with the difference that the Papacy supported instead of opposing it. Like Henry VI and Frederick II, Charles maintained and even increased the absolutism of the Crown in Sicily; like them, he endeavoured to subject the whole of Italy to his control; and like them, he dreamed of extending his power to the Orient. Rome became alarmed by the progress of this ally in whom she had hoped to find a tool, and who was now imposing his will upon her and involving her in his policies. But in order to escape his control she would have to find a rival to oppose him, who would of necessity obtain support from the Ghibellines and the malcontents of Sicily, who were recruited from among the partisans of the hateful Hohenstaufens. Moreover, troublesome though he might be, Charles was a zealous son of the Church; he had restored the privileges of the Sicilian clergy, and his designs upon Constantinople, now that the Latin Empire had at last disappeared (1261) and the Palaeologi had restored the schism, might serve to re-establish the union and the obedience which were among the essential objectives of the Papal policy. The Emperor Michael was not unaware of the dangers that threatened him. He secretly fomented in Sicily the unrest which the high-handed behaviour and arrogance of the Frenchmen who had followed the new king thither were aggravating day by day. His intrigues were actively supported by Pedro III of Aragon, who had married one of Manfred's daughters, and cherished the ambition of becoming his father-in-law's successor.

Spain, in which country the advance of the Christian kingdoms against the Musulman States had made constant progress since the beginning of the 13th century, while Barcelona was beginning to play an active part in the trade of the Mediterranean, now appears for the first time on the political stage of Europe. Her geographical situation being what it was, she was bound, as soon as she was strong enough, to pursue a maritime policy, and to play her part with the rest on the waters of the inland sea whose western extremity was closed by her own shores. Pedro of Aragon went to work both cleverly and vigorously. The revolt which broke out at Messina in 1282, and to which posterity has given the name of "the Sicilian Vespers," was largely due to his instigation. It rapidly spread over the whole island. Charles despatched to Sicily the fleet which he had been preparing for the attack upon Constantinople. It was destroyed by the Aragonese admiral, Andrea Loria, off Trapani, in the battle which made a glorious beginning for the history of the Spanish navy. Charles died shortly afterwards, in 1285, before he could succeed in suppressing the insurrection. His son Charles II followed him, and despite his efforts, and the support of the Pope, he was at last obliged to abandon the island of Sicily to the Spaniards. There were thenceforth two kingdoms of Sicily, one, beyond the Strait of Messina, belonging to the House of Aragon, while the other still acknowledged the Angevin dynasty, which established itself in Naples.[3]

While Charles of Anjou's intervention in Italy testified to the increasing prestige of France, it could not be regarded as part of the French policy. St. Louis left his brother's hands free; but did nothing to support him, as he considered that Sicilian affairs were alien to the kingdom. The case was altered under his successor Philip the Bold (1270–1285). Before his time the conduct of the kings of France had been shaped exclusively by their anxiety to consolidate the kingdom, to preserve it from foreign influences, and to group the various parties under their control. Their great enemy, indeed their only enemy, had been England, and if they had sought allies in the outer world, it was only in order that they might triumph over England more completely in their own country. They had succeeded in their task, and France had become a great power. St. Louis had employed his forces only to safeguard peace; Philip the Bold entered upon a policy of expansion which certainly owed something to the ambitious and restless spirit of his uncle, Charles of Anjou. In 1272, on the death of Richard of Cornwall, he allowed Charles to persuade

[3] A definitive peace between Frederick of Aragon and Robert of Anjou was signed in 1302.

him to become a candidate—or rather to allow his candidature to be discussed—for the crown of the King of the
Romans. If his candidature had been successful it would
have involved France—to the advantage of the King of
Sicily—in the inextricable entanglement of Germany's quarrels. Fortunately, the election of Rudolph of Habsburg prevented the realization of this plan. One result of this election was to inspire in Rudolph an infinite condescension
toward the House of France. Charles took advantage of
this to make him renounce all his claims to Sicily, and
Philip to obtain from him in 1281 the protectorate of the
Bishopric of Toul. Naturally, so much benevolence merely
encouraged the king to extend his power still further
beyond the frontier of the Empire. Already, in 1272, he
had obtained an oath of fealty from the Archbishop of
Lyons. In the Low Countries he supported the Count of
Flanders, Guillaume de Dampierre, in his conflict with the
House of Avesnes, helped him to obtain the County of
Namur, and used his interest to procure the Bishopric of
Liége for one of his sons, thereby making the influence of
France felt wherever the Flemish interest had penetrated.
The Count of Hainaut, Jean d'Avesnes, sought in vain to
interest Rudolph in his cause, and implored him in virulent
terms to fall upon the Low Countries, where his enemy the
Count of Flanders was insolently deriding the blunted
sword of the Empire. As a matter of fact, the German
suzerainty over these wealthy countries was already a thing
of the past, and it seemed that it would soon be replaced
by that of France.

This expansion of the Capetian power toward the north
and the east, into territories which their geographical situation, their customs, and, to some extent, their language naturally oriented toward France, was the inevitable consequence of Germany's weakness. It was so natural that it
was bound to follow from the moment when France no
longer encountered, behind the artificial frontier which she
had crossed, the resistance of a State superior to her in
strength, and determined to keep what the old Carolingian
treaties had attributed to her in the 9th century. In order
to succeed in his designs, Philip the Bold had only to take

advantage of the circumstances, and of time, both of which were working for him. But conditions were very different in the south of the kingdom. Here the Pyrenees had set a barrier between the countries and the peoples on either side which political ambitions and conquerors had always, in the end, to recognize. Clovis had never crossed the Pyrenees, and although the Arabs had done so later, they were soon driven back again. The Spanish March which Charlemagne had constituted beyond the mountains had before long detached itself from France. All that remained of it was the ill-defined rights of suzerainty of the kings of France over Catalonia and of the kings of Aragon over Languedoc. St. Louis, for the sake of peace, had replaced this confusion by clarity. Since the conclusion of the Treaty of Corbeil the Pyrenees had delimited political rights as definitely as they divided the adjacent countries. One may ask why Philip the Bold should have resolved once more to unsettle so satisfactory an arrangement and to meddle in Spanish affairs. No danger threatened him from beyond the mountains, and there was no question of claiming any rights or protecting any interests. The dynastic problems which had occasioned his intervention in Navarre and Castile since 1275 were merely pretexts. He made use of these pretexts because he wanted to make war: the sort of war that in the days of Louis XIV was described as a war of magnificence, and which we should call a war of hegemony. Having the power, he made use of it to enforce his will, with no other object in view than the glory of his crown. This, I believe, was the first war of pure political ambition to be recorded by the history of Europe. However, it may be that we should attribute his unwarrantable interference in Spain to his desire to support the Sicilian designs of Charles of Anjou, to whom the House of Castile was hardly less hostile than that of Aragon. At all events, this holds good of the Aragonese campaign of 1283. After the Sicilian Vespers the Pope, having excommunicated the King of Aragon, offered his kingdom, which was a fief of the Church, to the King of France, for one of his sons. Philip's choice fell on Charles de Valois, and he crossed the Pyrenees in order to win for him the throne of Pedro II. He did not succeed in winning it, for he died during the campaign.

What St. Louis had achieved was completely ruined. His son, at his death, left France involved in the affairs of Italy and Spain, while England, having emerged from the troubles of Henry III's reign, was on the point of once more taking up arms against her, at the solicitation of her new enemies. Yet if the position of France was not so stable as it had been twenty years earlier, it was more brilliant. She had considerably enlarged her frontiers at the cost of the Empire, and had crossed the Pyrenees; despite the Sicilian Vespers, with the accession of Charles II of Anjou a French dynasty was finally installed in Naples, and shortly afterwards one of its branches was established on the throne of Hungary.[4] In the Europe of the 13th century France had no rival. Nowhere else was there a kingdom so extensive, so well situated, thanks to its outlets upon the North Sea and the Mediterranean, and as populous; and with the exception of England, there was no other country with so robust a political constitution.

2. The French Civilization

Intellectual hegemony is not always accompanied by political hegemony. Germany had exercised the latter in the 11th century, without possessing the former, since a people can impose itself upon another by force without at the same time imposing its civilization. Countries whose power was really insignificant, like the Italy of the 15th century, may propagate their manners, their ideas, and their art in the outer world by the mere manifestation of their superiority. France, in the 13th century, had the good fortune to be superior to the rest of Europe both as a State and as a society. Her strength merely rendered more rapid and more irresistible a moral ascendancy which was of much earlier date, and which had nothing in common with the military and political achievements of the monarchy.

If we observe the general state of European civilization after the Carolingian period, we see that nearly all its es-

[4] See p. 201.

sential characteristics made their appearance in France earlier than elsewhere, and also that it was in France that they achieved their most perfect expression. This applies to religious as well as to secular life. The Order of Cluny, the Order of the Cistercians, and the Order of the Premonstrants had their birth in France; the Order of Chivalry was a French creation, and it was from France that the Crusades obtained their most numerous and most enthusiastic recruits. It was in France, too, at the beginning of the 12th century, that Gothic art suddenly rose as from the soil and imposed its supremacy on the world, and in France the first *chansons de geste* made their appearance. All these coincidences were not merely fortuitous. That so many eminent personalities should have existed in one country, that the basin of the Seine, from the 10th century onwards, should have been the scene of so many achievements and so many innovations, means that there must have existed there, as in Greece, in the Attica of the 5th century, an environment which was peculiarly favourable to the manifestations of human energy. And it is a fact that the two great social forces which operated, on the ruins of the Carolingian Empire, to constitute a new Europe—the monastic and the feudal system—were nowhere so active and so predominant as in Northern France. Of course, there were monks everywhere, and vassals everywhere, but only in Northern France had the old order of things disappeared so completely as to give them full scope and perfect freedom of action. Hence the monastic orders and the knightly caste, which Europe naturally borrowed from France as the evolution which had produced them gradually made its way into other countries. Hence the extraordinary enthusiasm of the Frenchmen of the North for the Crusades: that is, for the completest imaginable manifestation of a society which was dominated at once by the religious and the military spirit. And hence, again, evoked by the same ideas and the same feelings, the simultaneous birth of Gothic art, which transformed religious architecture, and of the feudal *épopée*, which was the beginning—at first in France, and then, through imitation of France, in the rest of Europe—of literature in the vulgar tongue.

Thus the ascendancy of French civilization long ante-dated the ascendancy of the French monarchy. It began at a time when the Capetians were still living in the shadow of their great vassals. It would be perfectly accurate to say that both civilization and politics had a feudal character when they first made their appearance in France. We must not forget that the monastery of Cluny was built by the Duke of Burgundy, and that the Counts of Flanders and the Counts of Champagne were among the most ardent patrons of the Clunisian movement, and also of the Cister-cian and Premonstrant Orders. Moreover, the heroes whose deeds were celebrated by the *chansons de geste* were the ancestors, actual or mythical, of the princes who built the monasteries. These heroes were feudal barons, and the vir-tues which the *chansons* extolled were courage, fidelity and piety. Their finest type of hero, Roland, was the ideal knight as imagined by the sons of those who had fought in the First Crusade. During the course of the 12th century this feudal civilization embellished and purified itself. The life of the court, with its refined and conventional manners, which the Middle Ages very exactly describe as "courteous manners," was first developed, not in the entourage of the king, who long continued faithful to the Carolingian tradi-tion, but in the princely residences. It was there that the rules and the ceremonial of chivalry were established; there the sentiment of honour had its birth; there the worship of womanhood first made its appearance; and there a litera-ture developed to which Rome and Brittany contributed motives, to its great enrichment, while the various lyric forms of the *langue d'oc* made their way into the *langue d'oil*. And already this blossoming of the feudal life was not restricted to France alone. At the close of the 11th cen-tury it made its appearance in England, with the compan-ions of the Conqueror, and it appeared in the East wherever the Christians had established themselves. French was the language spoken in Jerusalem, Antioch, and Saint-Jean d'Acre. From that time until our own days French has been the international language of Europeans in the basin of the Eastern Mediterranean.

In Europe itself its progress, from the beginning of the

13th century, was extraordinary, and here the political power acquired by the monarchy very greatly increased the power of expansion which it derived from its social prestige. As in the 17th and 18th centuries, it became in every country, for the upper ranks of the aristocracy, a sort of second mother-tongue. In the regions where "Thiois" was spoken French tutors were employed to teach the French language to the sons of the nobility, as the indispensable complement of good breeding and "courtesy." Even in Italy, Brunetto Latini gave French the precedence over all other languages.

And even earlier than the French language, the literature of France made its way into all parts of Europe. From the Low Countries, about the middle of the 12th century, it spread into Germany, and from Germany into the Scandinavian countries. It was translated into or imitated in all the Germanic and Latin tongues. Every fresh example of French literature attracted attention and found readers; indeed, it is only through Norwegian translations that we have learned of the existence of certain French branches of the "cycle" of Charlemagne. The greatest German poets of the 13th century—Hartmann of Strasbourg and Wolfram von Eschenbach—are full of reminiscences and paraphrases of French poems. To find a parallel to such prestige in the previous history of Europe we must go back, despite the fundamental difference of the times and societies in question, to the diffusion of the Greek language and literature in the Roman Empire from the beginning of the 2nd century before Christ.

The comparison is all the more exact inasmuch as, in the case of France as in that of Greece, it applies to art as well as to manners and literature. We have only to consider the conquest of Europe by Gothic architecture, for this epithet of "Gothic," which it owes to the disdain of the Italian humanists, was applied, as we know, to an essentially French creation. The invention of the pointed arch, at the beginning of the 12th century, somewhere on the confines of Normandy and the Île de France, had the effect, in a few years, thanks to the genius of French builders, of completely transforming the fundamental structure and the style of architectural monuments. Until then the methods of the builder's art had remained, in their essentials, what they were in antiquity. But now there was a sudden change. The conditions of equilibrium, the relations of buttresses and the pitch of roofs, of horizontal and vertical elements, of full and empty spaces, were revolutionized, and from this transformation was born the one great school of architecture which the history of art can place on an equality with Greek architecture. Notre-Dame of Paris was begun in 1163; the Cathedral of Reims in 1212; the nave of Amiens dates from 1220; the façade of Chartres from 1194. The admiration which such monuments evoked may be readily understood, and it was attested by the fact that the French architects were soon in demand everywhere. A French architect built the choir of Magdeburg Cathedral; another built the Cathedral of Lund, in Sweden. Villard de Honnecourt, whose sketch-book has happily been preserved for us, drew plans for buildings to be erected in all parts of Europe. Of course, the former pupils of the French architects did not confine themselves to mechanical reproduction. They adapted the new art to the materials at their disposal, modified it in accordance with their own genius, and to some extent harmonized it with the traditions of their own country. There is an English Gothic and a German Gothic, just as there is a Spanish Gothic and an Italian Gothic. But they are all the immediate offspring of the French Gothic, and none of them has attained the supremacy of its parent. The cathedrals of France may be inferior to those of other countries in respect of size, imaginative decoration, and luxuriance or resplendent materials, but in their harmony and their majesty they are incomparable: they are the Parthenons of Gothic.

The hegemony of France in the domain of literature and art in the 12th and 13th centuries is quite simply explained by the superiority of the French civilization. We cannot say quite the same of its intellectual hegemony, which made a much greater impression on the contemporary world. Here it was not the national but the clerical life of France that was in question. All the knowledge of the Middle Ages, if we make some exception in the case of law and medicine, was ecclesiastical, and its exclusive medium of expression was the Latin language. It was essentially universal and international. And yet its central point, its focus, was in France; or to be exact, in Paris. The two cardinal sciences of the epoch, those which dominated all the others—theology and philosophy—seem to have chosen, from the 12th century onwards, to make their home on the banks of the Seine. It was there that the scholastic method was evolved, which until the Renaissance dominated human thought as completely as the Gothic style had dominated art. It was there that the necessities of education created a new sort of Latin, which borrowed its syntax from the French: a dry and impersonal language, but incomparably lucid and precise; so that even the derision of the humanists could not deprive it of the glory of having been for three centuries not only the written, but also the spoken language of learned men in all parts of Europe. From Abelard to Gerson there was not a single thinker of any mark who did not either teach or study in Paris. The University, which had been created in the reign of Philip Augustus by the amalgamation of the masters and scholars of the various schools of Paris, exercised its irresistible and unexampled power of attraction to the very limits of the Catholic world. John of Osnabruck, at the close of the 13th century, awarded to France the monopoly of science; the Flemish poet Van Mearlant celebrated France as the land *par excellence* of the clergy; and we know that the University of Paris was the model by which Charles IV was inspired when he founded the University of Prague (1348), the prototype of the German universities. And the universal ascendancy exercised by Paris was matched, if one may say so, by the cosmopolitanism of the masters who taught in the University. They came not only from France, but from Germany (Albertus Magnus), the Low Countries (Siger of Brabant), Scotland (Duns Scotus), and Italy (Thomas Aquinas). In short, just as Rome was the headquarters of the government of the Church, Paris was the seat of its theological and philosophical activities. It was the keystone of its scholastic system.

What was the reason of this extraordinary destiny? Why

had Catholic science made its home in this northern city, although no literary or religious tradition seemed to justify the mission which had devolved upon it? No other explanation offers itself, beyond the peculiar character which had resulted in the choice of Paris as the residence of the royal court. The Carolingian traditions of the monarchy naturally predisposed it to interest itself in the ecclesiastical schools, and to accord them its protection. While the great feudal magnates had favoured the mystical foundations of the Church, the kings extended their patronage to its scholastic foundations. It is therefore not surprising that the schools of Paris should at a very early date have enjoyed a privileged situation. The progress of the monarchy, which from the beginning of the 13th century had enhanced the importance and the attractions of the capital, is sufficient explanation of the further developments. The national centre of France became the focus of the scientific life of Europe. It was not the French alone who broadcast through the world that proverbial saying of the 13th century, which was doubtless due to some student's play upon words: "*Paris absque pare*, Paris without peer."

The influence of French civilization in the 12th and 13th centuries was not everywhere felt with equal intensity. It attained its maximum in those countries to which it was carried by the Frenchmen who had settled there: in England and the Crusader communities in the East. Elsewhere it was introduced as a borrowed thing; it was imitated, became the fashion, and spread by contagion and example. But everywhere this influence was communicated only to the upper classes of society; to the nobles, in lay circles, and to the students and scholars among the clergy. In this respect it may be compared with the influence of the Renaissance in the 15th century; like the latter, it affected only the social aristocracy, or the aristocracy of intellect and learning. It is not difficult to understand why this was so. The France of the Middle Ages had not so far developed her economic life that she was able to propagate her influence by means of commerce and industry. In this domain she was far behind Italy and Flanders. Nevertheless, in Flanders, owing to the close proximity of the two countries, their political relations, and their commercial interests, the influence of French civilization affected even the bourgeoisie. The patricians of the great Flemish cities of the 12th century were more than half French; even employing French as their administrative language, and in business. The bilingual character which Flemish Belgium has preserved to this day dates from this period. It was not in any degree the result—as was the bilingual character of Bohemia, for example—of a foreign occupation; it was a natural and peaceful consequence of the fact that France was Belgium's next-door neighbour, and the best evidence of the power of attraction exercised by her civilization.

CHAPTER IV

Philip the Fair and Boniface VIII

1. *The Causes of the Crisis*

The death and the catastrophic failure of Frederick II (1250) ended the secular conflict of the Papacy and the Empire. Once that was ended, the Pope had no enemies. The universal power which he exercised over the Church was contested by no one. He was able to devote himself to the realization of the important aims of the pontifical policy: union with the Greek Church and the Crusade. For a moment it seemed as though the union of the Churches was on the point of being realized. The Emperor of Byzantium, Michael Palaeologus, hoping to obtain the support of the West against the Turks, declared that he was ready to recognize the primacy of Rome, and Gregory X, at the Council of Lyons, in 1274, was able to proclaim the end of the schism which for three hundred years had divided Christendom. But this was the triumph and the dream of a moment only. The Greek Church was too deeply rooted in the religious sentiment and the national tradition of the Eastern Christians to bow itself under the Latin yoke. It repudiated the Emperor's overtures. In 1281 Martin IV, abandoning hope, had once more to pronounce his anathema upon the schismatics. The end which had seemed to be achieved was as far from attainment as ever. The Crusade, which was solemnly announced in the Council simultaneously with the reconciliation with the Greeks, met with no greater success. Louis IX was the last Crusader. It is true that Charles of Anjou, inspired by political ambition rather than by religion, made preparations for an expedition which, if it had ever sailed for the East, would probably have been as unsuccessful as his brother's attempts. But the Sicilian Vespers compelled him to employ his fleet against Messina, and to apply himself to the defence of his threatened kingdom.

Thus the Papacy had arrived at its apogee only to witness the failure of its grandiose plans of once more receiving the Greeks into the bosom of the Catholic Church, and recovering the Holy Sepulchre from Islam. And even in the West its power was undermined. The hour of its victory was at the same time the hour that marked the beginning of its decline.

Of this there are various explanations. To begin with, now that the conflict with the Emperor was ended, the Papal cause, in Italy, was no longer confounded with that of the Guelfs, and above all, with that of the Lombard cities, which the Emperor had threatened equally with the Papacy. The Pope was henceforth merely an Italian sovereign, and his temporal power was reduced to the measure of his territorial interest. And this temporal power of the Popes was so inconsiderable that it could not successfully resist Charles de Valois, whose preponderance soon made itself felt throughout the peninsula; even in the States of the Church, even in Rome itself, where his title of senator made him the protector—which meant the master—of the people. But as though this was not enough, his power made itself felt even in the heart of the Curia. Formerly, in the days when the Popes were elected by the clergy and the people, the Roman barons had sought to rally the mob to their own candidate by means of violence or corruption. The creation of the College of Cardinals by Nicholas II (1059) had put an end to such practices, assuring liberty of election by removing it from the influence of popular riot. In 1179, as a further safeguard, Alexander III had decreed that in default of unanimity at least two-thirds of the cardinals must agree upon the choice of a candidate. It goes without saying that as the ascendancy of the Papacy in European affairs increased, the voting was swayed by political as well as religious considerations. However, since the cardinals were nearly all Italian, it was long since foreign interests had played any but a very secondary part in their deliberations. But the case was altered since the advent of Charles of Anjou. It was his constant preoccupation to assure himself of the support of a party in the Sacred College, and he did his utmost to secure the introduction of Neapolitan, Provençal and French cardinals on whom he could rely. His efforts were crowned with success. Clement IV, a Provençal by origin, and entirely devoted to Charles, furthered his designs by promoting the formation of an Angevin faction among the cardinals. Clement's death (1268) was the signal for the outbreak of a desperate conflict between these "Angevins" and their adversaries. It was only after three years of struggle and intrigue that they resigned themselves to the election of Gregory X (1271). It was not surprising that Gregory should wish to make an end of a state of affairs so damaging to the good government of the Church. It was he who was responsible for the institution of the Conclave, almost as it exists to-day. He decreed that on the death of the Pope the cardinals should assemble in a closed chamber, where they would have no communication with the outside world, being forbidden, under penalty of excommunication, to leave the Conclave before they had elected a Pope. However, these precautions did not prevent Charles de Valois, in 1280, from compelling the Conclave to elect the Frenchman, Martin IV, who eagerly seconded all his plans. After Charles's death the Angevin party, though less powerful, was no less active. The Conclave became a mere formality; Nicholas IV was elected only after a year's negotiations between the cardinals (1288), and when he died, in 1292, the quarrels broke out again with renewed force, so that after two years of fruitless agitation the cardinals finally decided, since no party was strong enough to force its candidate upon the others, to elect an aged hermit, ignorant of the world, whom the people regarded as a saint: the innocent sport of intrigues which would have disgusted him if he had understood them. The new Pope, Celestine V, knew hardly any Latin, and when he had exchanged the solitude of his

mountains for the Lateran Palace, where he was abashed
and bewildered, he did not realize that he was merely the
tool of the King of Naples, Charles II of Anjou, who, the
better to make use of him, installed him in his own capital.
Before long his one thought was to abdicate. The cardinals
asked nothing better than to take him at his word. He had
given them time to come to an agreement. On December
12th, 1294, they elected, in the place of the poor old man,
a Roman noble, Benedetto Gaetani, who took the name of
Boniface VIII.

In his person the last Pope of the line of Innocent III
and Innocent IV ascended the throne of St. Peter. His manifest aim was to restore to the Holy See the splendour, the
prestige, the moral authority, and the universal political
dominion which it had enjoyed in their time. The pomp
with which he surrounded himself on the occasion of public
ceremonies, the two swords which he had carried before
him, the crown with which he adorned the pontifical tiara,
were so many means of affirming the primacy in the Church
of the successor of St. Peter, and of reminding the world
that the temporal power was subordinate to the Church,
since, as part of the Church, it could make no pretension
to shake off the authority of the head of the Church. There
was nothing new in this, nothing that had not already been
pointed out by Nicholas I and Gregory VII, clearly formulated by Innocent III, and logically demonstrated by the
Scholastics. The famous Bulls addressed to Philip the Fair
contained nothing more than the doctrine concerning the
relations between the two powers as accepted by all the
theologians. Boniface had merely summarized and repeated
the principles of his great predecessors, without adding
anything to them.

Why, then, did they excite such a storm of indignation,
and result in catastrophe? Simply on account of their im-
mutability. They were not in accordance with political
realities; times were changed, and what the Pope, in conformity with tradition, promulgated as the essential truth,
now excited the opposition of the most advanced nations in
Europe, since both kings and peoples were agreed in re-

garding them as an insupportable encroachment on their most legitimate rights and interests.

One thing, indeed, must be understood: it was not only with France that Boniface VIII found himself in conflict. He found Edward I no more tractable than Philip the Fair, and the English Parliament repudiated his claims no less vigorously than the States-General in Paris. While current events so aggravated the conflict with France that it amounted to a complete rupture, it is none the less true that the pontifical policy aroused, at the same time, and for the same reasons, the opposition of the two countries which, from the end of the 13th century, possessed a veritable constitution.

Until then the Pope had had to contend against a single enemy only: the Empire, or rather the Emperor; and we must once more repeat that the question at issue between them was not comprehended within the limits of a single nation: it involved the whole of Christendom. Of course, in undermining the Imperial power the Pope was also undermining the power of the King of Germany. But German opinion, far from being incensed against him, regarded the impairment of the monarchical power with satisfaction, and the princes who represented this opinion, instead of opposing the enterprises of Rome, supported the Pope, and facilitated their success. Under Frederick II, it is true, the circumstances were somewhat different. The issue of conflict was the kingdom of Sicily rather than the Empire, and the kingdom of Sicily was a State; but it must be observed, in the first place, that this State was not independent, since it was a fief of the Holy See; and above all, it was not a national State. Its heterogeneous population, bandied about for centuries from one foreign conqueror to another, did no more than endure the despotic government which they inflicted upon it, and we cannot perceive that it ever displayed the slightest tendency to make common cause with them. The Sicilians had paid their taxes to Frederick II and had provided him with soldiers, but he was perfectly well aware that they cared nothing for his quarrel. He never for a moment thought of appealing to them for their opinion as to the legitimacy of his rights. He contented himself with the theoretical defence of these rights by legal experts.

How great was the difference between this absolute despot, this Hohenstaufen to whom a politic marriage had given Sicily, and the kings of England and France! In England, since the death of John Lackland, the liberties consecrated by Magna Carta had been consolidated. Under the long reign of Henry III (1216–1272) the barons and the burgesses, under the leadership of Simon de Montfort, had imposed on the Crown the control of a Council of State. Representatives of the cities sat beside those of the nobles in the national assembly, which the king pledged himself to convoke three times a year, and which in 1258 adopted, officially, for the first time, the name of Parliament, a name so glorious in the history of modern Europe. Its attributions were clearly defined under Edward I, and its essential prerogative, the basis of the first free constitution that the world had ever known—the prerogative of granting taxation—was formally acknowledged in 1297. Henceforth the nation and the sovereign were associated in the government of the country. Although the personal power of the prince was subjected to definite limitations, and although, alone among his European peers, he had to renounce the possibility of waging wars inspired by mere dynastic ambition, and apply himself solely to enterprises approved and subsidized by his people, yet, on the other hand, what strength he derived from this compliance! From the end of the 13th century English policy was truly, in the full acceptation of the term, a national policy. It was national both at home and abroad. Hence the striking contrast which it presented through the centuries, the contrast between unrest and intestine conflict at home, and a foreign policy which revealed a continuity of purpose, and a persistence and pertinacity in the execution of that purpose, peculiar to this country, where the enterprises of the Crown were necessarily those of the nation.[1]

This extraordinary strength, which gave such a modern character to the England of the late Middle Ages, was

[1] It should be noted that at the same time Simon de Montfort and the barons compelled the king to sanction the English liberties and to abandon his designs upon Sicily.

something unknown to France. France had another kind of strength, less deeply rooted, but for the moment equally effective, in the incomparable prestige of her king. For what France had become she owed exclusively to the monarchy. It was the monarchy that had liberated her from the particularism of the feudal system, had defended her against external enemies, had protected her nascent cities, and had endowed her with financial and administrative institutions which safeguarded the people against violence and exaction. Against the oppression exercised by an all-powerful dynasty England had created the guarantee of Parliament; against the abuses resulting from the feudal supremacy, France obtained protection from her king. Thus in France the king enjoyed the same popularity which in England was enjoyed by the Parliament. In either country the national sentiment was in harmony with the political constitution, and the two developed simultaneously. In England the distinguishing feature of this national sentiment was pride, a pious respect for the monarchy. It gave each of these two peoples its individual character, its collective temperament, so to speak; the product of its historic evolution, which we shall strangely misconceive if we seek to explain it by that mysterious factor of race which can be made to justify anything because it explains nothing.

Philip (IV) the Fair, who succeeded his father, Philip the Bold, in 1285, made a new addition to the kingdom on ascending the throne. His wife was the heiress of the Kingdom of Navarre, and, what was more important, of the County of Champagne, which was united to the royal domain. With the exception of Guyenne, in the possession of the King of England, Brittany, which had always maintained an independence which was not particularly embarrassing, on account of the outlying position of the country, and Flanders, all the great fiefs had now returned under the direct power of the Crown. Philip the Bold had allowed himself to be dragged by Charles of Anjou into a war of prestige against Aragon. His son made haste to end the war, and took great care not to waste his strength in furthering the Sicilian ambitions of the King of Naples. He kept it

intact for more useful and practical ends. To complete the
kingdom internally by annexing Flanders and Guyenne,
and to continue a vigorous policy of expansion in the east
and the north, to the detriment of the Empire, seems really
to have been the twofold aim of his policy. In this Philip
the Fair continued the tradition of his predecessors. What
distinguished him from them was the method which he employed. Before his reign the king had governed in the midst
of his court, and all the members of his usual entourage
were well acquainted with his affairs. This was no longer
the case under Philip the Fair. With him the old familiar
methods of the palace were replaced by secret intrigues;
he hid himself, so to speak, behind the ministers whom he
employed, dissimulating his influence to such a degree that
people asked, with a certain ingenuousness, whether his
policy was not simply the policy of his agents, and whether
he did not simply allow them to do as they thought fit.
This question might be asked in respect of all modern sovereigns who have not been men of genius, and the fact that
it has preoccupied the historians of Philip's reign is the best
evidence of the innovations which were introduced during
this reign in respect of the exercise of the monarchical
power. The king was henceforth so strong, so certain of
being obeyed, that he could safely confide the most important affairs to men of obscure birth, who had emerged from
the bourgeoisie or the *petite noblesse*, but who were rec-
ommended by their juridical or practical knowledge, while
the mediocrity of their fortune, and their hope of increasing
it in the service of the prince, were sufficient guarantee of
their devotion. It is true that before Philip's reign a certain
number of these new men had already made their way into
the councils of the Crown. Under Philip the Bold Pierre de
la Brosse, at first the king's physician and then his intimate
counsellor, had given great offence, and had ended on the
scaffold a career which was too brilliant to please the court.
But what had been merely an exception now became the
rule. All the men employed in the business of the government, entrusted by Philip the Fair with diplomatic missions, or the manipulation of the finances, were mere "clercs
de loi," like Pierre Flote, Enguerrand de Marigny, and

Guillaume de Nogaret, or Sienese bankers like the two brothers Guidi (Guy). With them a political personnel made its appearance, entirely distinct from the court, deliberating only with the king in private, and its members were the only persons who were in his confidence and were initiated in his designs. They were mere instruments in the hands of their master, who could break them whenever he chose. They knew that they were surrounded by ferocious hatred and that if they fell it might well be to mount the scaffold. Consequently, they contended zealously for the royal favour, and spared no one. Without class prejudices, and hostile to the privileges of the great nobles who despised them, they worked with a will for the establishment of absolutism, and here their conviction was in harmony with their passion for their interest, for the study of Roman law had taught them to perceive the political truth in absolutism. They were dry, abrupt, ironical, pitiless. It was not the king who spoke through them, but the anonymous monarchy, superior to all, subduing all to its power, and they served it with triumphant joy, proud to find the greatest seigneurs eager to solicit their protection and to pass in public for their creatures. It is not astonishing that Philip the Fair's policy, in the hands of such men, should have been characterized by frigid violence and a complete absence of scruples. St. Louis' ideal of justice and charity was replaced by exclusive consideration for the interests of the Crown. As its strength constantly increased, the monarchical power eventually refused to tolerate obstacles, and began to justify the means which it employed by the ends which it elected to pursue.

This at once becomes evident if we briefly consider the intervention of the Crown in the affairs of the Low Countries. Hitherto it had always supported the House of Dampierre against the rival dynasty of Avesnes, and had helped it to extend its influence over Namur, Liége, Guelders and Luxemburg. In this way it set up the power of one of its vassals in those portions of the ancient Lotharingia which were dependent on Germany, and its support of the Count of Flanders against the Count of Hainaut was part of its skilful policy of encroachment at the expense of the Empire. Jean d'Avesnes had vainly attempted to interest Rudolph of Habsburg in his cause. He could obtain nothing from him beyond some futile proclamations against Guy de Dampierre. It was daily becoming more obvious to the princes of the Low Countries that their traditional suzerain could no longer do anything for them, and that in their own interests they would have to seek the friendship of the King of France, by which the Count of Flanders had profited so greatly. Jean d'Avesnes, making a complete *volte face*, ventured to sound the French court. He found it quite prepared to welcome his advances. In 1293, breaking with his past, he definitely took his place among the protégés of the Capet dynasty. In this way Philip the Fair became the ally of the mortal enemy of the House of Flanders, whose suzerain he was, and to whom, according to feudal law, he owed comfort and assistance! But the feudal law was no longer invoked by the Crown except when it furnished the latter with pretexts for its pretensions; it repudiated, in the name of sovereignty, the obligations which this law imposed upon it. It had obtained from the Count of Flanders all the services which he could render it. Now that the vassal princes of the Empire were seeking its alliance, it was useless and even dangerous to increase the count's power in Lotharingia. The moment had come to show him that he was nothing without the support of the king, and to reduce him to the rôle of a mere instrument of the Crown.

The social unrest which was manifested in the Flemish cities from the middle of the 13th century offered the royal policy a fresh occasion to intervene, which it did immediately with extraordinary success. In the great industrial centres of Ghent, Bruges, Ypres, Lille and Douai, the masses of the workers—weavers, fullers, clothworkers, etc.—were inspired by a veritable class hatred of the patricians who constituted the municipal government. They accused the aldermen of administering the affairs of the municipalities to the sole advantage of the wealthy bourgeoisie, of sacrificing the workers to the interests of the rich wool and cloth merchants, and of reducing them to starvation wages. Strikes (*takehans*) had broken out, conspiracies had been discovered, and the exasperation of the people increased as the measures of precaution or defence taken against them were multiplied. In 1280 a general revolt broke out simultaneously in all the Flemish and Walloon cities, leading to veritable street battles in several of them. Guy de Dampierre had taken this opportunity of intervening. Incapable, unassisted, of dealing with the patrician municipalities, which for some time past had openly defied his authority, he adopted an attitude of great benevolence towards the lower orders, in order to induce them to defend his princely prerogatives. Threatened by the alliance between the count and the "vulgar," the patricians immediately sought a protector in the suzerain of their prince, the King of France. Already, in 1275, under the reign of Philip the Bold, the Thirty Nine of Ghent,[2] dismissed by Guy de Dampierre, had appealed to the Parlement of Paris. The Parlement had pronounced an equitable judgement. Convinced of the reality of the abuses of which they were accused, it nonsuited them, without giving its approval to the new organization which the count had set up in the city. But the legists of Philip the Fair had before long to replace the impartiality of the law by the *parti pris* of politics. Since they were guided only by the interest of the Crown, their object was not to try the issue between the count and the patricians, but systematically to support the patricians against the count. Everything possible was done to convince them that they could count absolutely on the king, and the protection accorded them was all the more effective inasmuch as the means to which it resorted were most humiliating to the count. Mere "sergeants" were despatched to the Flemish cities as "guardians," in the name of the Crown; the fleur-de-lys banner was flown from the city belfries, conferring upon them an immunity which enabled them to confront their seigneur and his bailiffs with flat defiance. The arrogant plutocracy which dominated the cities had nothing to fear now that it could take shelter beneath this formidable emblem of the royal power. Henceforth it could laugh at the efforts of the count and the "vulgar." It gloried

[2] Aldermen, representatives of the patriciate who governed the commune.

in the name of *leliaerts* (lily-men) which the people conferred upon it as a term of abuse. To the novel methods
of the pitiless policy now directed against him, Guy de
Dampierre, threatened from without by the alliance of
Philip the Fair with Jean d'Avesnes, and from within by
the king's protectorate over his great cities, could have devised no means of resistance, had not the war which had
just broken out again between France and England inspired
him with the hope of opposing force to force.

Since the beginning of the 13th century the English monarchy, engrossed in the civil commotions from which the
national constitution was one day to emerge, had found itself unable to continue the policy of expansion inaugurated
by Henry II. Amidst the mountains of the west the principality of Wales still maintained its independence, and in
the north the kings of Scotland paid no heed to the vassalage which had been imposed upon them by the great
Plantagenet. Such a state of affairs could not long continue.
The geographical unity of an island makes the introduction
of political unity a natural tendency. Moreover, the English
found the Welsh and the Scots highly dangerous and inconvenient neighbours, and when Edward I resolved to
subjugate them he had the enthusiastic support of the nation. Wales was united to the kingdom in 1284, though it
retained an autonomy of which the title of Prince of Wales,
borne by the heir to the crown, was thenceforth the sym-
bol. The war against the Scots was a more difficult matter.
Despite their diverse origin and their different idioms—
Anglo-Saxon in the Lowlands and Gaelic in the mountains
of the north and west—the Scots were inspired by a common love of independence. When their king John Baliol acknowledged the suzerainty of England and took the oath
of fealty to Edward (1292) their indignation was such that
Baliol was forced to break his oath and to take up arms
against the English. He might perhaps have hesitated if he
had not been encouraged in his attitude by Philip the Fair.
It had seemed to Philip that he ought to take advantage of
the moment when Edward was embroiled with Scotland
in order to strip England of her last continental possessions.
He gave orders for the occupation of Guyenne, and at the

same time concluded a treaty with Baliol, thus inaugurating that policy of alliance between France and Scotland which through all the fluctuations of European history made itself felt at intervals, century after century, uniting the two countries against the common enemy. However, the first results of this policy were unsuccessful. Edward, content with assuming the defensive in Guyenne, concentrated all his forces against Baliol, whom he took prisoner after defeating him at Dunbar (1296), and thereupon the stone on which the kings of Scotland were crowned was removed to Westminster Abbey, where it is to-day. For the time being the kingdom of Scotland had ceased to exist, and was merely an English province.

Edward was now able to deal with France. But an attack delivered by the English forces alone was hardly likely to be successful. He endeavoured to form a coalition against France: such as John Lackland, eighty years earlier, had formed against Philip Augustus. Greatly as the power of the monarchy had declined in Germany, Edward entered into negotiations with Adolphus of Nassau, or, to speak more exactly, hired his services, and induced him to declare war on the pretext that France had recently annexed certain territories of the Empire. But he based his hopes more especially on the princes of the Low Countries; for his plan was to attack France from the north—that is, on the only side which was not protected by natural frontiers. He was especially anxious to obtain the assistance of the Count of Flanders, and here the ground was already prepared for his advance by the harsh measures of Philip the Fair. On January 9th, 1297, Guy de Dampierre sent his challenge of defiance to his suzerain. The war began in June. Adolphus of Nassau, who had merely wanted to make sure of the good pounds sterling of England, did not put in an appearance. Edward disembarked in Flanders, but almost as soon as he had landed a general rebellion broke out in Scotland. From that moment his only anxiety was to withdraw from an expedition from which it was impossible to expect a favourable result. On October 9th he concluded a truce with the King of France, and made haste to grapple with the northern enemy. The threatened clash between the two great Western States was postponed. Guy de Dampierre, abandoned by Edward, who in 1299 signed a definitive peace in which he was not included, was left to confront the French army unaided. It did not take the French long to conquer his county, for its powers of resistance were disorganized by the Leliaerts (May 1300). The old count was treated as a traitorous vassal, and imprisoned, with his sons. Flanders was confiscated, and placed under a royal governor. It seemed that its annexation must soon be followed by that of all the Low Countries. The Count of Hainaut, Jean d'Avesnes, who had become the trusted ally of Philip the Fair, inherited the counties of Holland and Zeeland and inflicted a sorry defeat on the new King of Germany, Albert of Austria, who had advanced as far as Nimeguen in order to occupy the two counties. Already the French were beginning to regard the Rhine as the natural frontier of the kingdom. The power of the Capets had attained its apogee.

2. *The Crisis*

The events which have just been related were the occasion of a crisis which was to strike a deadly blow at the somewhat ill-defined arbitral power over the princes and the peoples which was claimed by the Pope simply because the princes and peoples belonged to the Catholic Church.

Having been on the point of waging war against each other, Philip the Fair and Edward I had vied with each other in the matter of military preparations, and the consequent expenditure. They had both imposed heavy taxes on the estates of the Church, as though they had been making preparations for a Crusade. There was naturally no lack of protests. Rome had been warned of what was happening, and Boniface VIII felt that he must take this opportunity of solemnly reminding the princes of the limits which theology assigns to the temporal powers. The Bull *Clericis laïcos* (February 25th, 1296) strictly prohibited laymen from imposing taxes on the clergy without the consent of the Pope, annulled all dispensations which might have been accorded in this connection, and threatened all transgressors with excommunication. The document was addressed to Christendom in general; neither the King of France nor the King of England was mentioned in the text, but no one could doubt that it was directed against them. As a matter of fact, it contained nothing that departed in any way from the principles constantly proclaimed by the religious authorities. Since the end of the Roman Empire the financial immunities of the clergy had been constantly extended, and for centuries had been considered as natural as its judicial immunities.

In the conflict which was now beginning it was not the Pope but the kings who violated tradition. The rôles allotted were exactly the converse of what they had been during the War of Investitures. Then Henry IV, in conflict with Gregory VII, had played a conservative part, defending his acquired prerogatives against claims that he considered revolutionary. Now it was Boniface VIII who was defending his acquired prerogatives, while the revolutionary claims were made by Philip and Edward. But in the dispute between Henry IV and Gregory VII the issue was debated on religious grounds, and for that very reason public opinion had supported the Pope. The issue between Boniface and the two kings, on the contrary, was debated on political grounds; the sovereign powers of the monarchy, the very existence of the State, and the most obvious interests of the nation were in question, so that this time public opinion, instead of supporting Rome, was bound to turn against the Papacy.

It was evident that the Pope had not expected that his claims would arouse such opposition. His whole course of behaviour goes to show that he was not aware that anything had changed in Europe since the days of Innocent IV and Frederick II, or that France and England, in 1296, were no longer what they had been a hundred years earlier. He had not realized that the prerogatives of the Crown were based on the consent of the peoples, and that the solidarity of the nation was so great, not only among the laymen, but also in the ranks of the clergy, that it was quite capable of defeating any attempt to intervene in the king's affairs, to paralyse his government, and imperil his finances or his military strength, in the name of the privileges of the

Church. If Philip and Edward had been abandoned by their subjects, as the result of religious scruples, or of mere indifference, they could have done nothing but humbly make their submission. What enabled them to triumph was the consciousness that they were supported by the assent of their peoples; that is, they had moral strength on their side, the only thing that could give them the victory in a conflict of this nature.

Neither king saw fit to discuss the matter. Edward regarded the Bull as null and void, and continued to levy the prohibited taxes. Philip took measures calculated to show the Pope how dangerous it was to meddle in his affairs: since his financial resources were threatened, he himself threatened the finances of the Pope. He prohibited the export, beyond the frontiers of the kingdom, of monies or letters of credit. Immediately all the revenues which the Papacy drew from France, and all those that were conveyed through France by the medium of the Pope's Italian bankers, were interrupted. The greater the Pope's need of money, the more highly developed his fiscal organization, the more overwhelming was such a blow. A century earlier such a counter-stroke would have been impossible, for the means of delivering it were lacking. But the arm of the French monarchy was now so long, and its administration so complete and well-disciplined, that the order was punctually obeyed. The State, being attacked, defended itself with its own weapons, and Europe witnessed the novel spectacle of a sovereign resisting the orders of Rome and opposing them by simple administrative measure. The thing was so unexpected that Boniface VIII did not know where to turn. His intervention in the Sicilian war, and the revolt of the Colonna in his own States, meant that he was in pressing need of money. Above all, France must open her frontiers. Before she would consent to do so he had to resign himself to making advances to the king which must have been very painful to a man of his arrogant nature. Without retracting the Bull he modified it to such an extent that it had no practical importance, and the canonization of St. Louis, pronounced in 1297, might be accepted as an act of homage to the House of France. The incident was hardly closed when another dilemma arose. Like his predecessors, Boniface VIII cherished the hope of uniting Europe in a new Crusade. Since the war between France and England, the two most powerful States of the West, rendered such an enterprise unrealizable, he offered his services as mediator to the belligerents. Out of respect for their susceptibilities it was understood that this was a purely private proceeding on his part. However, since peace was solemnly promulgated in a Bull, Philip regarded the latter as an encroachment upon his sovereign prerogatives and an affirmation of the temporal supremacy of the Papacy over his crown. He immediately gave expression to his resentment by openly giving his support to the Colonna.

Just as the situation was becoming intolerably strained, preparations were made for the great jubilee of the year 1300. This was the first solemnity of the kind that Europe had ever seen, and it was an incomparable triumph for the Pope. From all parts of Christendom the faithful flocked to Rome in their thousands and hundreds of thousands (it was said that they numbered two hundred thousand), to obtain the indulgences accorded to those who visited the tomb of the Apostles. The homage and veneration and affection which these enthusiastic masses lavished on Boniface VIII intoxicated him with pride. He forgot the misadventures of the last few years; and the spectacle of so many pilgrims prostrate at his feet deluded him into the belief that the kings and the peoples were equally ready to obey his orders. He was soon forced to realize that the sincerity of their religious fervour and their devotion to the Church were not so great as to induce them to sacrifice their independence and their dignity.

Edward I, taking advantage of his peace with Philip, had once more marched against the Scots. The Scots having appealed to Rome, Boniface VIII intervened, accusing Edward of violence and injustice, and claiming the right to judge between the two parties. He had addressed himself only to the king; the king decided to address himself to the nation, and in January 1301 Parliament was convoked and required to pronounce upon the Papal claims. Thus, this famous question of the temporal sovereignty and its limits, which had hitherto been discussed only by hermits, theologians, and legists, was now to be considered by the mandatories of a whole people. Their response was a categorical affirmation of the sovereign rights of the Crown. Prelates, barons, knights and burgesses were equally indignant with the Pope's interference in a war which was thoroughly popular, and which had been gloriously terminated by the battle of Falkirk (July 22nd, 1298). "Never," they replied, "shall we suffer that our king should submit to such unheard-of demands!"

Boniface ignored these words. At the moment when they were reported to him his relations with France had assumed such a serious character that he could not run the risk of complicating them by a quarrel with England. At the request of the Archbishop of Narbonne, who complained of the confiscation of certain fiefs which he claimed were held from his Church, the Pope had sent to Paris, as legate, the Bishop of Pamiers, Bernard Saisset. The arrogant language of the legate had offended the king. He concealed his indignation, and allowed the bishop to report on the result of his mission in Rome; and then, shortly after he had returned to his diocese, the king had him arrested, and accused, by Pierre Flote, his Chancellor, of *lèse-majesté*, rebellion, heresy, blasphemy and simony. An assembly of prelates and doctors having found him guilty, the Pope was requested to deprive him of his episcopal functions.

The Pope's reply to these proceedings was to demand the immediate liberation of Saisset, and to revive the prohibition which forbade the taxation of Church property, while he convoked an assembly of the French clergy in Rome, to deliberate with him upon the means of rebuking the king. At the same time he personally addressed the king in the Bull *Ausculta fili*, in which he reminded him that God had placed the successor of St. Peter over the heads of princes and States. "For this reason," said the Pope, "give no credit to those who would persuade thee that thou hast no superior. Who thinks thus deceives himself, and he who persists in this error is an infidel." Innocent III would not have spoken otherwise, and St. Thomas Aquinas, some

fifty years earlier, had expounded at length the theory
by which these words were inspired. But this time they
evoked the most passionate contradiction in the ranks of
the jurists and doctors. Pierre Dubois and Jean de Paris,
the author of the *Dialogue entre un clerc et un chevalier*,
repudiated with indignation the Pope's claim to intervene
in temporal questions. According to them, his competence
extended only to purely religious matters. They even went
so far as to debate the legitimacy of his Roman sovereignty,
and one of them (Jean de Paris) attributed the decadence
of the Church to the Donation of Constantine! Frederick II
and Pierre de la Vigne had already said almost the same
thing. These discussions, however, interested only the
learned, and the crisis would not have been very serious if
it had been restricted to a battle of pamphlets. But Philip,
like Edward a year earlier, and doubtless inspired by his
example, resolved that his quarrel should be the quarrel of
his people. France had no parliament. Never yet had the
delegates of the whole nation been convoked to advise the
Crown. This great debate, in which the very principle of
the king's sovereignty was at stake, was the occasion of the
first assembly of the States-General: the first, and a worthy,
example of those assemblies of which the last, five hundred
years later, was to proclaim the Rights of Man and in-
augurate the Revolution.

The delegates of the clergy, the noblesse and the bourgeoisie assembled at Notre-Dame de Paris on April 10th,
1302. Opinion had been adroitly manipulated by manœu-
vres which clearly revealed the spirit of the government to
which all means were lawful if they were successful. False
Bulls, insulting the king, and a false reply, insulting the
Pope, had been widely distributed: crude methods, but
characteristic of the period when policy was beginning to
feel the need of appealing to the support of public opinion.
Pierre Flote expounded the point in dispute before the
States. All the delegates, clergy and laymen alike, enthusiastically declared their approval of the king's attitude.
The clergy couched their reply to the Pope in the Latin
tongue; the other two orders replied to the cardinal in
French.

From this moment the Pope's was a lost cause. The States-General decided the question of sovereignty in favour of the Crown—that is, in favour of the State—and their verdict was delivered with much greater emphasis than that of the English Parliament of the preceding year. It was enough that a national assembly had spoken its mind; the result was attained for which the Emperors had striven through two centuries of exhausting campaigns, which had drenched Germany and Italy in blood. To the brutal force of the Germanic Caesars Rome, of old, had victoriously opposed her moral force; her resistance to their attempts to secure universal dominion had rallied the nations to her cause, and Italy, by joining her in her resistance to the Hohenstaufens, had at the same time fought for her own liberty. To-day the ancient allies of Rome were deserting her because she in her turn was threatening their liberty and independence. In Germany there was no solidarity between the people and the policy of the Emperors, but the whole of the French people was behind the policy of its king. What was to be done with this declaration of war on the part of a whole people? To whom could the Pope appeal? To England? But in this particular France's quarrel was also that of England. What was more, it was that of all the nations. For unlike the Emperors, France did not propose to offer violence to the Papacy or to oppress it to her own advantage; she merely demanded that the Papacy should not arrogate to itself the right of intervention in her government; she was threatening no one; she laid claim to nothing but her own temporal autonomy, and every State, in its own interests, was bound to hope for her success. Boniface VIII consequently found himself isolated. By the irony of history, not knowing where to turn, he appealed to the King of Germany, Albert of Austria, whose election he had hitherto refused to recognize; and now, in his necessity, extolling that Imperial majesty which his predecessors had so sorely humiliated, he reminded Albert that the Empire enjoyed primacy over all kingdoms, "and that the French lied in saying that they had no superior, since they were in law subordinate to the Emperor." The Bull *Unam sanctam,* which he published on November 18th, 1302, was

Rome's last solemn affirmation of her primacy over the temporal power. It contains a long exposition of the traditional theory of the two swords, and the subordination of all princes to the successor of St. Peter, *ratione peccati*.

Thus the contradictory claims of Church and State were in absolute conflict. And there matters might have rested. For the declaration of principles contained in the Bull was henceforth merely a harmless manifestation. But Philip the Fair had determined to overthrow his adversary. It was in his power to employ a terrible weapon against him. And it was not his policy to spare the enemy.

The Pope's personal situation in respect of the king was indeed most unfavourable. The king's orthodoxy was so complete and so evident that it was impossible to launch against him the formidable accusation of heresy which had been brought against Frederick II. On religious grounds his position was unshakable, and the Pope's was not. The election of Boniface, which had taken place during the lifetime of his predecessor, and thanks to the abdication of the latter, had been so singular that his enemies had not failed to invoke it, long ago, as a reason for regarding it as null and void. The Colonna kept on repeating that the Pope was merely an intruder, and it was so much in Philip's interest that he should be an intruder that the king was quite willing to believe, or to pretend that he believed, that the Colonna were right. In June 1303 a fresh assembly of the States-General approved of his intention to submit the question to a general Council. This was a good beginning, and the partisans of the Crown were careful not to let the matter drop. The University of Paris, and many of the monasteries and cities, vied with one another in demanding the Council, while the government canvassed the foreign States in favour of this project.

However, Nogaret was sent to Italy in order to get into touch with the Colonna, seize the person of the Pope, and if possible force him to abdicate. On August 15th he took him by surprise at Anagni. Violence had no effect on the old man. Threatened with death by the Colonna, he remained immovable, confronting his furious captors with proud majesty, and remaining worthy of himself even in calamity.

But this last blow had shattered him. Liberated by a popular rising, he returned to Rome only to die there, on October 12th, 1303.

The problem was not solved by his death. The king's appeal to the Council was felt as a threat by his successor. Benedict XI (1303–1304) did not live long enough to solve this distressing problem. Clement V (1305–1314) avoided it only by involving the Papacy in a crisis which finally destroyed the incomparable prestige which it had enjoyed in the 13th century.

His election, to which the cardinals resigned themselves only after eleven months of deliberation, was in itself a signal defiance of Boniface's contention. For the new Pope was a Frenchman, and in electing him the Conclave had submitted to the will of Philip. It very soon realized that it had placed on the throne of St. Peter a pontiff who was incapable of forgetting that he was born a subject of the King of France. Clement V was not content with filling the Sacred College with the relatives and protégés of his sovereign; impressed with the pre-eminence which his country had acquired in Europe, he was insensible to the majesty of Rome, and to the tradition of twelve hundred years which had made the city of the Emperors the city of the Popes. For this Frenchman *aurea Roma* was merely a city like other cities, with an unhealthy climate and a dangerous and fickle population; no doubt he thought it greatly inferior to Paris. Was not the Papacy wherever the Pope might be? What did it matter whether he lived in the Lateran and pontificated in St. Peter's? Clement V took up his residence in Avignon, and there his successors remained until 1378. Avignon, of course, was a possession of the Roman Church. But surrounded as it was by the domain of the King of France it was actually in France, and the outer world was not deluded. In deserting the banks of the Tiber for those of the Rhone, the Popes derogated from the position which they had occupied for the past century, between God and the kings, and degraded themselves, if not always in fact, yet at least in appearance, to the rank of protégés and instruments of the French Crown. This was the final consequence of the policy of Boniface VIII! What mattered henceforth the attacks made upon his memory? For some years Philip continued to intimidate the Pope. Having forced him, in 1312, to pronounce sentence against the Templars, whose wealth he coveted, he spoke no more of the matter. What remained henceforth of the arrogant declarations of the Bull *Unam sanctam,* and what likelihood was there that the Popes, when in future they addressed the kings of France, should ever again adopt such a tone? It is true that the propositions contained in the Bull still held good. In theory the claims of the Papacy had never been refuted. In reality they were merely harmless declamations; at all events, as far as France was concerned. And this was all that Philip required. In politics the practical result is all that need be considered, and this had been more decisive, and, above all, more rapidly achieved than anyone would have ventured to hope. In the clash between the Church and the National State the latter had shown itself the stronger. The Papacy was tottering, in its turn, on the ruins of the Imperial power which it had overthrown. It was almost as though in leaving Rome for Avignon it had endeavoured to conceal its humiliation by seeking a less conspicuous stage.

Thus the 13th century saw both the apogee of the Papal power and its decline. At the very moment when, triumphing over the Empire, it believed itself in a position to assume control over Europe, to unite the Continent against Islam, and to impose its tutelage on all the peoples, the economic and political transformations which had taken place, almost unnoticed by Rome, rendered the realization of the Papal designs impossible. The lofty ideal which the Papacy had conceived in a period of agricultural and feudal civilization no longer responded to the social realities. Faith was no less ardent and no less general than of old, while the discipline of the Church was enforced more completely than ever before. But the Crusade was now regarded merely as an impossible chimera, while the progress of trade and of urban life had profoundly modified men's habits and their way of life. At the same time, the constitution, in France and England, of national States, which could not subsist without an autonomous administration and an independent policy, was bound to end in the conflict which was so disastrous to Boniface VIII. And yet, during the brief reign of St. Louis, it had been possible to realize the Christian policy. This was the greatest moment of the 13th century, a moment of calm in the continual tempest into which the tumultuous forces of life were sweeping humanity.

BOOK TWO

The European Crisis

(1300–1450)

*The Avignon Papacy, the Great Schism, and the
Hundred Years' War*

CHAPTER I

General Characteristics of the Period

1. *Social and Economic Tendencies*

Nothing more involved and bewildering and more full of contrasts can be imagined than the period extending from the beginning of the 14th to about the middle of the 15th century. The whole of European society, from the depths to the surface, was as though in a state of fermentation. While the Church, harassed to begin with by its exile in Avignon, and then by the Great Schism, and finally by the quarrels of the Popes and the Council, was shaken by convulsive movements, of which the heresies of Wycliffe and Huss were the most formidable manifestations—while France and England were at war—while the Empire was finally disintegrating amidst the quarrels of the rival houses contending for the crown of Germany—while in Italy, more dismembered than ever, every type of State and every imaginable policy might be observed—while the Slav States were reacting to the German advance, and repulsing it—while the Turks, profiting by the intestine quarrels of the West, were invading the Balkan peninsula, and were soon to seize Constantinople, the peoples were perturbed by social insurrections, excited by the hasty quarrels of the parties, or the prey of a general unrest which sometimes found expression in tentative reforms, and sometimes by the oppression of the weaker classes by the more powerful. A spirit of restlessness was abroad, affecting men's minds as well as their policies; even religion was not immune; it was a restlessness that almost amounted to mental confusion. The world was suffering and struggling, but it was hardly advancing. For the only thing of which it was clearly conscious was the fact that all was not well with it. It longed to escape from its ills, but it did not know how it could do so. No one had anything to offer in the place of the tradition that weighed upon it and from which it could not liberate itself. Though they were badly shaken, the old ideals still survived; one finds them everywhere, modified, no doubt, or impaired, but still unchanged in any essential. In their fundamental characteristics the Church, the State, and the social and economic constitution remained, throughout these hundred and fifty years, what they had been at the close of the 13th century. The same may be said of art and science. Gothic architecture and the Scholastic philosophy still had enough vitality to produce interesting work, but the period of their masterpieces was past. Everywhere the world was in labour, but it produced only abortive births. There was a definite feeling abroad that it was waiting for a spiritual renewal. But the dawn was slow in coming, though here and there a gleam was visible. The men of this period were restless, nervous, melancholy. Not one of them achieved true greatness. Compare John XXII or Clement VII with Innocent III or Boniface VIII; Charles V with St. Louis, Charles IV with Frederick II! These, no doubt, were singular or attractive personalities, but personalities of the second class, not one of whom could be regarded as the embodiment of his age, for the thing most conspicuously lacking in this period of instability was a really specific character, an ideal which might inspire it and which it might strive to attain.

What is really new about this period, what strikes one immediately upon a general survey, is its revolutionary tendencies. They were nowhere triumphant, but they were felt in every department of life. The State and the Church were no more secure against them than was society. All the traditional authorities were criticized and assailed: the popes and kings no less than the landowners and the capitalists. The great masses of the people, who had hitherto endured or supported the power of the State, were now rebelling against it. No previous epoch had ever furnished so many names of tribunes, demagogues, agitators, and reformers. But there was no coherence in all this unrest, and no continuity. There were numerous and violent crises, but they were dispersed and of brief duration; the symptoms of a social unrest which was felt more acutely in some regions than in others, and which, according to the region, expressed itself in different ways. If we wish to realize the progress and the extent of this unrest, we must look for it, first of all, in the simplest and most general phenomena of social life—that is, in phenomena of an economic order.

But here we shall discover no essential novelty, nothing to be compared with the effect of the revival of trade and the rise of the cities.

The frontiers of Europe had not been extended since the foundation of the Italian settlements in the East, and of the German cities on the Baltic; and there had been no further increase of population since the end of the 13th century and the first part of the 14th.

Venice in the South and Bruges in the North remained the two busiest commercial centres: Venice as the point of contact between East and West, and Bruges the connecting link between the trade of the North and that of Italy. The Germans of the South had their "fondaco" in Venice, just as the Germanic Hansa had its factory in Bruges.

In Italy a true system of capitalism was evolving, though it was hampered by the more and more restricted economic demands of the cities.

The towns engaged in the Flemish weaving industry in the North, and Florence in the South, were still, as in the 13th century, the two great centres of industry and the export trade. Cotton was only beginning to make its appearance. No technical progress was manifested. Machinery and methods were still very much what they were in the days of ancient Egypt. The curing of herrings, first introduced in Holland, during the 14th century, seems to have been the only novelty of any importance to be recorded.

It is true that the circulation of men and goods had undergone some development. While the roads were still generally defective navigation was increasing in importance: larger ships were built, and they made longer voyages. From the beginning of the 14th century the galleys of Venice and Genoa made their way to Bruges and to London. On the Atlantic coast the Basques and the Bretons maintained an active coastal trade. The cogs of the Hansa cities sailed to all parts of the North Sea and the Baltic. Holland and England were so far interested only in local navigation.

The circulation of money was even more noticeable than that of manufactured and other products. This explains why, from the end of the 14th century, gold coins were regularly struck in France, Flanders, Poland and Hungary. Under the influence of the Italian merchants, who had already brought it to a high pitch of perfection in the 13th century, the minting of money was undergoing still further improvement.

The bill of exchange with acceptance made its appearance in the first half of the 14th century. Pegolotti wrote the *Practica della Mercatura*. Book-keeping by double entry seems to date back to 1394. But however notable these improvements may have been, they were not enough to constitute the point of departure of a new era of economic history. They undoubtedly betray a tendency toward the development of capitalism and the improvement of trade and commerce, yet if we consider the period as a whole we shall readily perceive that one of its most obvious characteristics was its hostility to capitalism, except in Italy.

The explanation of this must be sought in the evolution of the bourgeoisie; that is to say, of the class responsible for the entire commercial and industrial activity of Europe. Apart from very rare exceptions, of which the most conspicuous was Venice, from the end of the 13th century, the preponderance of the patricians in the cities was replaced, more or less completely, by that of the handicrafts, trades and professions.

Even if the artisans could not obtain political control of the local government, they could at least influence the organization of the municipal economy. This means that from being under the control of the great merchants it came under that of the small producers, and that henceforth the spirit which inspired it underwent a corresponding change.

In the beginning, the guilds or trade fraternities were free associations of artisans following the same calling, who combined for the defence of their common interests. As far as their aims were concerned, they could quite accurately be compared with the voluntary syndicates or trade unions of our own days; their most important function was to regulate competition. Every newcomer, under penalty of ostracism, had to affiliate himself to a guild. It will be understood that in the beginning such a situation must have given rise to disputes and conflicts between the syndicated confraternities and those recalcitrant workers who refused to sacrifice their liberty. The municipal authorities were as much concerned as the artisans themselves to make an end to such disturbances. In order to do so, they only had to give the trade organizations a legal status: or in other words, to transform them from voluntary into obligatory syndicates recognized by the communal authority. The oldest examples of this transformation date back to the 12th century; by the beginning of the 14th century it was general, and as the same causes everywhere produced the same result it took place all over Europe. Henceforth, in every city, each trade was the monopoly of a privileged group of masters. Only those could exercise it who had been officially admitted as members of the group. In its main features the organization was everywhere identical. Between the French *corps de métier*, the Flemish *ambacht*, the English "craft," the Italian *arte* and the German *Zunft* there were only superficial differences, due to the differences of national customs, or the degrees of autonomy which the corporation enjoyed in respect of the urban power. Among the Germanic as among the Latin peoples its nature was the same. Here again, as in all the fundamental phenomena of European life, the national element was expressed only in externals; the essential phenomenon was the consequence of necessities to which, under the same circumstances, human nature is everywhere subject.

Everywhere the trade corporation had its chiefs (deans, syndics, *vinders*, etc.), who were clothed with official authority; everywhere it drew up professional regulations and saw to it that they were observed; everywhere it enjoyed the right of assembly; everywhere it constituted a moral personality, having a treasury and common premises, and everywhere the hierarchy of its members was the same. The craftsman entered the guild or corporation as apprentice, was promoted to the rank of journeyman, and finally became a master.

Generally speaking, we must envisage the master as the head and proprietor of a workshop, in which were employed, under his orders, one or two journeymen, and an apprentice. In him we have the most perfect type of the artisan—that is to say, the small producer working in his own home. The raw material which he elaborated was his own property, and he sold the finished product at his own exclusive profit. The consumers on whom his livelihood depended were the burgesses of the city and the peasants of the surrounding countryside. The petty character of his industry and the small amount of capital involved were thus in proportion to the restricted nature of his market. If he was to live at all he had to be protected against competition; not only the external competition of the foreigner, but also the local competition of his fellow-craftsmen. To prevent such competition was the first object of the corporation. In order to assure the independence of the masters it restricted their liberty, subjecting it to curious regulations. The economic subordination of each member guaranteed the security of all; hence the circumstantial prescriptions by which the artisan was encompassed. He was forbidden to sell his wares at a price below the tariff fixed by the regulations; he was forbidden to work by artificial light; he must not use tools of unusual form, or modify the traditional technique, or employ more journeymen or apprentices than his neighbours, or allow his wife to work, or such children as were not of age; and lastly—and this prohibition was absolute—he must not advertise his wares or praise them to the detriment of those produced by others. Thus each worker was given his place in the sun, but it was a place very strictly delimited, and it was quite impossible for him to emerge from it.[1] But no one ever dreamed of doing so. For when a man's livelihood is secure his desires are moderate. The corporations provided the *petite bourgeoisie* with a framework admirably adapted to its character. Without a doubt, it had never been so happy and contented as under their régime. For this class, but for this class alone, they had solved the social problem. By safeguarding it against competition they also protected it against the intervention of capitalism. Until the French Revolution the craftsmen and petty manufacturers were obstinately faithful to the corporations that so well safeguarded their interests. Few economic institutions have been so tenacious.

The first half of the 14th century was the period when the handicrafts attained their apogee. But as they evolved, the two essential features of their constitution—monopoly and privilege—naturally became more and more prominent. Each group of artisans racked its brains to increase, and to go on increasing, the protectionism that surrounded it like the walls of a fortress. The admission of new members was made more difficult; apprenticeship became more protracted and more exacting; promotion to the rank of master became more costly, so that the poor journeyman could hardly hope to achieve it. A sort of industrial Malthusianism began to make its appearance, which surrendered the local market to a small number of masters, and the absence of competition among them simply meant that the consumer was exploited. The sudden check in the increase of the urban population which was a general phenomenon about the year 1350 was undoubtedly due to this corporative exclusivism, which was gradually making it impossible for people to leave the country and establish themselves in the cities. But in the cities themselves, in the ranks of the bourgeoisie, what complaints and protests were heard! What indignant reproaches were bandied about be-

---

[1] Capitalism is not in itself opposed to the tendencies of human nature, but its restriction is. Economic liberty is spontaneous. The trade corporation suppresses liberty because it threatens the majority. It presupposes, of course, that this majority exercises political power.

tween the different trades, each condemning in the others
the excesses of the monopoly which it felt to be justifiable
in its own case alone! At the same time, the original spirit
of fraternity was replaced, among the craftsmen, by an
increasing opposition of interests between the masters and
the journeymen, who were more and more reduced to the
status of mere wage-earners. Riots broke out; there were
strikes; and in many regions "compagnonnages" of journeymen were formed, mutual associations of workers organized
to defend their interests against the employers. In short,
from the beginning of the 15th century the abuses of the
system were so evident that there were those who demanded the abolition of the corporations and the liberty
of the handicrafts.

The situation was much more serious in those cities
which were the centres of the textile industry, such as Florence in the South and the Flemish and Brabançon cities
in the North, which carried on a regular export industry.
The kind of trade organization which was suitable for
craftsmen whose livelihood depended on the local markets
was obviously unable to satisfy the needs of workers engaged in mass production for an unrestricted market. It
could not possibly afford protection against the influence
of capital to the weavers, fullers and clothworkers, masters
or journeymen, who crowded the lanes and alleys of Gand,
Bruges, and Ypres, or the *vicoli* on the banks of the Arno.
Here the artisan was necessarily subordinated to the rich
merchant who provided him with wool, and to whom the
manufactured product was delivered after the various ma-
nipulations which it had to undergo. As to its external form,
the cloth trade presented the same aspect as the other
trades; here, as elsewhere, the home industry was predominant. But in this case the employer himself was merely
a wage-earner employing other wage-earners. Further, the
workers in the cloth trade, instead of numbering only a
few dozen or a few score, as in the trades which provided
the bourgeoisie with the necessities of life, numbered hundreds and even thousands. But the great industry which
employed all these workers was subject to crises. If a war
broke out, if the export of English wool was forbidden,

unemployment supervened, with all its miseries. Even in normal times there were incessant disputes as to wages, whether between the merchant-manufacturers and the heads of weaving-sheds or workshops, or between the latter and their journeymen. Thus, the condition of the workers in the cloth industry in those cities where the industry provided the basis of a considerable export trade was very like that of the modern proletariat. And they were an organized proletariat. For, like the artisans properly so called, they were grouped together in corporations; and although the incredible demands of wholesale trade prevented them from ruling the market and regulating prices and wages, these corporations did at least enable them to oppose too excessive exploitation and to provide for mutual aid in times of crisis.

The political result of these corporative organizations was naturally to wrest the government of the cities from the patrician oligarchies who were in power in the 13th century. It was no longer possible for a few "lineages" of landowners and merchants, sitting in the city council, to do precisely what they chose in the matter of regulating trade and commerce, and assessing taxes and personal contributions, etc. They did not surrender their position without resistance. Their government had been, in the full force of the term, a class government, and they obstinately clung to their privileged position. The whole of the 14th century was filled with the conflict of the *grandi* and the *piccoli* for the possession of municipal power. It is natural to compare these conflicts with those which were provoked in the 19th century by the question of the parliamentary franchise. In each case the masses, refused the right to manage their own affairs, persisted in their demands. The fundamental cause of the two crises was the same. However different men's manners, sentiments and ideas may have been, what the patricians were defending against the claims of the handicrafts was the same preponderance which the property-owners' Parliaments of our own time defended so long and so obstinately against the demand for universal suffrage. The whole of the 14th century, like the whole of the 19th, was shaken by the struggles of democracy. The democracy of our days, however, takes the form of a régime which safeguards the political rights of every citizen. In those petty States, the cities of the Middle Ages, the conception of democracy was proportionately restricted; it was as narrow as the limits of the city, and it could not have been otherwise. Society was too subdivided, subject to too many clashes, too localized to permit of the emergence of the concept of general liberty. The city was a little enclosed world, living for itself, indifferent to the feelings and the interests of classes which were alien to it. The artisan was as strictly bourgeois as the patrician, and quite as exclusive in his feelings toward all who did not inhabit his commune. He knew nothing of the levelling spirit of proselytism, as indifferent to local groups as it is to juridical classes, which the spectacle of the modern democracies has accustomed us to regard as inherent in any popular régime. Fundamentally, democracy as he conceived it was merely a democracy of privileged individuals, since the bourgeoisie itself, as compared with the inhabitants of the countryside, was a privileged class.

However, the pure democratic régime was triumphant in only a few cities. In most cases some sort of compromise was arrived at. The patriciate, voluntarily, or under pressure from the mob, made way for the corporations, and constitutions came into force of which we may say, despite innumerable differences of detail, that they organized a sort of representation of interests. Once the opposing interests had achieved equilibrium, these constitutions, as a general thing, became congealed into fixity. It is certainly a fact that urban legislation was much more active and more fertile of innovation in the 13th than in the 14th century. These democracies of privileged *petits bourgeois* were characterized by egoism and protectionism. Urban politics became even more exclusive than before where, as in France and in England, it was not compelled to reckon with the State. Its aim was the achievement of complete political liberty, of the free city, as it already existed in Germany. Economic progress was naturally affected by such a programme. Capital, encompassed by suspicious and fumbling legislation, could develop only beyond its control, in the domain of inter-urban trade. Here men still made their fortunes, though less frequently than in the previous century. The local patriciate no longer played a part in the development of capitalism, and became a class of *rentiers*. By the side of the patriciate new men were making their appearance, who taxed their ingenuity to evade the regulations of protectionism; but it will be time to consider their activities in our survey of the following period.

However, all the cities were not of the same type, nor were they inspired by the same spirit. They were not all controlled by the *petite bourgeoisie*, and where the export industry produced a proletariat they offered a very different spectacle. In Italy, the upheavals of the Florentine democracy afford a striking example of this difference. In Florence the system of trade corporations could not establish itself as readily as elsewhere. The workers in the woollen industry and other manufactures for export were too numerous; and special provision had to be made for them. As a matter of fact, from 1282 onwards the *nobili* were excluded from the government of Florence by the constitution, which confided the power of government to six *priori delle arte*, chosen from among the twelve great corporations, one for each of the six wards of the city; and they were changed every two months. This was a government of merchants and manufacturers, a government of the *popolo grasso*. But the *popolo minuto* was socially oppressed. In 1341 it supported Gauthier de Brienne, who overthrew the ruling plutocrats and set himself up as tyrant. Two years later he was overthrown in his turn. The *popolo grasso* then returned to power, but was violently expelled in 1378 by the democratic revolt of the *Ciompi*,[2] led by the guilds of the wool-carders, but it once more returned to power in 1382.

The same sort of thing happened in the Flemish cities. From the beginning of the 13th century the weavers and the fullers had been complaining of the oppressive government of the patriciate. The patriciate looked to France for support, and the battle of Courtrai was in reality a social

[2] The name given to the inferior guilds in Florence.

victory for the artisans. But the new régime, which depended on the support of the wool-carders, was unable to hold its own; inevitably the merchants came to the top again. And so, during the whole of the 14th century, there was a series of convulsions and upheavals. The workers had vague dreams of an impossible communism. There were Flemish workers among the followers of Wat Tyler, as there were later among the Hussites, and in the sect of the Adamites. Gand, above all, where the weavers were in greater strength than anywhere else, was distinguished by its sullen violence. Under Louis de Maele their audacity reached its height. For six years, despite amazing vicissitudes, they held their own against the prince, the nobles, and all "good folk who had anything to lose." From all parts of Europe the suffering proletarians fixed their gaze upon Gand. There were cries of "Vive Gand" in Paris and Rouen. It was felt that they were threatening the entire social order, and at Roosebeke (1382) the King of France inflicted upon them a terrible defeat. The weavers of Gand were certainly the most ardent protagonists of democracy to make their appearance in the 14th century. But all their energy could achieve nothing. It was impossible for them to escape from the capitalism under which they suffered. The factors which gave rise to that capitalism were beyond their reach. Constantly rebelling, they were constantly defeated. The other trades turned against them. The fullers, who were even poorer, and whom they oppressed, made common cause with their enemies. The result of their efforts was to make the merchants and businessmen look to the princes for support, and to take steps to remove the industry from the cities to the countryside.

While these internal commotions or transformations were occurring within the cities, they were acquiring a political importance in the outer world which they had never before possessed, and which, as a matter of fact, they had never sought. The increasing expenditure which war imposed upon the State or the princes compelled the latter to find some new means of replenishing their treasuries; for now that bands of mercenaries and fleets were playing a greater part in warfare, it was becoming more costly than ever.

The old sources of revenue were insufficient. It was possible to borrow from the Italian bankers. And the princes did raise money from them, but this involved them in onerous obligations. It was possible to debase the currency, but this again was a dangerous expedient. To decree a fresh impost was not possible; at the most, fresh *tonlieux* could be imposed. There was no financial absolutism about the juridical State of the Middle Ages. Consequently, the only thing to be done was to apply to the Third Estate—that is, to the cities—and to ask them to open their purses. They were willing enough to do so, but they demanded guarantees. The State knew only how to spend; it did not yet understand how to create resources for itself. It was completely dependent on taxation, and a taxation that was a drain on its wealth. From the beginning of the 14th century the necessity of taxation dominated the prince's policy, and compelled him to accede to the demands of the cities and the Estates, which wrested privileges from him, and would presently even claim the right to participate in his power; in the Duchy of Brabant the Charter of Cortenberg, the Walloon Charter, and finally the Joyous Entry; in the Pays de Liége, the Peace of Fexhe, and in the County of Flanders, the Constitution of the Members of Flanders, all originated in this way; and in France the same predicament provoked the disturbances of the epoch of Étienne Marcel. The States-General of 1355 attempted to restrict the rights of the Crown; in 1413 the Ordonnance Cabochienne was forced upon the king by the trade corporations of Paris; and in England the parliamentary influence of the cities was constantly increasing. The 15th century was the epoch in which the bourgeoisie began to play a political as well as a class rôle. It took its place beside the clergy and the *noblesse*.[3] In Aragon too, under Pedro IV (1336–1387), the cities began to impose their will on the Crown. That taxation came from the cities was evident in Spain, where, under Alphonso XI of Castile (1312–1358), the war against the Moors compelled Burgos

[3] It was in the 14th century that the financiers began to acquire political importance.

to introduce the *alcabala*, which was then extended to cover the whole kingdom.

The financial needs of the princes made the 14th century a century of parliamentarianism, or shall we say, a century of Estates. In Belgium there were annual assemblies of the Estates in all the provinces. In France they insisted on meeting despite the opposition of the Crown. And every assembly of Estates was always to the advantage of the Third Estate. It was the Third Estate alone which supported the institution and profited by it, because it disposed of the finances. And it was the Third Estate alone which made conditions and demanded guarantees.

But the Third Estate was itself merely a class of privileged persons, and beneath it was the majority of the nation, the Fourth Estate, which was never mentioned, though it bore the burden. Undoubtedly its condition was much less tolerable after the 14th century than it had been for two hundred years. We have seen how the rise of the cities, by unsettling the economic status of the countryside, shattered the domainal system, releasing great expanses of territory and great numbers of the rural inhabitants. At that time the rural classes gave evidence of unusual energy. They cleared uncultivated ground, they emigrated, and yet the population was rapidly increasing. But there was an end to all this during the first half of the century. Emigration no longer offered an outlet; the available land was occupied (in Eastern Germany), and the cities were closing their gates. Meanwhile taxation was heavier than ever and was still increasing. Moreover, there was a surplus of workers, so that the situation of the peasants was most unfavourable. The nobles took advantage of this, endeavouring to re-establish their old feudal rights, and, in a general manner, to exploit the peasants, for the old patriarchal relations of the domainal epoch no longer existed. In maritime Flanders a terrible rebellion broke out, which lasted from 1324 to 1328. The peasants hunted the chevaliers, and refused to pay their tithes. A true social hatred finds expression in the *Kerelslied*. This terrible rising ended in the massacre of Cassel, and in wholesale confiscations. In France, the so-called revolt of the Jacques in 1357—which, I admit, may have been partly the result of the sufferings caused by the war—gave evidence of a profound hostility between the rural masses and the noblesse, which must have had causes of a more general kind. The English rebellion of 1381, which is that concerning which we are best informed, was due to attempts on the part of the nobles to re-establish the old *corvées*, in order to avoid paying the higher wages which were one of the consequences of the Black Death. In Germany we shall find no popular movement of this kind until the beginning of the 16th century. However, since the end of the 14th century the condition of the peasants had been growing visibly worse; especially, it seems, in the South. The nobles took advantage of their need of land in order to oppress them.[4]

Generally speaking, people began to despise the peasant as a helot who stood outside society. There were no more charters of rural franchises in the 14th century, except in a few new countries, such as Northern Holland. The cities, too, oppressed the rural districts, taking care that no industries should be practised there. All through the 14th century Gand was organizing expeditions which destroyed the looms and the fullers' vats in the villages and country towns. And the monasteries no longer extended the old social protection over the "villeins," but added to their wretchedness by their exaction of the tithe.

As for the nobles, they too were passing through a serious crisis. They had retained the ancient forms of chivalry, but the spirit was no longer present. It had vanished with the end of the Crusades. I cannot find that anything remained of the old idealism, apart from certain outward gallantry. Fidelity to the seigneur was now merely a word. The chief preoccupation of the chevalier was now his fief. Homage (that noble word) now meant little more to him than registration. What did survive was the military character of the

----

[4] The victory of the men of Schwis, Uri and Unterwalden over Duke Leopold of Austria in 1315 cannot be regarded as a social insurrection. These were free peasants fighting to preserve their independence. The rising was more nearly analogous to the struggle of the Frisians against the Counts of Holland, which ended in the battle of Stavoren (1345).

noble class. But this often assumed the aspect of mercenary military service. The knights of the Rhine valley, Austria, and Hesbaye, began to hire themselves to the King of France. Knights-errant began to make their appearance, fighting on all fronts and for all causes; Froissart has given us the portraits of many such. These were professional soldiers, who were not very far removed from the *condottieri* —leaders of bands, experienced captains to whom war was a lucrative calling. Du Guesclin, one of the most typical of these knights, was a pure soldier. The literature of the *chansons de geste* came to an end or was rewritten. What men of this class read was narratives of campaigns, fought for no matter what or whom, but yielding handsome profits, and there must be feasting and women, as described by Froissart. At heart these knights were adventurers: very valiant men, but also violent and greedy. They were fond of sport: we see them engaging in tournaments, and in Lithuania, in the winter, in man-hunts, and even in expeditions like that of Nicopoli, where they were defeated by the Turks (1396). Some also went to break a lance in Granada.

In countries where manners were still more brutal than elsewhere, as in Germany, matters were even worse. Here the *Raubritter* made his appearance, a sort of bravo who made use of the pretext of *Fehden* (private wars) to hold the adjacent countryside to ransom; a brutal bandit, robbing the merchants; a village tyrant, oppressing the peasants who lived beneath his castle walls; who fled before the Hussites or the Swiss peasants.

For it was no longer by this military noblesse that battles were won. Artillery, which was first heard at Crécy, still played only a secondary part in any campaign, but the infantry was gradually recovering the position which it had lost since the Carolingian epoch. At Courtrai it destroyed the French chivalry; the Swiss infantry had been winning battles since 1315; the foot-soldiers were the backbone of the English army, where they were formed into companies of archers; and the tactics of Johann Ziska, leader of the Hussites, was based on the infantry. Thus, despite appearances, the part played by the noble and the knight was constantly diminishing. It is very significant that the purest military figure of the time, Joan of Arc, was a peasant. And while, from the military point of view, the nobles were in retreat, they were not distinguishing themselves in other respects. They played no part in the government, and they were not becoming more cultivated. Obviously the services which they rendered were not commensurate with the position which they occupied. And this is all the more striking inasmuch as their position was more advantageous than ever. The upper ranks of the clergy, and the chapters, became the monopoly of the younger sons of noble families. The democratic character of the Church was disappearing. Consider the type of canon represented by Jean Le Bel and Froissart; think of bishops like Adolphe de la Marck! In the upper ranks of the ecclesiastical hierarchy there was a stupendous moral and intellectual decadence; in accordance with the tastes of society, the clergy were becoming worldly.

If we examine them closely, shall we not see among the nobles, considering them as a whole, a tendency analogous to that which we may observe in the patriciate of the bourgeoisie? Neither class was undergoing any further development; they were digging themselves in, so to speak, in the position which they had acquired. Their only care was to preserve their privileges and their property. They were no longer capable of idealism, and hardly of disinterestedness. Consider the great examples of devotion in the 14th century: the "Bourgeois of Calais," Étienne Marcel, van Artevelde: there was not a nobleman among them. There were no such figures in the 14th century as Simon de Montfort, Villehardouin, or Joinville. Manners were embellished by a veneer of elegance, but under that they were brutal. We have only to read Froissart to see that these nobles loved money above all things. On the whole, they were brutal sensualists. Not one of them was distinguished for his piety or his beneficence. And here I am speaking of those who played some part in the life of the world. The others hunted, looked after their estates, and oppressed the peasants. It is surprising to discover how completely sterile were the nobles of the 14th and the beginning of the 15th centuries, despite their numerical strength.

However, a new social stratum was beginning to spread over the old basis of the feudal chivalry. In the 14th century we see the first traces of what may be called the *noblesse de cour*. In the 13th century it hardly existed. Then, of course, as always, the king's entourage consisted of nobles. But their position was independent of the court. They frequented the court as the king's companions. They did not constitute his household. There was a royal household in the Frankish epoch, a somewhat heterogeneous mixture of dignitaries and servitors, whose names have been preserved in those of the great officers of the Crown. But as soon as the monarchy became powerful they disappeared, or were transformed into functionaries, or merely ornamental personages. The hereditary nature of their duties, which bound them to the king, was abolished. They began as members of the king's domestic staff, who were not freemen; in the feudal period they became metamorphosed into great hereditary officers, only to disappear upon the reconstitution of the monarchical power. But the powerful monarchy which had demolished the ancient court since the 12th century had to create a new court for itself.

It would seem that the nucleus of this court consisted not of nobles, but of commoners: councillors, servants in charge of the king's plate and his wardrobe, etc., with a few clerks. But was the king to be surrounded by plebeians? The court is a resort of the nobility. Consequently the king proceeded to ennoble his officers and his functionaries. This was a new nobility, entirely different from the old military chivalry. It was now conferred for civil services, and intelligence or learning, rather than for military service and valour. And this new nobility was entirely dependent on the sovereigns. In the beginning any knight could "arm" another. It was no longer so in the 14th century. The king alone was the source of nobility, and so he remained until the end of the *ancien régime*. From the end of the 13th century, anyone who was ennobled was ennobled by the king alone. The nobles of the robe—such as the Chancellor Rolin, Jacques

Cœur, and many another—took their place beside the nobles of the sword.

Here was a novel factor of very great social importance. To my thinking, it saved the noblesse, which was decaying as a military caste, and could not enrich itself, because it constituted a juridical caste, which was becoming more and more a closed social category. In the persons of these new-comers it received fresh recruits, and they were commonly very wealthy recruits, thanks to their participation in the government. It despised them, but it was they who saved it.

Here again we note the influence of tradition. In point of formation, and in respect of its occupation, the *noblesse de robe* was a kind of lay clergy. It had nothing in common with the old nobility in whose ranks it now installed itself. Why then did the new nobility enter the old? Because there was no other place for it in the society of those days. It could not, on coming to court, remain in the ranks of the bourgeoisie, which would have continued to influence it and to detach it from the prince. Could it enter the ranks of the clergy? A few of the new men did so, and were rewarded with bishoprics and cardinals' hats. But for the rest there was no society available but that of the nobility, for the plebeian class consisted only of peasants. Thus, by a process which was necessary though it was not natural, the high government officials became a sort of annex of a social class whose origin was purely military. The social habits and interests of the new class merged themselves in those of the old. And with this the nobility acquired a more comprehensive status. Henceforth it included the entire élite of the nation. To be an *homme convenable* a man must be a member of the noblesse. The consequences of this fact were hardly preceptible in the 14th century and the beginning of the 15th. They were to be incalculable later, and even to this day there are many States which have not yet shaken them off. The Renaissance was powerless to dissolve this social bloc. This was reserved for the modern democracies. However profound the influence of the bourgeoisie might be in the State, the noblesse, during the whole of the *ancien régime*, retained its primacy of social rank,

and every man who emerged from the bourgeoisie endeavoured to enter it.

2. The Religious Movement

The 13th century saw the Catholic Church attain its
apogee. It presented the grandiose spectacle of a government endowed with all its organs, so powerful that not
only could it victoriously resist the attacks made upon it,
but every victory left it still more powerful. In form this
government was a monarchy, which was strongly reminis-
cent of the Roman Empire in whose midst it was born, and
it had retained the capital, the language, and, with necessary modifications, the law and the administrative traditions of the Empire. And again, as in the Roman Empire,
its head, the Pope, was uplifted above the rest of mankind,
a sacred personage, whose commands were laws, and who
was amenable to no man's judgements. However, it was not
this that gave the Papacy its extraordinary vitality. This it
derived from the religious society whose enthusiastic support it enjoyed, which lived in close communion with it
through its faith, and from whose ranks it was continually
receiving an afflux of fresh recruits, a perpetual source of
rejuvenation. Piety was continually inspiring the masses to
establish new monastic orders, adapted to the needs of the
period, which, subject to its guidance, furnished it with the
spiritual army which it needed to discipline or defend the
Church: Clunisians in the 11th century, Cistercians and
Premonstrants in the 12th, Franciscans and Dominicans in
the 13th. To enable him to deal with heresy the Pope had
his police, the Inquisition. And he had only to appeal to
the peoples for help, and immediately thousands of champions of orthodoxy leapt forward to massacre the infidel.
Lastly, all education was under his control; the learning of
the universities was no less obedient to his influence than
the zeal of the religious.

But it is evident that about the middle of the 13th century the Church had attained the maximum of its power.
It had ceased to grow, and presently began to decline. The
principal cause of this decline must be attributed, as we

have already seen, to the attitude which lay society had adopted in respect of the Church. On the one hand, the national States, in their need of independence, shook off the tutelage of the Papacy; on the other hand, the more active and laborious peoples, mainly concerned with their economic interests, and becoming inaccessible to the naïve idealism of the Crusades, were also beginning to escape from the exclusive control of religion. Evidently the Church was ceasing to be the sole mistress of the faithful, or rather, its influence upon men's souls was no longer without a rival. Its authority was no longer all-powerful because it no longer imposed itself spontaneously on every aspect of political and social life. Without intention, without being really conscious of what they were doing, men were gradually turning away from the influence of the Church. And the Church was not aware of this desertion. Although its moral strength and its political influence were diminishing, it surrendered none of its pretensions, none of its hopes. Even after the disaster suffered by Boniface VIII, even after the exodus of the Pope to Avignon, even during the conflict of the Popes with the Council, it remained obstinately faithful to the ideal of the Crusades, and continued to claim supremacy over the peoples and their kings. It even revived the old quarrel with the Empire, and John XXII excommunicated Louis of Bavaria (1324) as Innocent IV had excommunicated Frederick II—but what a difference between this performance and the grandiose drama of the 13th century! However loud the accusations of the two parties, the rest of Europe remained indifferent. The monks, jurists, and theologians were involved in the quarrel, but the States stood aside. The Minorite Friars, whose doctrine of evangelical poverty had been condemned by the Pope, went over to Louis of Bavaria, who found it impossible to refuse these strange auxiliaries, and, tormented by scruples, allowed them to involve him in the accusations of heresy which they hurled against John XXII. However, in the midst of the battle of pamphlets the omnipotence of the pontiff, which was violently debated, provoked certain words which should not be forgotten. The *Defensor Pacis* of Marsilius of Padua, which was presently translated into

French and Italian, expounded ideas of which we may note the first traces in the entourage of Frederick II and Philip the Fair. But only now were they fully developed, and they amazed the world by their boldness. For Marsilius the pretensions of the Papacy were merely an intolerable usurpation, as incompatible with the interpretation of the Holy Scriptures and the usages of the primitive Church as they were disastrous to the peace of the world. The Pope was merely a bishop like any other. His entire mission consisted in preaching the faith and administering the sacraments. All interference in the temporal domain, all jurisdiction over laymen should be refused him. And expatiating on this question, Marsilius defined the Church: the community of all those who believe in Jesus Christ. Before Wycliffe and before Huss, he declared that the layman belonged to the Church no less than the priest, and he categorically insisted that the "clerks" should be subject to the secular power in all temporal relations. Of course, we must not exaggerate the influence of these declarations. It is not apparent that they produced any practical effect. They had, as yet, only the importance of a symptom, and in religious as in social questions, contemporaries do not usually notice the symptoms which precede a crisis.

How far can Marsilius of Padua have been influenced by the religious tendencies of his age? There is, at all events, between the mysticism of his day, and his conception of a Church which should comprise both the laity and the clergy, a concordance which must doubtless be attributed to that mysterious harmony which may be observed, at this time, between the various manifestations of the intellect. In its profoundest and most spontaneous features the piety of the 14th century was essentially mystical. In its efforts to attain to God the Church no longer sufficed it. Without hesitation, it took flight towards Him; it sought to contemplate Him face to face in the intimacy of the consciousness, without the intermediary of the priest. Moreover—and this is a peculiarly characteristic innovation—it no longer expressed itself in the tongue of the Church. Nearly all the mystics—Eckhardt († 1327), Tauler († 1365), Ruysbroek († 1381)—wrote in the language of the people, thus for the first time giving religious thought a secular form, and so undermining the prestige of the clergy, who had hitherto enjoyed the sole monopoly of religious ideas.[5] At all events, it is certain that the clergy, whether regular or secular, no longer had the same influence over the faithful as of old. It is true that the ascetic ideal of monasticism was still attracting many novices to the convents, but monasticism was no longer regarded by all as the highest and most perfect form of Christian life. Mysticism took alarm at the fact that a conventual rule necessarily imposes constraint upon spiritual liberty. It preferred solitary contemplation, as a voluntary practice, or such congregations as were exempt from perpetual vows, like the *béguinages*, or the community of the Brothers of the Common Life, founded by Goert Groot († 1384). Here piety could still expand beyond the boundaries which the Church had created to confine it. For neither the Béguines nor the Bégards nor the Brothers of the Common Life were religious Orders. They did not consider that the secular life was incompatible with devotion, or that it was necessary to flee the world in order to enter into relations with God. Thus the most original and most active manifestations of piety in the 14th century were to be found outside monasticism. As for the latter, it made no further progress. It founded no new Orders, unless we give this name to a few communities which were so closely related to the Franciscans that it is very difficult to distinguish them from the latter, and in any case they played only a very secondary part.[6]

This spread of mysticism in the lay community was doubly perilous for the Church. To begin with, it represented a danger to orthodoxy. Without the curb of a rule and the permanent control of authority, the contemplative life might easily cross the frontiers of the Roman dogma. The danger was all the greater inasmuch as these naïve zealots were without theological training, since most of them came from the ranks of the people or the *petite bour-*

---

[5] Cf. Bridget, Catherine of Siena, Gerson, Vincent Ferrier, Pierre de Luxembourg.

[6] For example, the Carthusians.

geoisie. As a matter of fact, during the whole of the 14th century they constantly attracted the attention of the Inquisitors, and sailed very close to the perilous reefs of heresy. The Pope even went so far as to condemn the religion of the Béguines as suspect. During the Black Death of 1347–1348 bands of penitents, urged onward by a sort of ecstatic delirium, went from city to city, exciting the people, like Oriental fakirs, by their singing, their dancing, or their public flagellations. In Italy, France and Germany obscure sects appeared which seemed to have preserved something of the doctrines and the dreams of the Albigenses; they were known as "Spirituals, Apostolics, Friends of God." All these mystics—and this was the second danger to the Church—aspired to lead the world back to evangelical poverty. This question of poverty troubled the whole of the 14th century. Among the workers in the manufacturing cities, and the English rebels in 1384, it gave rise to communistic aspirations, which the secular power proceeded to stifle. But even more widespread, and even more difficult to contend with, was the criticism of the religious authorities, beginning with the highest of all, the Papacy. For the more completely the Church had adopted the monarchical form, the more zealously it surrounded its head with pomp and luxury. In respect of the artists which it attracted and employed, the majesty of its ceremonies, the number of its servants, the expert hierarchy of its bureaucrats, and the abundance of its revenues, the court of Avignon was so far in advance of the royal courts, even those of France and England, that the very comparison was impossible. And the cardinals who were gathered about the Pope vied with one another in point of magnificence and luxury. The fiscal system of the Papacy, which even in the 13th century was so highly developed, was still further extended, and strove to find new resources which would meet the increased expenditure. From the pontificate of John XXII it subjected the ecclesiastical hierarchy to a system of expedient taxes and dues, though it was difficult to persuade the pious that this was not tainted with simony. By the creation of *Reservationes* and *Provisiones* the Pope now had at his disposal, in all parts of Christendom, a quantity of benefices, which he could confer at will in return for payment. The natural consequence was that the Curia was besieged with applications, and the system was further extended by which ecclesiastical dignities were obtained by favour or in return for payment. Little attention was paid to the merit of the candidates, nor was it asked whether they possessed the requisite qualities for the post which they coveted. We have only to take a random glance at the episcopal catalogues of the 14th and 15th centuries in order to make some singular discoveries. Firstly, we observe the great preponderance of Italians and Frenchmen; then we shall note how short a time they commonly continued to officiate; and lastly, we shall see that nearly all belonged to the *haute noblesse*. Here we perceive the inevitable results of the system. Not only did it award the highest positions in the hierarchy to the younger sons of great families—not only did it introduce into many dioceses prelates who were unfamiliar with the manners and language of the faithful—but it also had the result of multiplying the translations from one see to another, each such transfer being, for the Curia, a source of taxes in proportion to the revenue of the vacant see (annates). It is not surprising that St. Bridget implored Gregory XI († 1378) to destroy the "lupanar" which the Holy Church had become.

To the offence which such practices gave to all pious souls, may be added the discontent of all those whose interests they injured, or who felt them as an affront to their national self-respect. The higher clergy and the princes of Germany were filled with indignation when they saw that the Curia was systematically favouring the Italians and the French, and that the heavy taxes imposed upon their dioceses mostly went into the pockets of foreigners. But Germany, dismembered and divided as she was, had no effective power, and her complaints merely attested to her impotence. It was otherwise in England. From the close of the reign of Edward III Parliament entered upon a vigorous campaign against the Curia's self-arrogated right of taxing the national Church and refusing to reserve all dignities and benefices for subjects of the king. The hostility to France excited by the war was extended to the Pope, whose partiality for that power was only too visible since he had left Rome for Avignon. In 1376 the "Good Parliament" demanded the suppression of the *Reservationes* and *Provisiones,* the expulsion of the pontifical collectors, and a law forbidding the exportation of money. Already voices were heard in the Commons demanding the secularization of the properties of the English Church.

It was in the midst of this political agitation that Wycliffe began his activities. It was almost inevitable that this agitation should have directly influenced his religious ideas. In him we see for the first time that concordance, or rather, that unconscious alliance of speculation and practice, of a tendency to universality and anxiety for the welfare of the nation, which was afterwards to characterize the genius of so many English thinkers, and which may doubtless be explained by the strong national solidarity with which the English people had been endowed by circumstances, long before any other European people.

Wycliffe was the first to tread the path which was to lead to the Reformation. He had nothing in common with the heretics who had troubled the Church before his time, and whose doctrines had their essential foundation, like that of the Albigenses, in the dualism of flesh and spirit. Wycliffe, who was utterly unlike them, brought nothing to Christianity that was not already there. He did not rebel against Christian dogma nor against Christian morality, but simply against the Church, and even more than against the Church, against the Papacy. The only head of the Church, he taught, was Christ. His word, recorded in the Bible, sufficed for the salvation of those who had faith. Now the Bible knew nothing of that powerful and religious hierarchy which the Church had become. Its ideal was poverty; it made no difference between the priest and the layman, from which one must conclude that the priests, like the rest of the faithful, were amenable to the secular laws and could not claim any privilege. England was absolutely independent of the Pope, for the temporal power of her king, like the spiritual power of the Church, was derived directly from God. As for the Pope, far from being the representative of Christ on the earth, he was actually the Antichrist.

Before the people could practise the true religion it must go back to the Bible, with which it was no longer familiar; so, in order that the people might know the Bible, the reformer undertook to translate it into the vulgar tongue, inaugurating, by this great achievement, the history of English prose.

Hitherto England had been so orthodox that by great good fortune there had been no need to introduce the Inquisition. No people had been more docile to the teachings of the Church than the English, although, since the reign of Edward I, it had plainly manifested its intention of preventing the Church from exerting any influence in the political domain. By uniting, in his campaign against the Papacy, the religious and the political aspect of the matter, Wycliffe could not fail to interest in the religious question all those who were deeply interested in the political question. Within a few years he had enthusiastic supporters among both the nobles and the burgesses, while many members of the lower clergy accepted his doctrines, and as "simple priests" spread them among the people, surprising and attracting their hearers by the evangelical simplicity of their manners and the strength of their convictions. And in proportion as his influence increased, the reformer became bolder and more radical. He even went so far, in the name of the Bible, as to deny the Transubstantiation of Christ in the Communion. The Chancellor of the University of Oxford, and the Archbishop of Canterbury, might vainly accuse him of heresy, and his enemies might hold him responsible for the great agrarian rising of 1381, but the attitude of Parliament was so obviously favourable to Wycliffe that no one dared to persecute him, and in 1384 he died peacefully in his own parish of Lutterworth. It was only after the advent of Henry of Lancaster (Henry IV), that the king, desiring to obtain the support of the Pope for his new dynasty, turned against Wycliffism, or, to use the term employed by the adversaries of the reformers, against the sect of the Lollards.[7] At the very beginning of his reign —1399—he introduced the first law which ever condemned

7 "Lollium" means a noxious weed.

heretics to be burned at the stake in England, and which forbade the translation of the Bible into the national tongue, and sent Lord Cobham, the protector of the Lollards in the House of Lords, to the stake (1417). These violent measures hampered the movement without suppressing it. Until Protestantism made its appearance, the disciples of Wycliffe never ceased to influence the religious thought of England and to prepare it for the great transformation of the 16th century. Moreover, just as they were subjected to persecution in their own country, enthusiastic emulators, at the other end of Europe, took up the passionate defence of their doctrine. Transplanted into Bohemia by John Huss, this doctrine, becoming associated with the outburst of nationalistic passions and democratic instincts, was to shake the very foundations of the Church and of Germany.

At the very moment when it seemed that the Papacy should have concentrated all its forces to resist its enemies, it flung itself into the famous crisis which is known as the Great Schism, and which for forty years was to rend Western Christendom in twain (1373–1417). This catastrophe was due to no religious cause. The double election which was its point of departure would doubtless have remained an incident of no particular significance, but for the fact that the European States, actuated by political interest, arrayed themselves in two hostile groups, one subject to French and the other to English influence, both envenoming the schism and seeking to derive advantage from it. But it should be clearly understood that although secular policy drove the States to take sides in the schism, and although it exploited the schism and delayed the possibility of agreement, it was incapable of originating it. The old Carolingian conception, which by associating the Pope and the Emperor in the government of the Church, had formerly enabled the Emperor to appoint Antipopes, had lost its last representative by the death of Frederick Barbarossa. The Church had triumphed so completely over the Empire, had so completely shaken off any temporal intervention in its government, had encompassed the pontifical elections with so many guarantees of independence, and was so profoundly venerated by the faithful, as an authority divine in its essence, that the very idea of forcing a Pope upon it by violence, and in opposition to the traditional rules of the Conclave, would have been inconceivable. In France and England at least, at the end of the 13th century, the State had been able to repudiate the interference of the Church in its own affairs, but it could not and did not dream of subjecting the Church to its own intervention. All that the State desired was to secure the neutrality or benevolence of the Church, and to prevent the Church from acting, with all the enormous strength of its hierarchy, in opposition to its designs or interests; and even, if it were possible, to find in the Church an ally against its external enemies. The kings of France had skilfully profited by the sojourn of the Papacy at Avignon to secure these advantages. Their attitude to the Papacy had been completely different from that of the Emperors, in the days when the Empire still stood for something. Unlike the Emperors, they did not claim to possess the least right to share in the government of the universal Church, and their relations with the Church were purely external, as those of one power with another. The line of demarcation between the spiritual and the temporal power had always been a cause of contention between the Pope and the Emperor, because both the Pope and the Emperor were inside the Empire. For the King of France, who was outside the Empire, the line of demarcation was very clear. It was drawn by the independence of the king in his kingdom. And the Pope derived too many advantages from the king's protection to dream of spoiling the good relations between the monarchy and the Papacy by reviving old quarrels. Though he maintained all his claims in respect of the kings of Germany, he no longer mentioned them to Paris. He surrounded himself more and more with French cardinals and, as we have already seen, a good proportion of the benefices of which he disposed so generously was reserved for Frenchmen. And so harmony reigned between the Church and the State, each avoiding any cause of conflict. There was actually a concordat between them, unwritten, but none the less real. The relations between the king and the Pope were still further facilitated by the fact that in France the question of the temporal power of the Papacy did not arise. Avignon and the County of Venaissin were of so little importance that the king did not dream of contesting the Pope's possession of them. It seems to me that this has been too little remarked; I think it is evident that the *modus vivendi* of the Pope and the King of France during the sojourn at Avignon (1314–1377) was in many respects an anticipation of the modern age, and a mutual accommodation of Church and State.

But this situation was profitable only to France. This fact was very evident to the outer world, which spoke of this period as that of the "Babylonian captivity." The idea that the Pope should no longer dwell beside the tomb of the Apostles was intolerable to pious souls. The non-French States were infuriated by this long succession of French Popes: Clement V (Bertrand de Got), John XXII (Jacques d'Euse de Cahors, 1316–1334), Benedict XII (Jacob Fournier de Saverdun, 1334–1342), Clement VI (Pierre Roger, 1342–1352), Innocent VI (Jean Birel, 1352–1362), Urban V (Abbé de St. Victor de Marseille, 1362–1370), Gregory XI (of the Roger family, 1370–1378).[8]

Avignon, of course, was merely a temporary home, in which the Papacy seemed inclined to linger. But it could not remain there permanently. John XXII was elected in 1316 only after he had promised to restore the Holy See to Rome. But there were very serious troubles in Italy, by which the Papacy was not unaffected. King Robert of Naples (1309–1343), who had succeeded Charles II, had received his crown at the hands of the Pope in Avignon, and had defeated the expedition led by the Emperor Henry VII. But before long Rome was in a state of anarchy. In 1347 Cola di Rienzo was appointed tribune, and during the few months of his dictatorship he dreamed once more of restoring the Roman Empire. The territory of the Church was in a state of decomposition. Innocent VI sent Cardinal Albornoz to Italy as Vicar-General (1353), to reconstitute the Papal State. Cola joined him, but was killed by the

---

[8] These were all Provençaux, doubtless owing to the influence of the Angevins of Naples.

people. At Naples, after Robert's reign, a war had broken out between his daughter Joanna and King Louis of Hungary, who laid claim to the crown as a member of the House of Anjou; and hostilities continued until 1350.

Urban V (1362–1370), the best of the Avignon Popes, who reacted against the luxury and abuses of the Papal court, was anxious to return to Rome, as he actually did in 1367. The city was half depopulated, and many of the ancient monuments had fallen into ruin. The "Great Companies" of disbanded mercenaries were ravaging the country. The Emperor Charles IV came to Rome and remained in Italy until 1369, without doing anything more than fill his purse by punishing a few cities. In the midst of this anarchy the Emperor of Constantinople, John Palaeologus, came to implore the support of the Pope against the Turks. The situation was so lamentable that in 1370 the Pope returned to Avignon, where he died in the following year.

His successor Gregory XI (1370–1378) was also to take the road for the Eternal City. The voices of St. Bridget and St. Catherine of Siena were raised so loudly, and carried so far, that the Pope could not pretend that he did not hear their objurgations. But his return was demanded even more imperatively by the political situation. Bologna had just been taken. The Florentines, hitherto the most faithful allies of Rome in Italy, combined with the other Tuscan cities against the government of the "legates." The Pope left Avignon in 1376. He died in March 1378, without having brought order out of anarchy. For the first time since the election of Boniface VIII, seventy-five years earlier, a Pope was about to be elected in Rome. It was impossible that the people should not demand a Roman Pope. The cardinals, assembled in Conclave, deliberated amidst the clamour of the mob, with which mingled the tocsin of St. Peter's. The Vatican was surrounded by armed bands. It was a revolutionary "day." It ended in the election of Cardinal Bartolomeo Prignano, Archbishop of Bari, who on his coronation took the name of Urban VI, 1378–1379. But the French cardinals who had collaborated in the election had acted only under the influence of terror. Some of them protested; the rest soon quarrelled with the Pope, who announced that he wished to reform the Sacred College, and make an end of the financial abuses which were the origin of its wealth. On the top of this came the urgent entreaties of the King of France, Charles V, and the downfall of Naples. No more was needed to make them declare the election of Urban null and void. On September 20th they assembled at Fondi and gave their suffrages to Robert of Geneva, Bishop of Thérouanne. The name of Urban, adopted by his competitor, spoke of Rome; he chose a name which spoke of Avignon, styling himself Clement VII (1378–1394).

Of old, whenever two Popes had disputed the right to wear the tiara, the question of legitimacy had been capable of a plain answer. One of the two Popes, forced upon the Church by the Emperor, was obviously a mere intruder, from whom Christendom resolutely turned away. But how, on this occasion, was the true successor of Peter to be discerned? Who were in the right—the cardinals who acknowledged Urban, or those who had voted for Clement? The theologians of the universities debated the matter; and pious souls, with equal conviction, addressed their prayers to heaven on behalf of the Roman Pope (as did Catherine of Siena), or on behalf of the Avignon Pope (and among these were Vincent Ferrier and Pierre de Luxembourg). But as in all problems of law which are really political problems, the solution was furnished by political interest. France, and all the States which gravitated around her— Naples, Scotland, Castile, Aragon—pronounced for Clement. This was enough to make England support Urban. He was also acknowledged by the Emperor Charles IV, in virtue of the traditional connection between the Empire and Rome. The States of the North, Bohemia and Poland, followed suit, without taking much interest in the question. The King of Hungary, being the enemy of the Queen of Naples, who was for Clement, gave his support to the opposite party. Thus, in a dispute which involved such serious consequences for the Church, Christendom refused to be guided by other than considerations of temporal expediency. The Papacy, so triumphant only a century earlier, suffered the humiliation of perceiving that the obedience of the faithful was subordinated to the interests of the various governments concerned. And not only did it accept this situation, but it consecrated it, so to speak, by its attitude. In order to retain his political supporters, each of the Popes manifested a singular condescension where they were concerned. The arrogant declarations by which their predecessors had claimed to dispose of kingdoms were things of the past. Now the question was which of the two contending pontiffs could show himself the more accommodating in his treatment of his adherents. As for the peoples, they passively imitated the attitude of their princes unless they were at war with them, when they gave their support, in a spirit of opposition, to the Pope of the opposing party.

In the midst of all this confusion, the abuses from which the Church had been suffering, more and more visibly, since the beginning of the 14th century were bound to undergo aggravation. The court of Rome, like that of Avignon, subjected the Church to an exploitation which was all the more intensive inasmuch as half Christendom had now to provide each of these courts with as much revenue as had formerly been furnished by the whole Christian world. The system of *provisiones, annates,* and *reservationes* was applied in the extremest manner, while simony, nepotism and favouritism became deplorably prevalent. The hierarchy was more and more at the mercy of money.

Such a situation was indefensible. Had it been prolonged it must undoubtedly have ended in the ruin of the Church. The success of Wycliffe in England was significant. And in Bohemia, John Huss, inspired by Wycliffe, was beginning to rouse the people (1403). But in opposition to these revolutionary reformers, the ancient University of Paris, that home of conservative theology, was ardently seeking the solution compatible with orthodoxy. On the one side were Pierre d'Ailly, Gerson and Clémangis; on the other, Wycliffe and Huss. This was the great religious conflict of the beginning of the 15th century. One might be tempted here, in accordance with a convenient formula, to invoke the racial element: the Latins being on the side of the Church, and the Germans opposing them. In this case, the Germans and the Slavs. But the attitudes of the different

parties are very readily explained. In England, as we have
seen, the increasing difficulty of that country's relations with
the Pope naturally tended to make her accept the Wyclif-
fian theology, and Huss merely borrowed Wycliffe's theses,
while basing them on Czech nationalism. In France, on the
contrary, since the Papacy had been resident in Avignon,
the State could but support it. It had no motive for breaking with the Papacy; and the people were in no sense hostile
to it. It was quite possible to correct abuses, re-establish
discipline, and restore piety without overturning everything, without denying the whole past and suddenly going
back to the Bible and primitive Christianity. An oecumenical council could deal with the question, and at the same
time put an end to the schism, and give the Church the
reforms of which it stood in need. Unfortunately, neither
of the two Popes would give way to the other. The States
were unable to come to an agreement under which they
would proclaim, to one Pope or the other, a general "sub-
traction of obedience," which would compel them to yield.
France did her very utmost to end the schism, but she was
hampered by her intestine quarrels. The assassination of
the Duke of Orleans, when the country came under the
influence of the Duke of Burgundy, Jean Sans Peur, forced
her to adopt a more definite attitude. For Jean, since the
Flemings over whom he reigned were in favour of Rome,
was greatly embarrassed by the quarrel, and did his very
utmost to force a solution. The cardinals of the two parties,
feeling that they were supported, grew bolder. In 1409 they
at last convoked a General Council, which opened its proceedings at Pisa on March 25th.

It was an unheard-of innovation in the Church that a
Council should assemble in obedience to a summons from
the cardinals. The revolutionary spirit which was abroad
in lay society had evidently spread to the religious community. The two Popes, Gregory XII (Rome) and Benedict
XIII, protested equally, and did their utmost to wreck the
proceedings of the Council. But the Council had resolved
to proceed to extreme measures. On June 5th it solemnly
declared that Pietro de Luna (Benedict XIII) and Angelo
Corrario (Gregory XII) were notorious schismatics and

heretics, deposed them both, and declared the Holy See to be vacant. Ten days later the cardinals gave the tiara to Alexander V (1409–1410). They then dispersed, leaving the reformation of the Church to a future Council. The outlook appeared more gloomy than ever, for neither Gregory nor Benedict acknowledged the validity of the sentence which had been pronounced against them. There were thenceforth three Popes contending for the government of Christendom. And as though it was not enough that the government of the Church should be undermined, it was at the same time torn by heresy, thus recalling the spectacle of the Carolingian decadence, when the sons of Louis the Pious were contending for the crown while the rising feudality was undermining the political constitution of the Empire.

Wycliffism had found in John Huss an apostle who was even more ardent than the founder of the doctrine, and whom circumstances were to render much more dangerous. Just as the success of Wycliffe in England was explained, as we have seen, by the political discontent which the Papacy had provoked in that country, the success of Huss was due to the increasing hostility of the Czechs of Bohemia to Germany since the middle of the 14th century.[9] The national sentiment was in favour of each of these reformers, but it favoured them in a very different manner, which is naturally explained by the composition of the two peoples. In England, where the population was homogeneous, Wycliffe had the support of all those who resented, in the Papacy, the unwarrantable interference of a foreign power. In Bohemia, where the Czechs lived side by side with the immigrants whom Germany had been pouring into the country since the 12th century, Huss was supported by the entire Slav portion of the nation, which greeted in him the reformer who had liberated it from a Church which it regarded, above all, as the Church of the Germans. From the very first, Huss relied on the sole support of his Czech-speaking compatriots. The religious zeal with which he in-

[9] As to this hostility and its origins, see p. 130 et seq., and p. 190 et seq.

spired them by his eloquence and his conviction was intensified by the full force of the nationalistic passions of the people, so that we have the singular spectacle of a theologian who had become so completely the apostle of his people that no authority would have dared to think of resisting him. The excommunication launched against him, and the interdict placed on the city of Prague (1412), did nothing to check his propaganda, which was already beginning to recruit supporters in Poland, Hungary and Croatia.

It seemed that the only thing that could save Christianity was the task of ecclesiastical reform which the Council of Pisa had adjourned to a later Council. John XXIII (1410–1415), who had just succeeded Alexander V, convoked a new Council in Rome (April 1412), but this was soon compelled to disperse, owing to the invasion of the city by the King of Naples, Ladislas. At the proposal of the King of Germany, Sigismond, who was happy to assume an importance which would not have been his had not France and England been absorbed in their quarrel, Constance was selected as the site of a new assembly, which opened its sessions on November 5th, 1414. After three years of deliberations and negotiations it succeeded in putting an end to the schism. John XXIII was deposed, Gregory XII was induced to renounce the tiara, and Benedict XIII, who refused to, was condemned as a heretic and schismatic. On November 11th, 1417, Martin V was elected, not by the Conclave, but by a commission of cardinals and delegates of the nations represented in the Council. The unity of the Catholic government was at last re-established. As for the reformation of the Church "in her head and in her members," of which the best minds of the day were so desirous, it was hardly begun. Little more was done beyond mitigating in some degree the power which the Curia had arrogated to itself in respect of the distribution of benefices. On the other hand, the Council felt that it had crushed the Bohemian heresy by condemning John Huss to be burned at the stake. Provided with a safe-conduct by Sigismond, he had gone to Constance in the hope of converting the fathers to his doctrine (July 6th, 1415). His disciple, Jerome of Prague, was also condemned and put to death

a few months later. Both died as martyrs, and their sufferings had no other result than to serve the cause which had
cost them their lives. They fanned the religious and national
enthusiasm of the Czechs to a paroxysm. Their hatred of
the Church and their hatred of Germany increased simultaneously. Was not Huss the victim at once of the Council
and of Sigismond? How could they regard the safe-conduct
which he had received from the king as other than a proof
of the monarch's abominable perfidy?

Hitherto the followers of Huss had confined themselves,
like their master, to professing the ideas of Wycliffe. A certain number of them remained faithful to these ideas: these
were the Utraquists, so called because they communicated
"in the two elements." But the mass of the people, under
the spur of religious passion, suddenly pushed the doctrine
to its extreme consequences. Since the Bible proclaimed the
Word of God, it must be obeyed in everything, not only
in such matters as regarded the soul, but also in all that
related to the body. Hence the ecclesiastical organization,
no less than the civil organization, ought simply to disappear. The Kingdom of God must be established in this
world, by reconstituting the whole of humanity in accordance with the Holy Scriptures. Such was the enthusiastic
dream of a young people, a people full of illusions, and
history shows no pendant to their behaviour save that of
the Russian Bolsheviks of 1917. They set to work immediately, under the conviction that the Czech nation was the
Chosen of the Lord. The Catholic clergy was dispersed, its
property confiscated, and the churches and monasteries
were destroyed. A patriarchal constitution, on the lines of
the Old Testament, was given to the people, and on the
site of the castle of Kozihradek, where Huss had passed
his last years, the Holy City of Tabor was built, from which
the New Hebrews received their name of Taborites. The
sudden death of the King of Bohemia, Wenceslas (August
16th, 1419), left them a free field, the more so as his successor was the hateful Sigismond, who had played the
Judas to the martyr of Constance. The revolution was thus
in full control of the country. The Germans of Bohemia,
who had remained faithful to the Church, bowed their

heads to the storm. However, from all parts of the world exalted mystics, members of the associations of Bogards, or of the proletariat of the industrial cities, hastened toward this country in which the Kingdom of God had been proclaimed, and their communistic aspirations, or their paradisiacal visions, gave rise to some singular sects amidst the Biblical rigorism of the Taborites. The sect of the Adamites, founded by a Belgian weaver, affords a curious example of the exaltation of their adepts. The disciples of the new Adam, who settled on an island in the river Nezarka, professed to live there, in a state of the completest communism, the life of the Garden of Eden. Like the first of our race, they wore no clothes, and their morals were as primitive as their costume. They soon caused such a scandal that John Ziska, in 1421, had them massacred.

The faith of the Hussites was too ardent to allow them to neglect the duty of propagating it. As early as 1419 Bohemia had become a centre of fervent propaganda, from which a revolutionary religion poured forth its fiery doctrines like a stream of lava. The adjacent Slav regions, Poland, Moravia and Silesia, where the language of its apostles was readily understood, and where the masses of the people were living wretchedly under the oppression of the nobles, immediately provided it with thousands of adepts. It even made some progress among the poorer inhabitants in the German regions of Austria. And its prestige appeared more dazzling than ever in the light of its triumphs. The victories of John Ziska and Procopius over the German chivalry sent against them by the Pope and Sigismond inevitably reminded the faithful of the victories of David or of Gideon over the Amalekites.[10]

The Hussite peril was invoked by all those members of the Church who were calling for the assembly of a new Council. Martin V succeeded in temporizing; his successor Eugenius IV (1431–1437), yielding to circumstances, and to the general opinion, convoked the Council, which opened its sessions at Basle in July 1431. It had to deal with two important problems: the Bohemian heresy, and

[10] See p. 191.

the reform of the Church. Events enabled it to solve the first of these problems.

The religious and social radicalism of the Taborites ended by provoking a definitive rupture between them and the Utraquists. Almost the whole of the nobility had gone over to the side of the Utraquists, and at Lipan, on March 30th, 1434, they won a bloody victory for their cause. Bohemia, exhausted by the war, asked for nothing more than peace, and the negotiations which were opened between the Council and the Utraquists ended at last in a somewhat obscure solution, with which the two parties decided to content themselves (1436). The difficulties were evaded rather than solved. All the efforts, all the enthusiasm, all the bloodshed, profited, in the end, only the Czech nobles, who divided the property of the convents among themselves. At the cost of the spoliation of the Church, the nobles were reconciled with it. They thereby acquired such power that little danger was to be feared henceforth from the discouraged sectators among the people. Their further discomfiture was left to time.

As for the reformation of the Church, there was at first some reason for believing that this time it would really be accomplished, in accordance with the programme which had formerly been expounded at Constance by men like Pierre d'Ailly and Gerson. The majority of the fathers were apparently resolved to replace the monarchical constitution of Catholicism by a conciliary constitution. Even more emphatically than at Constance, they proclaimed the superiority of the Council over the Pope, and vigorously thwarted the efforts of Eugenius IV to dissolve the assembly. Not content with suppressing the financial abuses of the Curia, correcting the morals of the clergy, requiring ecclesiastical dignitaries to reside in their sees, attacking simony, and forbidding plurality of benefices, they manifested, in respect of the Pope, so revolutionary a spirit of defiance and criticism that dissension finally crept into their ranks. This dissension was skilfully exploited by Eugenius. The Emperor John VII Palaeologus and the Patriarch of Constantinople had just arrived in Italy, once more seeking to obtain the aid of the Occident against the Turks, and once more promising in return the union of the Greek Church. The Pope immediately convoked the Council in Ferrara, and then in Florence, to deliberate on this proposal; the last expedient of despair, which men could pretend or persuade themselves to take seriously. A certain number of the fathers answered his summons, and the proclamation of the union on July 5th, 1439, was regarded as a brilliant success —but the Eastern Church repudiated it four years later. The opposition, which had remained in Basle, was henceforth discredited. It sought to mask its weakness by violence. On June 5th, 1439, it deposed Eugenius IV and appointed in his place Felix V, whom no one in Europe took seriously, and who was the last of the Antipopes. Persisting in its hopeless opposition, the Council dragged out its obscure existence for ten years longer, finally dissolving on April 25th, 1439. Felix V abdicated and resumed his rank among the cardinals. The great crisis through which the Papacy had been passing was terminated, and by its victory. Of the work of the Council nothing survived. The Church had preserved its monarchical form; after so much effort, so many hopes, everything was as it had been in the beginning.

And yet something remained as the result of all this agitation, and for a moment it had seemed that this new factor would give Catholicism a new form. It was something that no one in the Church had ever desired: the increasing independence of the States in ecclesiastical affairs. The quarrels between the Popes and the Council had enabled the princes, whom both parties were equally concerned to humour, to restrict the intervention of Rome within their frontiers, and to acquire a certain amount of influence in the recruiting and disciplining of the national clergy. The Pragmatic Sanction proclaimed by Charles VII in 1438, and in which we may see the germ of the famous Gallican franchises of the Church of France, was the most noteworthy result of these conjunctures. The Papacy remained supreme within the Church. But the Church was no longer what it had been in the Middle Ages. It no longer extended its authority over the temporal as over the spiritual domain. To a certain extent it turned inward upon itself, and, so to speak, decided to specialize in its religious rôle. Following the Emperor, the Pope in his turn disappeared from the stage of the world as a universal power. From the middle of the 15th century there were to be no more Antipopes. However, after the deposition of the King of Bohemia, George Podebrad, by Paul II, the quarrels of the kings would no longer be submitted to Papal arbitration.

The Hundred Years' War

1. *To the Death of Edward III* (1377)

Since the close of the 13th century France had no longer
exercised the uncontested hegemony which she had enjoyed from the time of Philip Augustus to that of Philip
the Fair. She could not have retained this mastery over Europe unless her civilization had continued to progress, while
her political power remained undiminished. But the progress of her civilization came to a standstill, and her political
power began to decline. Neither her art, nor her literature,
nor her science, whatever interest they might still possess,
produced anything essentially new. As for the strength and
prosperity of the nation, they were both compromised by
the formidable crisis of the Hundred Years' War.

As a matter of fact, this great conflict spread far beyond
the frontiers of Western Europe. The two States immediately concerned were so powerful that it was impossible
that their quarrel should involve only themselves. As a
matter of fact, all the princes were dragged into it, and by
virtue of the alliances which it provoked among them, or
the extent to which it influenced their conduct, it assumed
a European importance. In a Europe whose equilibrium
had been upset by the political preponderance of the Papacy it was, for good or for ill, a centre of attraction, or at
any rate, the cardinal event, which impressed a few common motives and tendencies on the restless confusion of the

period which it dominated. A war so long and so bitterly contested was possible only between France and England. They alone had governments disposing of sufficient resources, and peoples endowed with a sufficient national unity, to endure such an ordeal without perishing. But it is appalling to compare the vast expenditure of effort with the futility of the results obtained. Fundamentally, this conflict between France and England was like that of the Popes and the Councils: it was essentially abortive. After all the shedding of blood, after all the misery and devastation, the two adversaries found themselves still more or less at the point of departure, so that the Hundred Years' War had been merely a futile and terrible calamity. It is only too easy to say, after the event, that it could not have been anything else. It is perfectly obvious that the kings of England could not possibly have conquered the Crown of France. And yet this was precisely the end which they had proposed to themselves. Apart from this, they had no urgent motive for going to war. Above all, the English people had no motive for going to war. For France was not threatening or even incommoding England. Neither England nor France had as yet become a maritime nation. Nowhere did their merchants come into contact as rivals, as they were to do later, or as the merchants of Genoa or Venice had done, in the ports of the Levant, since the 13th century. Guyenne, still the Continental possession of the kings of England, meant no more to the English people than the Kingdom of Hanover was to mean in the 18th century. It is quite comprehensible that France might have attacked England in order to recover this province, the last remnant of the Angevin possessions, which was still an obstacle to the unity of the kingdom—but it was not France, it was England that provoked the war. The pretext of the war was Edward III's claim to the crown of the Capets. But one cannot see that this interested England as a nation; indeed, it was against the national interest. The alliance between France and Scotland affords no better explanation of the origin of the conflict. It is, in fact, only too clear that by complicating the conquest of Scotland with a war in France, this conquest was rendered infinitely more difficult, and even impossible. In short, from whatever point of view we regard it, the Hundred Years' War is seen to have been a useless war, a needless war, in the sense that it was not provoked by any vital necessity. As a matter of fact, it must be regarded merely as a war of prestige. And this, precisely, explains the passion with which the English people followed its kings into this war.

The Parliamentary constitution had become further consolidated under Edward I (1272–1307). In 1297 the king formally acknowledged the right of Parliament to vote on questions of taxation. The reversion of his successor, Edward II (1307–1327), to the exercise of personal government provoked, as under Henry III, a popular rebellion, led by the barons. The king's ill-success in Scotland, where he was confronted by Robert Bruce, who had taken up arms again, and who defeated him at Bannockburn (June 24th, 1314), made him hateful to the people. In 1326 the malcontents gathered about the queen and the heir to the throne. Parliament proclaimed the deposition of the king (January 7th, 1327). Thus the reign of Edward III (1327–1377) began, like that of Edward I, with a fresh victory of the nation over the Crown. But by admitting the accomplished fact, as his grandfather had done, and by frankly co-operating with the Parliament, Edward III turned this national victory to the advantage of the Crown. The more he allowed Parliament to intervene in his policy, the more popular this policy became. The approval of the Lords and the Commons (it was only during Edward's reign that they were divided into two chambers) made them conscious of their solidarity with the king's undertakings. Whatever they might cost, the honour of the nation was henceforth engaged in them, and was one with the honour of the king. Parliament, of course, did nothing to encourage the king to make war upon France. Indeed, Edward seems to have been so uncertain of its attitude at first that he began by borrowing the money necessitated by his preparations from the Florentine bankers. But his bankruptcy in 1339 compelled him to address himself, henceforth and until the end, to his faithful Parliament. His quarrel had thus become the quarrel of his people. England felt that her honour was engaged in her king's war, and she continued the war in a sentiment of national pride, the most powerful of all incentives. No one, of course, from the beginning of this war could have imagined what it would lead to. Certainly the English had not expected to find in France a self-esteem and a national passion like their own. Having begun a war which would admit of no compromise, because it aimed at nothing less than giving their king the crown of France, they were obliged to go on to the bitter end, and to lay down their arms only when forced to do so by sheer exhaustion.

But how can we explain the fact that France was not able to repel Edward's aggression immediately and decisively? It would seem that all the advantages were on her side. Not only had she the great advantage of defending herself on her own soil, but her population was certainly two or three times greater than that of England, and she was very much wealthier. Moreover, the defeats which she had suffered at Crécy, Poitiers, and Agincourt were not in any way decisive. Serious though they may have been, they did not annihilate her forces, nor did they prevent her from continuing the campaign. The causes of her weakness must be sought elsewhere. They must be sought in the disorders to which she was a prey from the middle of the 14th century; which were explained, at least to a great extent, by the nature of the French State as it was constituted from the reign of Philip Augustus to the reign of Philip the Fair.

This State, as we have already seen, was essentially monarchical. There was no independent political power beside the king; there were only functionaries or councils, and none of these were derived, like the English Parliament, from a source which was distinct from the Crown. The royal authority, which from reign to reign had extended itself farther and farther, and had amalgamated the portions detached by the feudal princes, manifested itself essentially in affording protection and administering justice. The king was the attorney of his kingdom, the first justiciary in the land, the guardian of his subjects. It was from this that he derived his social function, and this was the foundation of his popularity. The State over which he presided was essentially based upon the idea of law. Its principal functionaries were the bailiffs, officers of justice: its most important central organ, the Parlement of Paris, was a court of justice. And the popular sentiment that cherished the picture of St. Louis dispensing justice under the oaks of Vincennes was in complete accordance with the reality. Philip the Fair had always upheld this conception of the monarchy, and his conflict with the Pope was fundamentally a dispute concerning the juridical sovereignty of the king.

But the State, in order to maintain itself, had greater and greater need of financial resources. Now all that was left of the ancient Roman fiscality, the old taxes transmuted into fines, had passed, since the 10th century, into the hands of the great vassals. The court had nothing to depend on apart from its domains and their revenues. To this may be added the revenue from the coinage, which had been to a great extent withdrawn from the great vassals since the reign of Philip Augustus.[1] The court also had recourse to borrowing. But this was not enough. It would evidently be necessary to resort also to taxation. But there was no tax which the court could collect. Hence the expedient of monetary depreciation under Philip the Fair, the taxation of the clergy, which made the Pope go to war, the suppression of the Templars, which was a scandal, and dealings with the Italians which went far to drain the Treasury. The idea that the State could impose a tax upon its subjects did not occur to it, for this was not a legal notion. The notion that the State could extend its competence so far as to draw upon the private fortune of those whom it protected had not yet arisen. From the financial point of view the evolution of the State was backward as compared with its development from the juridical point of view. Indeed, at the close of the 13th century the State had not really progressed beyond the conception which confused the public finances with the revenues of the king.

[1] The *taille* (tallage) was not properly a tax, but a permanent due.

This was naturally the cause of extreme embarrassment on the outbreak of the Hundred Years' War. In order to pay the armies, to hire mercenaries, and to subsidize allies, the King had to contract debts, and the disorder of his finances was soon so great that he had to appeal for assistance to the subjects whom he dared not tax, convoke the States-General, and ask them for money. The result was a terrible crisis. It meant the outbreak, when the country was at war, of a sort of revolution, which reminds one of the rebellion in England at the time of the Great Charter. But in France the situation was much more serious; for in that country the national cohesion which the Norman conquest had given England did not exist. The monarchy, which had reunited the *membra disjecta* of the country, caused a general commotion by addressing itself to the people.

It was a terrible muddle. The Orders of the States-General could not come to a mutual understanding. The Third Estate, which had money and was supported by the cities, wished to introduce reforms which the monarchy would not accept. The princes profited by this contingency to recover the influence which they had lost. The conflicts of the parties excited the political ambitions of the seigneurs of royal blood. Étienne Marcel mobilized the Burgundians and the Armagnacs. If we except the restorative reign of Charles V, we may say that from the States-General of 1355 to the reign of Louis XI France was the victim of a double intestine war: that of the Third Estate against the king, and that of the princes against the Crown, both being really due to the fiscal crisis which was rendered necessary by the constitution of the kingdom: a crisis of confidence, so to speak, which was necessary in order to replace the Capetian conception of the State by a more complete conception: a crisis in which it seemed as though the State was on the point of foundering amidst the disasters of the war.

During the years which preceded the great war there was nothing to indicate the approach of such a crisis. The three sons of Philip the Fair, who, lacking male heirs, succeeded in turns to their father, Louis X (1314–1316), Philip V (1316–1322), Charles IV (1322–1328), profited by the position which he had bequeathed to them, but did nothing to improve it. No new problems arose. The Papacy, established at Avignon, was henceforth full of consideration for the Crown; France was at peace with England, whose king, Edward II, in conformity with the stipulations of the Treaty of Montreuil, married Isabelle, the sister of the three kings. The only war was a war with Flanders, which dragged on for a few years, to be concluded, under Philip V, by the Treaty of Paris (1320), which ceded to the kingdom the Castellanies of Lille, Douai and Orchies, while the heir of the county, Louis de Nevers, married a member of the royal family.

On the death of Charles IV, therefore, the kingdom was in a state of profound tranquillity. Even the extinction of the Capetian dynasty did not give rise to any difficulty. On the death of Louis X his daughter's claim to the crown had been waived, so that on ascending the throne Philip of Valois was merely profiting by a principle which had been proclaimed twelve years earlier, in conformity with the ancient Frankish law, accepted without dispute by the whole nation, and so manifestly unassailable that Edward III, the grandson, through his mother, of Philip the Fair, made no protest at the decisive moment. Moreover, his rights, even in the female line, were second to those of Jeanne, the daughter of Louis X, and wife of Philippe d'Evreux, to whom the new king, as a measure of prudence, ceded the kingdom of Navarre, to which the so-called "Salic law" did not apply so clearly as it did to France.

His reign opened under favourable auspices. When the Count of Flanders appealed for his assistance against the great insurrection of the bourgeois weavers and peasants of maritime Flanders, who since 1325 had been fighting, respectively, against the nobles and the patricians, Charles won a victory at Cassel, on August 23rd, 1328, which put an end to the revolt. The following year, Edward III took the oath of vassalage, in respect of Guyenne. War seemed so improbable that the king, with the concurrence of the Pope, made preparations for a Crusade, or rather, the French expedition to the East, which was to sail in 1332.

In England the reign of Edward III had begun less

favourably. The further military successes of the Scots forced him to recognize (1328) the independence of their country, so that their king, Robert Bruce, broke the bond of vassalage to which Edward I had subjected these tenacious adversaries. Fortunately for King Edward, Baliol's revolt against David Bruce, the successor of Robert Bruce (1331), enabled him to restore the broken bond. He declared for Baliol, defeated the troops of the legitimate king at Hallisdown Hill (1333), and forced him to take refuge in France, where Philip VI welcomed him as Louis XIV was one day to welcome James Stuart. Baliol made haste to safeguard his situation by ceding Berwick to the conqueror, and acknowledging the suzerainty of England over the kingdom which the English had won for him (February 1334).

The sympathy with which David Bruce was received by the French court was felt as an insult by Edward III. He retorted by lavishing proofs of confidence upon Robert d'Artois, the mortal enemy of Philip VI, receiving him in London with great display. His claims to the crown of France, whether he believed or not in their validity, presently made him incline to the idea of resuming the war which his grandfather had been obliged to terminate so suddenly in 1297. Young and active, and popular since his victory over Scotland, he allowed himself to be carried away by ambition. But like all very ambitious persons, he was prudent, and he would risk nothing until he had every chance of success. Following the example of Edward I, he first of all set about securing the alliance of the princes of the Low Countries. The most important of these, the Count of Flanders, Louis de Nevers, proved to be as faithful to Philip IV, who had saved him from a popular insurrection, as Guy de Dampierre, in 1297, was ready to break with Philip the Fair, who had helped the patricians in their conflict with him. But on the other side of the Scheldt, in the ancient Lotharingia, now divided into flourishing principalities, which since the great interregnum had enjoyed complete independence under the nominal suzerainty of the Empire, it would be easy to recruit supporters, provided they were well paid. Thanks to the Florentine bankers, who allowed him the most generous credit, Edward could spend without counting the cost. He gave *carte blanche* to Count William II of Hainaut and Holland, whose daughter Philippine, the patroness of Froissart, he had married in 1328, and it did not take him long to make arrangements, in return for cash payment, with the Duke of Brabant and others of less importance—the Counts of Guelders, Clèves and Juliers. Just as in 1297 Edward I had bought the support of the King of Germany, Adolphus of Nassau, Edward III thought it best to hire the services of the Emperor, Louis of Bavaria. He hoped, no doubt, that this unfortunate man, recently excommunicated by John XXII, would find in his rancour against the Avignon Papacy a motive for avenging himself on France.

To the English coalition Philip VI opposed, in the Low Countries, an old ally of France, the Bishop of Liége, and John, the blind King of Bohemia, with whom he was connected by marriage, but who brought with him only a few knights from his County of Luxemburg. In Scotland he supported the partisans of David Bruce, who took up arms again.

Hostilities began in 1337. The French made surprise attacks on Guernsey and on Portsmouth, which they burned; and the English attacked a body of Flemish troops on the island of Cadzant. In the following year, July 22nd, 1338, Edward III disembarked at Antwerp, with the intention of doing great things. But his allies were completely lacking in enthusiasm. Louis of Bavaria did not move; he contented himself with bestowing upon Edward the title of Vicar of the Empire. The Duke of Brabant and Guillaume III, Count of Hainaut-Holland, who had just succeeded his father, were plainly trying to wriggle out of their engagements. In order to drag such auxiliaries into a conflict which for them was merely an opportunity of exacting subsidies it was necessary to pay through the nose, and Edward, overburdened with debts, went bankrupt, ruining his Florentine creditors. Fortunately, in order to compel the Count of Flanders to come over to his side, he had repeated the tactics which had already proved effective in dealing with the count: he prohibited the export of wool, which was indispensable to the cloth trade of Gand, Bruges, and Ypres. Despite the crisis provoked by this measure, Louis de Nevers had remained unshakable in his loyalty to France. But the trade corporations and the merchants of the cities had no intention of allowing themselves to be ruined or starved, and since their prince preferred the cause of his suzerain to theirs, they undertook to work out their own salvation. Gand, where the corporations of the cloth trade had for some years been in power, took over the government of the county, under the direction of a wealthy burgess, Jan van Artevelde. Artevelde got into touch with Edward; the embargo on wool was raised, and in order to dispel the scruples which might have deterred the burgesses from abandoning Philip VI, their suzerain, Edward went to Gand, where he was solemnly acknowledged, in the market-place, as King of France. Thus the solidarity of their interests brought about an alliance between Edward's monarchical and dynastic policy and the bourgeois and economic policy of the Flemish cities, an alliance to which Flanders was to show herself unshakably faithful. In this essentially industrial country, where the bourgeoisie was predominant, politics, sooner than anywhere else in the North of Europe, were subordinated to economic considerations.

The entry of Flanders into the English alliance assured Edward of a solid base in the north. Hitherto the war had consisted of operations along the French frontier: skirmishes and the burning of villages. Meanwhile the cardinal envoys from Avignon sought vainly to negotiate a peace, which Edward discussed only in order to gain time. Operations of the magnitude of which Edward had dreamed were about to become possible. He hastened to England to demand from Parliament the subsidies which his bankruptcy had rendered indispensable, and which were granted him, in view of the existing situation. On June 23rd, 1340, his fleet won a brilliant victory over the French fleet off Sluys; then, accompanied by the Flemish militia, and with the aid of the princes, encouraged by this splendid victory, he proceeded to besiege Tournai (July 22nd–September), but the siege was unsuccessful, and ended in the Truce of Esplechin, which was several times renewed during the following years.

Thus, despite the assistance of Flanders, the plan of attack from the north had failed. Van Artevelde was killed in 1345, during a rising fomented against him by the weavers of Gand. The coalition of the princes was dissolved. Louis of Bavaria, without returning the money which had been paid to him, actually went over to Philip VI, but he was no more effective as his ally than he had been as Edward's. As regards the situation of the two belligerents, that of France appeared to be more favourable. She had profited by the truce to extend her eastern frontier. In 1343 she bought, for cash payment, the Dauphiné from the Dauphin Humbert II, whose title was thenceforward borne by the heir to the crown.

The truce did not prevent Edward III from going to Brittany, to the help of the Countess of Montfort, who was disputing the Duchy with Charles of Blois, supported by France, or from sending the Earl of Derby to make war upon Gascony. In 1346 he suddenly landed in Normandy. This was the beginning of a complete change of policy. A new system of tactics, based on the rôle of the archers on the battlefield, gave the English a series of brilliant victories. Moreover, the purely natural composition of Edward's army must have given him the same advantage, over an adversary whose troops were largely foreign mercenaries, as the Spanish armies enjoyed in the 16th century. The battle of Crécy (August 26th) proved the quality of his army. Despite the advantage of numbers, the French suffered a defeat *moulte grande et moult horrible* (Froissart). The King of Bohemia, the Count of Flanders and a number of other great seigneurs were among the dead. The victor profited by this unhoped-for success to besiege Calais, which was taken after a siege of eleven months, and was not restored to France until 1558. A few weeks after the battle of Crécy, David Bruce, driven across the Scottish border, was defeated and taken prisoner at Nevil's Cross (October 17th). The English were triumphant everywhere. But both sides were equally in need of a breathing-space. On the Pope's intervention a truce was concluded in Sep-

tember 1347. This, owing to the appearance of the Black
Death, was prolonged into the following year, and being
repeatedly renewed was terminated only in 1355.

Both sides had profited by this period of repose, and had
made preparations for a decisive action. Thanks to the subsidies granted by Parliament, the English had mustered
three armies: one in Guyenne, another in Brittany, and a
third in Normandy. The new King of France, Jean II the
Good[2] (1350–1364), had decided to convoke the States-
General, which had furnished him with the means of
equipping 30,000 men. These he led against the Black
Prince, who was ravaging Guyenne. The battle of Mau-
pertuis, near Poitiers, on September 19th, 1356, ended in a
catastrophe even more overwhelming than that of Crécy.
Jean himself was taken prisoner and sent to England as a
captive.

In France this disaster immediately provoked the first of
the crises with which the monarchy was repeatedly confronted until the middle of the 15th century. The States-
General of 1355, in which the influence of the bourgeoisie
was predominant, led by the Provost of the merchants of
Paris, Étienne Marcel, had demanded, in return for voting
the taxes required by the king, a considerable voice in the
government. They had stipulated that they themselves
must levy and administer the new taxes, and they demanded guarantees in respect of their right to assemble in
the future, and the introduction of administrative reforms.
A great victory would doubtless have enabled the king to
stifle an opposition which his misfortunes rendered irresistible. This opposition was all the bolder inasmuch as it was
encouraged by the King of Navarre, Charles the Bad, an
ambitious and unscrupulous prince, who was all the more
inclined to embroil the situation inasmuch as only a state
of turmoil would enable him to advance his pretended
claim, as the son of Jeanne D'Evreux, to the crown of
France. Thus the French monarchy found itself, in the middle of the 14th century, suddenly obliged to reckon with

2 Jean I was the posthumous son of Louis X, who lived only a
few days, and was succeeded by Philip V.

the bourgeoisie which had formerly helped it to fight against the feudal seigneurs and establish the unity of the kingdom. Unassailed and undisputed for a century past, the monarchy was asked to share its power with the nation. France, after the battle of Poitiers, was in the position which had been occupied by England a hundred and fifty years earlier after the battle of Bouvines. In both cases financial disorder and defeat provoked a revolution. It is not surprising that this revolution should have occurred much later in France than in England. The political and national unity which is a necessary condition of a revolution had been suddenly forced upon England, at the end of the 11th century, in the days of the Norman conquest, while in France it was not achieved until the reign of Philip the Fair, after long-continued efforts. But the difference presented in this particular by the history of the two countries was not a mere chronological difference. In England the resistance to John Lackland was organized by the barons: that is, by the military class, behind which the rest of the nation was gathered, complaining of the same grievances and demanding the same rights. There was nothing of the kind in France under Jean the Good. There the bourgeoisie—that is to say, the commercial and industrial class—headed the movement. Now between this bourgeoisie and the nobles no understanding was possible. The privileges of the one class were opposed to those of the other, giving rise to a mutual hostility, which the disasters of Crécy and Poitiers, for which the bourgeoisie held the chivalry responsible, increased to a maximum. It was too late, in the middle of the 14th century, for another Simon de Montfort to emerge from the ranks of the French feudality. If a few *grands seigneurs* supported the efforts of the Third Estate, this was only by reason of personal interest, resentment or ambition, and on the first opportunity they abandoned the allies whom they despised. The same may be said of the clergy. Its representatives were concerned only to defend their prerogatives and immunities. In short, between the English Parliament and the States-General of France the contrast could not be greater. The English Parliament confronted the king with the united representatives of the various classes of the nation, who deliberated together, and by mutual agreement gave expression to their will; the States-General, composed of three orders which debated and voted separately, constituted in reality three distinct assemblies of privileged persons, incapable of agreement, so that their disagreements and their conflicts offered the Crown only too easy a means of evading their intervention. Moreover, in the course of the 13th century the competence and the attributions of Parliament were in all essentials determined by custom, so that it became an indispensable organ of the government. The States-General, on the contrary, were merely an institution adapted to the circumstances, an *ultima ratio* to which recourse was had only at a time of financial distress. Every one of their convocations corresponded with a crisis of the Treasury: they were assembled only that they might be asked for money. And it was precisely this fact that gave the bourgeoisie the preponderant rôle in the States. For since it did not enjoy the financial immunities of the nobles or the clergy, it was the bourgeoisie above all that was called upon to make payment, and it was natural that in return for the taxes which it voted it should stipulate for certain guarantees. As far as can be judged from the sixty-seven articles submitted to the Dauphin by Étienne Marcel, its ideal was to inspire the administration of the kingdom with the same spirit of control and legality which prevailed in the urban administration. The agents of the king, above all the financial agents, must no longer be irresponsible in respect of the taxpayers. The government must accept the permanent collaboration of the States-General and associate them in its activities. But when Marcel spoke of the States-General he was thinking before all of the bourgeoisie, and especially of the Parisian bourgeoisie. From the time of this first encounter between the King of France and the nation, Paris actually assumed the leadership of the movement, and no one dreamt of disputing its position. The importance of Paris as the capital, which it owed to the Crown, was now exploited by the people of Paris against the Crown. The royal city was so truly without peer, it so far surpassed all the other cities of the kingdom, by its population, its wealth, and its activity—and also by its turbulence—and it was already so truly the centre of the country, the focus of universal attention, that from the middle of the 14th century its tumults shook all France, the voice of its tribunes was heard by the whole nation, and its riots were "historic days" (*journées*). The Dauphin understood this so fully that he introduced a tactical expedient which was often employed afterwards, down to the 19th century: he decided to remove the States-General from this turbulent centre and to assemble them at Compiègne (1358). This merely exasperated the Parisian opposition. Civil war seemed on the point of breaking out. Marcel negotiated with the King of Navarre and the King of England, and he was exhorting Gand and the Flemish cities to unite their efforts to his in opposing "wicked and foolish enterprises, in such a manner that we may all live in full liberty," when the explosion of the Jacquerie led to the dénouement of the crisis.

The burden of the new taxes, accompanied by the excesses of the troops of mercenaries disbanded after Poitiers, who were dispersing in all directions and living on the country, had driven the peasants of Champagne, Picardy, and Beauvais to extremities. The defeat of the nobles at Crécy and Poitiers had dispelled the dread with which the peasants had regarded them. They attributed their distress to the cowardice of the nobles. They felt, confusedly, that the privileges of the nobles could be justified only by their military rôle, and this they had just shown themselves incapable of fulfilling. Suddenly they envisaged the gentleman as the enemy of the people. Bands of peasants armed with iron-bound cudgels proceeded to scour the country and to attack the châteaux. Their first successes emboldened them. Before long there was a general rising among the peasants. Yet there was no general plan of revolt. There were no recognized leaders, and no precise claims were advanced. It was a reaction of despair, an explosion of rage. The startled bourgeoisie, in the shelter of its walls, watched the movement without taking part in it, doubtless intending to profit thereby if it should succeed. But how could it have succeeded? The heavily-armed knights whom the English archers had defeated could not fail to overcome these "villeins, black and stunted and poorly armed" (Frois-sart, v, 105), who were killing their children, violating their wives, and burning their manors. Their superiority was like that of regular troops over a mob of strikers. After the first moment of confusion the nobles took the field, and the re-sult was a massacre. The decimated "Jacques" returned to their villages, convinced of their impotence. There were no further rural insurrections in France until the French Revolution.

This insurrection brought the nobles over to the side of the Dauphin, snapping the very feeble bonds which here and there united some of the party of the nobles to the party of the bourgeois reformers. Marcel's enemies grew bolder. A conspiracy was hatched against him, and on July 31st, 1358, he was assassinated, just as Jan van Artevelde, be-tween whose policy and his own there was a striking resem-blance, had been assassinated fifteen years earlier. His death did not put an end to the assembly of the States-General. The Dauphin could not dispense with their as-sistance in the exhausted condition of the country. Edward III, in 1359–1360, besieged the city of Reims and advanced as far as Burgundy without encountering any resistance. It was imperative that peace should be concluded. It was signed at Bretigny (near Chartres) on May 9th, 1360. Ed-ward received Gascony, Guyenne, Poitou, Calais and the County of Guines in full sovereignty, plus three millions of gold, in return for which he renounced his claim to the rest of France. England thus once more became a Continen-tal power, to the detriment of France. The situation was strangely like that which obtained in the time of the first Plantagenets. The area of the kingdom had been dimin-ished until it was almost what it had been at the beginning of the reign of Philip Augustus.

This fact alone is enough to show that the results of the Peace of Bretigny were indefensible. A French State was not like the territorial possessions of the houses of Bavaria, Luxemburg and Austria, a mere juxtaposition of countries and peoples which the dynasties could amalgamate as easily as they could dismember them. It was as definitely based on geographical unity as it was on national unity and solidarity of interests. Rescued by the kings from its state of feudal subdivision as soon as the agrarian economy on which this subdivision was based had disappeared, it had crystallized round them through successive reigns, and the only reason why the action of the monarchy had been so prompt and so fruitful was that it was in correspondence with the nature of things. The annexations which had of necessity been conceded to Edward III were obviously only a temporary sacrifice. It was as impossible that England should be able to retain her new French provinces as it would have been for France to take and retain possession of Kent. The Peace of Bretigny was plainly no more than a truce. What hope could there be that France would accept as lasting a situation which was not only humiliating to her, but which constituted a permanent menace? And how could England retain, against the will of the population, conquests as extensive as her own territory?

Charles V (1364–1380), who succeeded his father Jean II in 1364, could not hope to break the peace which had barely been concluded. The kingdom was exhausted by taxation, and more than ever victimized by the companies of mercenaries who were living on the inhabitants. The king very skilfully succeeded in relieving his subjects of the nuisance of these mercenaries by employing them against England. Henri de Transtamarre, who was fighting Pedro the Cruel, an ally of Edward III, in Castile, had appealed to France for help. Du Guesclin received orders to march to his assistance at the head of the companies. Pedro the Cruel was defeated (1369), and a treaty of alliance was concluded between Charles V and Henri de Transtamarre, so that an enemy threatened the flank of the English possessions in Aquitaine. At the same time the king's diplomacy won another success in the north. The Count of Flanders, Louis de Maele, the son of Louis de Nevers who was slain at Crécy, had abandoned his father's policy and adopted an ambiguous neutrality, which, as it compelled both France and England to treat with him, had procured for him a situation which was all the more advantageous, in that having no male descendant, he was able to keep the two belligerents in suspense by negotiating with both for the marriage of his daughter Marguerite. In this conflict between the two bidders, Charles V was victorious. In return for the restitution to Flanders of Lille, Douai and Orchies, ceded in 1320, Louis consented to the marriage of his daughter (June 29th, 1369) with the King's brother, Philip the Bold, who in 1361 had received the Duchy of Burgundy as his appanage. It seemed that the "Flemish question" which had so greatly preoccupied the Crown since the reign of Philip Augustus was on the point of being solved, since the succession of the powerful County was assured to a royal prince.

Charles V now felt himself strong enough for a frontal attack upon England. A revolt against the Black Prince in Guyenne served him as a pretext for denouncing the Peace of Bretigny. The States-General hastened to grant the necessary subsidies, and the war, energetically waged by Du Guesclin, resulted in an uninterrupted series of successes. In 1372 the fleet of Castile defeated the English fleet off La Rochelle. On land the English had retained hardly anything more than Calais, Bordeaux and Bayonne when Edward III died, in 1377, two years after the Black Prince, bequeathing the crown to the Black Prince's son, Richard II, a child of nine; and three weeks later another child, Charles VI, inherited the crown of France on the death of Charles V.

2. The Burgundian Period (1432)

The two regencies, which began almost simultaneously in France and England, were equally stormy. Though the actual happenings on either side of the Channel were of a very different nature, they were influenced by the same motives: the discontent of the people, due to the heavy burden of war taxation, and the ambition of the royal princes invested with the regency.

The reign of Richard II is memorable on account of the great rural insurrection of 1381. The fundamental cause of this rising, like that of the Jacquerie, was the poverty of the rural population, whose sufferings were as little regarded by Parliament as they had been by the States-

General. How should the political assemblies concern themselves with the troubles of the people, since they consisted only of the representatives of the privileged classes? Parliament regarded the people much as the governments of landowners, at the beginning of the 19th century, regarded the industrial proletariat: as the unprivileged multitude, on which the social edifice rested, and which received attention only when its commotions shook the society which was based upon it.

In England, as everywhere, the situation of the peasants was much improved in the 13th century. But during the first half of the 14th century progress was arrested by the action of the general causes which have already been indicated. The greater cost of living and the increased wages which were a consequence of the ravages of the Black Death led the nobles, in 1350, to insist that Parliament should pass a law reducing the wages of agricultural labourers to the tariff obtaining in 1347 (Statute of Labourers). Emboldened by their success, they thereupon endeavoured to re-establish their old domanial rights, to revive the system of *corvées*, which had fallen into desuetude, and once more to degrade the peasants to the status of serfs attached to the soil. If we consider that all these wrongs were aggravated by the increasing burden of taxation we can understand what a ferment of hatred must have filled the minds of the people. The religious movement provoked by Wycliffe led to the final catastrophe, just as in the 16th century the Lutheran propaganda led to the outbreak in Germany of the Peasant War. Of course, neither Wycliffe nor Luther urged the masses to rebel, but both reformers, by undermining the people's respect for religious authority, taught them to revolt against the social order which was the cause of their sufferings, and which the traditional Church had taught them to respect. It was in this particular that the English rebels of 1384 differed from the Jacques of France in 1357. The Jacques were driven to revolt only by their poverty; the English rebels were all the more formidable in that they were spurred onward not merely by poverty, but also by the feeling that they were the victims of a Church and a society both of which were corrupted by the love of riches. They had at their head not only journeymen like Wat Tyler, but also poor priests like John Ball, whose Lollardist preaching had inspired so many poor folk with passionate hopes of a naïve communism.

But the peasants could not hold their own against the nobles, those steel-clad policemen. Like the Jacquerie, their rising ended in a massacre, and like the Jacquerie it was not repeated.

However, the war with France resulted in a series of defeats. The English allowed the men of Gand to be crushed in the battle of Roosebeke, and in the following year the English expedition against Ypres, under the command of the Bishop of Norwich (1383), was a pitiable failure. In 1388 the English had to resign themselves to accepting a truce, which was renewed for twenty years in 1396. These reverses increased the dissatisfaction with the king's government. Richard had hardly emerged from the tutelage of the regency when he attempted to undermine the increasing authority assumed by Parliament during the reign of Edward III. The only result of his efforts was that in 1384 he had the humiliation of seeing his counsellors condemned to death. The opposition had been led by his uncle, Thomas of Gloucester. The king joined forces against him with his other uncle, John of Lancaster, with the result that Gloucester was accused of high treason; he also succeeded in obtaining from Parliament a permanent tax, which he found highly advantageous, as henceforth he was able to abstain from convoking that formidable assembly. This new attempt to restore the personal power of the Crown in England, which followed the unsuccessful attempts of Henry III and Edward II, was no more successful than the latter. How could the king have got the better of Parliament, the organ of the triple strength of the nobles, the clergy and the burgesses? He seems to have had some vague notion of seeking support from the Lollards, and from the mass of the people, who were still seething with rebellion. However, when Henry of Lancaster, after the death of his father, summoned the nobles to take up arms against the king, no one raised a hand to defend the monarch. In 1399 Parliament, making use for the second time of the right which it had arrogated to itself under Edward II, deprived him of the crown, which it gave to Henry of Lancaster (1399–1413), although he was not the next heir.

The new king found himself in the situation which in 1689 was that of William of Orange on succeeding to James II. Parliament, to which he owed the throne, expected guarantees, which he hastened to give. In order to conciliate the spiritual lords he made a clean break with the Lollards, introduced the Inquisition into England, and forbade the translation of the Bible into the vulgar tongue.

War with Scotland and a rebellious Wales made it impossible for him to satisfy the bellicose aspirations of the nobles and to break the truce which had been concluded with France. It was reserved for his son Henry V to reopen this fruitless struggle, and to win fresh victories, as brilliant and as ephemeral in their results as those of Crécy and Poitiers had been.

While Richard II, Henry IV and Henry V succeeded one another on the throne of England, the long regency to which the youth of Charles VI (1380–1422), and presently his insanity, condemned France during his reign resulted in a return of the commotions and the rivalries which Charles V had interrupted, though he had not removed their cause. The king's uncles, entrusted with the government during his minority, were chiefly concerned to exploit their position to their personal advantage. Louis of Anjou, whom Queen Joanna of Naples had recently appointed her heir, busied himself with making preparations for an expedition into Italy, while Philip of Burgundy turned an anxious gaze upon Flanders, his future heritage.

Since the Black Death the increasing cost of living had not been balanced by an increase of wages, so that the industrial populations of the cities were in a state of the most dangerous unrest. The weavers, who were the most numerous, the best organized and the boldest of the clothworkers, were everywhere assuming a threatening attitude, and were posing as the champions of the poor against the rich. Year after year the social antagonism increased, still further excited by the communistic mysticism which had so many adherents in the ranks of the proletariat. In 1379

the weavers of Gand succeeded in seizing the power of government, and were immediately imitated by their comrades
of Bruges and Ypres. In this region of Flanders, where the
wealthy employers had so long been predominant in the
cities, and had reduced the majority of the workers to the
condition of wage-earners, the latent economic conflict between employers and employed broke out into a veritable
class warfare. The rebels were by no means content with
demanding political rights. What did they actually want?
They themselves could not have explained very clearly
what they wanted, for what they wanted was that indefina-
ble State which was at once the objective of the grossest
appetites and the purest love of justice, an ideal which
alternately consoled or exasperated the unfortunate. The
immediate effect of their victory in the three great cities
was to assemble against them, and to gather about the
Count, all those "who had something to lose": merchants,
employers, courtiers, wealthy artisans—the defenders of the
order which protected their property against the revolution
which was threatening them. The weavers of Bruges and
Ypres were unable to resist the coalition of their enemies.
But the weavers of Gand remained indomitable. Their city,
blockaded by the chivalry of Louis de Maele, who dared
not make a direct attack, attracted the impassioned interest
of all who suffered under the rule of the rich and powerful.
The trade corporations of Liége sent provisions to Gand;
the men of Malines followed its example and revolted, while
in France the people of Paris and Rouen rose to the cry of
"Vive Gand." A veritable social contagion was spreading
from the heroic city. It was starving, but it had no thought
of surrender. Philip van Artevelde, whom Gand chose for its
leader, encouraged the rebels to make a supreme effort. Under the walls of Bruges they offered battle to the army of
Louis de Maele, and, against all expectations, cut it to
pieces. Once more Gand was the mistress of Flanders, and
everywhere the weavers once more laid down the law in
the Flemish cities.

Philip the Bold, by invoking the necessity of dealing
drastically with the centre of so contagious a rebellion, had
no difficulty in persuading the court to despatch an expe-

dition which would assure him of his heritage. The men of Gand and their adherents were defeated at Roosebeke, and Louis de Maele resumed possession of his County. He had just inherited from his mother Artois and the Franche Comté of Burgundy, so that on his death in 1384 Philip became the possessor of these territories, as well as Flanders. Combined with his Duchy of Burgundy, they gave him a power which no vassal of the Crown had ever before possessed. However, his dazzling position was regarded merely as a victory won by the policy of the Crown. The result at which Charles V had aimed was achieved. Flanders was now ruled by a prince of the blood. Did not this mean the definite rupture of the English alliance, and was it not the prelude to a closer union in the future?

Philip did not fail to profit by the conjuncture which identified his own interest with that of the kingdom. From the beginning of the 13th century it had been the policy of the Crown to endeavour to subject to its influence all the princes of the Low Countries. Nominally vassals of the Empire, they had really been quite independent of it since the great interregnum, and were entirely indifferent to its quarrels. Just as the whole economic life of their territories was oriented upon the Flemish coast, so their policy was wholly Occidental. Turning their backs on the Empire, their sympathies were given now to Paris, now to London, according to their interests of the moment. The advanced civilization of these regions, the general diffusion of French manners, the similarity of the institutions which analogous economic needs and the general preponderance of the bourgeoisie had bestowed upon the various principalities, had saved them, despite the fact that in the north the population was Flemish and in the south Walloon, from the racial conflicts which in Eastern Europe had broken out, with all the brutality of instinctive hostility, between the Slavs and the Germans. Thus the dynastic amalgamations of various originally independent territories effected during the 13th century were of a durable nature. Since 1286 the union of the Duchies of Brabant and Limburg, and since 1250 that of the Counties of Hainaut, Holland and Zeeland, had constituted, as it were, the prodrome of a movement of unification which was to undergo still further development. At the very moment when Philip the Bold took possession of Flanders the extinction of the petty local dynasties had given these territories to two of the houses which were struggling for preponderance in Germany. The House of Bavaria had inherited the Counties of Hainaut, Holland and Zeeland in 1345, and in 1355 the marriage of Jeanne, the heiress of Brabant and Limburg, to Wenceslas, the brother of the Emperor Charles IV, enabled the House of Luxemburg to anticipate the future possession of these two fair provinces. But engrossed as they were in their German quarrels, neither of these two houses was capable of giving effective support to their representatives in the Low Countries. Philip the Bold, on the other hand, who, under his nephew Charles VI, was able to make use of the resources and the troops of the government, quickly prevailed over both houses. In 1385 he contrived a double marriage: his son Jean married Marguerite of Bavaria, and William of Bavaria, Count of Hainaut, married his daughter, while in order still further to safeguard the alliance, which was in reality a protectorate, he made the king, Charles VI, marry Isabella of Bavaria, the daughter of the Duke of Hainaut-Holland. Three years later, the Duchess of Brabant being at war with the Duke of Guelders, he persuaded Charles VI to lead the French army against this ally of England. The only result of the expedition was to give the Duchy to Philip. Wenceslas of Luxemburg having died some little time before this, the Duchess of Brabant tore up the convention by which she acknowledged the Luxemburgers as her heirs and secured the succession to Philip, who ceded it to his second son Antoine, in order not to offend the Brabançon sentiment of autonomy. Thus, when he died in 1404 the influence of his dynasty was enormously increased in the Low Countries. But these regions were so wealthy, and their political situation was so advantageous, that before long the dynasty took root there, when, forgetting its French origin, and actuated by an ambition which naturally identified itself with the interests of its northern subjects, it became naturalized among them. Charles V, by assuring his brother's possession of Flanders, had hoped to recover it for the Crown. But by the irony of history the marriage of 1369 was the beginning of that Burgundian power which was presently to become the cruellest enemy of France.

Already, under Jean the Fearless (1404–1419), the successor of Philip the Bold, we see the beginning of the evolution which was to make him, the son of a pure-blooded Valois, above all things a Burgundian prince. There can be no doubt that the interest of his northern possessions, and above all of Flanders, determined his political principles. In the interests of Flemish industry he was obliged to humour England, and he began to conciliate that country from the very beginning of his reign, and as the Flemings acknowledged the Pope of Rome he did all that was in his power to bring about the end of the schism. At the same time he set to work to improve the position of his house in the Low Countries. He brought about a marriage between his nephew Jean of Brabant and Jacqueline of Bavaria, the future heiress of Hainaut-Holland. In 1408 he extended his influence as far as the Meuse by aiding the Bishop of Liége, John of Bavaria, against the Liégeois rebels, whom he cut to pieces at Othée.

This increase of the Burgundian power in the north constituted such a direct threat to France that she could not look on unmoved. The king being insane and incapable, his brother, the Duke of Orleans, forced the government to adopt an attitude which was entirely hostile to Jean the Fearless. On November 23rd, 1407, his rival had him assassinated. This was the signal for the outbreak of a civil war which had only awaited some such occasion.

The defeat of the men of Gand at Roosebeke in 1382 had decided the fate of the Parisian insurrection. Returning to his capital victorious, the king made it clear that he was the master. He abolished the franchises of the city and put an end to that era of reforms and convocations of the States-General which had begun with Étienne Marcel. The opposition was defeated, but it was more exasperated than ever. It only awaited a leader to take up arms again. Jean the Fearless, seeing that the partisans of the Duke of Orleans were making ready to oppose him, under the leadership of the Count of Armagnac, immediately allied his cause with that of the urban democracy. He posed as the champion of the people against the exploitation of the nobles and the court, and affected demagogic manners, so that the cry of "Vive Bourgogne" replaced the cry of "Vive Gand" which had resounded through the streets of Paris twenty-five years earlier. Thus the dynastic policy which in the Low Countries had made the Duke the enemy of the Liége artisans placed him in France at the head of the Parisian artisans, and led him to support all their claims and to work hand in hand with the butcher Caboche, allowing his slaughterers to massacre the Armagnacs. When the States-General, which had not assembled for thirty years, were convoked in 1413, he supported all the reforms demanded by the "Cabochiens," being anxious above all to remain popular with the masses. As for the interests of the kingdom, we find no trace of them in his policy. In the following year, when Henry V took up arms against France, he preserved a neutrality so benevolent that it came near to being an alliance.

The state of disorganization into which France had fallen rendered her incapable of vigorous resistance. The king being insane, and the bourgeoisie hostile, while the Duke of Burgundy pursued his own ends, the burden of the war rested on the Armagnac party, as though the war with England had been merely an episode of the civil war. The disaster of Agincourt (October 25th, 1415) gave Normandy to the English. The French wished to negotiate. The claims of the victor were so exorbitant that Jean the Fearless, who had merely wished to see France and England neutralize each other, made approaches to the Dauphin, round whom the Armagnacs had rallied. But men's passions were too unbridled to subordinate themselves to the national interest. On September 20th, 1419, on the occasion of their meeting at Montereau, a blow from an axe avenged the murder of the Duke of Orleans.

At the very moment when the House of Burgundy was becoming reconciled to France, this crime led it to conclude an immediate alliance with the English. For sixteen years the son of Jean the Fearless, Philip the Good (1419–

1467), strove to overthrow the kingdom, with an energy
inspired by the spirit of vengeance and directed by political
interest. For although he placed his troops at the disposal
of England, it was on condition that England should give
him a free hand in the north, and help him to conquer the
Low Countries as he was helping England to conquer
France. The popularity which his father had enjoyed
among the bourgeois facilitated his task. The States-General did not fail to recognize Henry V as the successor of
Charles VI. The Dauphin, without energy, or military
talent, or popularity, and whose troops were both insufficient and lacking in confidence, was soon obliged to fall
back along the Loire. The death of Henry V, and that of
Charles VI, which occurred a few months later in 1422,
enabled the English and the Burgundians to proclaim
Henry VI, a child only a few months old, King of France
and England, the proclamation being made in Paris. After
seventy years of war the end pursued by Edward III and
bequeathed by him to the ambition of his successors was
at last attained. The Duke of Bedford was invested with
the regency and entrusted with the final conquest of the
kingdom. The future of the Dauphin, who had withdrawn
to Bourges, and who on the death of Charles VI had immediately assumed the royal title of Charles VII, appeared
extremely precarious.

However, it was far less precarious in reality than it
seemed. The advance of the English in the north had been
favoured by the Burgundian alliance. But Philip the Good
evidently could not allow his troops to operate too far from
the Low Countries, where he was pursuing an increasingly
active policy. On the other hand, Bedford and his brother
Gloucester, the Regent of England, found it hard to agree,
with the result that there was an immediate decrease of
vigour in the conduct of the campaign. Lastly, and above
all, the national feeling of the French had to be reckoned
with. The proclamation of Henry VI as King of France had
not aroused any popular indignation. The people either
ignored it, or regarded it as null and void. For the French
there were not two kings in France: there was only one
legitimate and possible monarch, only one appointed by

God and by tradition: the heir of the late king, Charles VII. Neither the miseries of the war, nor the burden of taxation, nor dissatisfaction with the government, nor the insanity of the last king, and the scandals provoked by the flagrant misconduct of the queen, had undermined the people's feeling for the dynasty. This feeling was as universal and as deeply rooted as their religious sentiments, and even in the remotest parts of the country, even among the descendants of the poor Jacques who were massacred in 1358, a veneration was felt for the king almost like that which was paid to the saints. This monarchical piety does not explain Joan of Arc—the superhuman cannot be explained—but it was, so to speak, her point of departure, the indispensable condition of her career, just as faith is the indispensable condition of martyrdom. Without it the heroic and visionary soul of the Domrémy shepherdess would never have heard the voices that determined her destiny. Those voices would never have spoken had she been born in the ranks of the nobility or the bourgeoisie, where the idea of the monarch was allied with too many considerations of interest or of politics. The exalted, simple, pure and ingenuous conception of the king entertained by Joan was possible only in a child of the people. Joan of Arc was no more than the sublime expression of the national sentiment of the French peasants, a sentiment which was blended with their religious faith, and which their memories of the good king St. Louis had indissolubly associated with the monarchy.

By its very unlikeness to that of the Armagnacs of the court, her popular royalism must have contributed greatly to the extraordinary influence which she exercised over the best of Charles's soldiers—over La Hire and Dunois. As for the nation, discouraged and disillusioned, the deliverance of Orléans (1429) gave it the sudden stimulus that restored its confidence and energy. The Pucelle dispelled the last remnants of party quarrels. Men began to hope again, and they recalled the old prophecies which announced that a virgin would save the kingdom. It needed no more than this pure apparition: France was herself again, and ready to confront the English and the Burgundians. The brief career of the "Bonne Lorraine" restored the latent energies of the people. Her capture at Compiègne in 1441, and her execution at Rouen in 1442, did not check the work which she had begun. Though the king showed little enough energy, though he took little advantage of the circumstances, he could now be certain that his cause would be victorious. Moreover, Bedford, paralysed by Gloucester, was not conducting the campaign with any vigour. And when in 1435 Philip the Good at last concluded a peace with Charles VII, so that henceforth France had to deal only with the English, the final result was only a question of time. In 1435 Paris opened her gates to the royal troops, and the "King of Bourges" at last took possession of his capital. Then, when the war, interrupted by a truce, was resumed in 1445, it was one series of victories. In 1449 Rouen was recaptured. In 1450 the victory of Formigny gave the French the whole of Normandy; Bordeaux and Bayonne were theirs in 1451, and finally, in 1453, after the battle of Chatillon, the enemy evacuated the last positions which he still occupied in the south of the kingdom. Of all the English conquests, Calais alone was left, and the empty title of King of France, which figured on the English currency even in the 19th century. The only lasting result of the Hundred Years' War was the creation, on the northern frontier of the kingdom, of a powerful Burgundian State. Philip the Good, in assisting the English, was really working for himself. He took effective advantage of Charles VII's weakness, reaping the results of the policy initiated by his grandfather and his father, and united under his power the various territories of the Low Countries. He purchased the County of Namur in 1421. In 1428 he was acknowledged by Jacqueline of Bavaria as the heir to Hainaut, Holland and Zeeland; in 1430 he succeeded his cousin Jean IV as Duke of Brabant and of Limburg; and when he concluded the Peace of Arras it was only in return for the cession by the King of Artois and the towns of the Somme. The following years brought him the possession of Luxemburg, and the protectorate over the ecclesiastical principalities of Liége and Utrecht.

But this State must not be regarded as one of those mere

collections of territories such as the Houses of Luxemburg and Habsburg were at this time assembling in Germany, and which, being held together merely by the fragile tie of dynastic union, fell to pieces as rapidly as they were made. Although its populations were heterogeneous, their general civilization and the interests were the same. If the peoples themselves had not tended to unite, nothing would have been easier than to prevent their union, for the rights invoked by Philip in respect of his succession to Hainaut, Holland and Brabant were, to say the least of them, doubtful. The Emperor Sigismond protested furiously against this annexation of Imperial fiefs to the Burgundian power, and urged the States to resist it. They did not listen to him, because the dynastic ambition of the prince was in accordance with their own desire, so that in the unification of the Low Countries the nation itself supported the plans of the dynasty.

In respect of its admirable geographical situation, the length of its sea-coast, the number of its cities, and the industry and wealth of its inhabitants, the Burgundian State had no equal in Europe, save Italy. But for France its creation was a check to the plan which she had pursued, from reign to reign, since the beginning of the 13th century, of subjecting to her influence these wealthy countries that lay upon her northern frontiers. It was only to be expected that once France had recovered from the terrible crisis by which Philip the Good had profited so greatly, she would never cease endeavouring to recover the preponderance which she had lost in the basins of the Meuse and the Scheldt. Her enemies just as obstinately disputed this preponderance, so that the creation of the Burgundian State created also that problem of the Low Countries which, until the 19th century, when it was finally solved, was to give rise to so many European crises that it served, so to speak, as a pressure-gauge in the international relations of the great powers.

CHAPTER III

The Empire. The Slav States and Hungary

1. *The Empire*

Germany, during the great interregnum, had assumed the political form which she was to retain down to modern times. It is not very easy to define her constitution, in which were comprised, without any real coherence, a monarchy which possessed none of the attributes of sovereignty, a multitude of ecclesiastical or lay princes, urban republics (Free Cities), and "immediate" (unmediated) nobles, enjoying complete independence, with a Diet (*Reichstag*) whose attributions were as ill-defined as its composition was bizarre. An anarchy in monarchical form: that perhaps is the best description of this extraordinary political entity, which had neither common laws, common finances, nor a common body of functionaries. It is strictly correct to say of it that it was a totality composed of parts which did not constitute a whole. Compared with France and England, it seemed amorphous, illogical, almost monstrous. The fact is that the mainspring of this strange mechanism, subjected too soon to an excessive tension, was broken. By the end of the War of Investitures it was evident that the monarchy, which everywhere else gave its form to the State, had no longer the strength to fulfil its task. Its Imperial ambitions had drawn it into adventures from which it had emerged half shattered, and while under the Hohenstaufens it gathered up what strength remained to it and endeavoured to take its revenge, this attempted recovery ended in a decisive catastrophe. After the election of Rudolph of Habsburg (1273) it was so completely devoid of prestige and authority that one may wonder why the electors still took the trouble to appoint a king. Perhaps it was really the Imperial ideal, the cause of its fall, which preserved its existence. The necessity of an Emperor, who no longer corresponded to any existing reality, was imposed by tradition. And since the King of Germany was the Emperor-designate, to suppress him would have been to abolish the Empire. He therefore continued to exist, and by the most paradoxical of destinies he retained his illusory monarchical power only in order to secure an Imperial power which had become even more illusory.

For since the death of Frederick II nothing remained of the Empire but the empty forms. The attitude adopted by the Papacy since Innocent III, and the formation of national States in France and England, finally deprived it of any further possibility of compelling Europe to acknowledge its temporal primacy. If this primacy was still acknowledged anywhere, it was in the schools, where the professors of Roman law continued to regard the Emperor, in theory, as the master of the world. It might also be invoked, from time to time, against a political adversary, as Boniface VIII invoked it in his conflict with Philip the Fair. Or some idealist might see in it, as Dante saw, a beautiful dream to which reality gave the lie. As a matter of fact it was a dead ideal, a relic of the past, and it would have been a majestic relic, if the weakness of the Emperors had not only too often contrasted too sharply with the memories which they evoked. The Emperor's precedence over other sovereigns was still recognized, as was his right to create nobles and to institute notaries in all countries. And this was almost all that was left of his old universal power. And he still derived some prestige from his relations with the Pope, with whom he was necessarily allied. In the 14th century these relations gave rise to an epilogue to the great conflicts of the past, and in the 15th century they enabled Sigismond to play what we may call—with a lack of reverence in some degree justified by his pretentious demeanour—the part of impresario to the Council of Constance.

Rudolph of Habsburg never found time, during his long reign (1273–1291), to go to Rome in order to receive the Imperial crown. Germany provided him with sufficient occupation. He did not need to be a great politician to realize that a restoration of the monarchical power in that country was impossible. The first condition of such a restoration would have been the hereditary nature of the Crown. It was useless to think of such a thing. Neither the Pope, nor the electors, nor the princes would have consented to it. The idea of rallying the cities to the cause of the monarchy was even more chimerical. It would have been possible only if they had felt the need of a protector, and they were not conscious of any such need. The princes were not powerful enough to imperil their position, and in the event of danger the regional leagues which they had concluded were a sufficient guarantee of their independence. Was there at least some hope of rallying the nation against a foreign power—of profiting by the encroachments of France on the western frontier in order to take his place at the head of the nation and make it accept him as its defender? To make that possible, Germany would have to be inspired by the nationalist ideal, and the country was quite devoid of any national feeling. Each thought only of himself, and the only frontier that gave him any anxiety was that of his own domain. In the midst of this universal egoism, Rudolph had no intention of devoting himself to the cause of the monarchy, which interested no one. Needy and burdened with a large family, he contented himself with profiting by the position which had been conferred upon him to attend to his own affairs, or rather, those of his house. Totally devoid of idealism, he felt that it would be a mockery to sacrifice himself and to leave the Crown as poor as when he had received it. The circumstances favoured his designs. The victory which he won over the King of Bohemia, Ottocar II, at the beginning of his reign, with the assistance of the King of Hungary (1278), left vacant the Duchies of Austria and Styria. He hastened to bestow them as fiefs on his son Albert. Thus a lucky chance had suddenly endowed the petty House of Habsburg with the wealthy Danubian duchies. This was the sole result of Rudolph's policy. Though he reigned without governing, at least he left his family well established, and provided with an example of the art of profiting by contingencies which it was to follow only too often in the future.

The electors had appointed Rudolph simply because he was weak and poor. Although he had disappointed them, they replaced him by a king who was still weaker and poorer, and gave the crown to Adolphus of Nassau (1291–1298). However, it was inevitable that the good fortune of his predecessor would induce him to proceed upon the same lines. But he was not, like Rudolph, favoured by chance. For the want of any better policy, he decided, in 1294, to sell to Edward I his services as ally against Philip the Fair. The encroachments of France on the German frontier sufficed to provide an honourable pretext for this bargain. But he was really as indifferent to these encroachments as he was to Edward's quarrel. What he really had in mind was to seize Thuringia, and the pounds sterling which he had received were employed merely in defraying the cost of a war by which he hoped to enrich his house. The electors were not disposed to countenance a second *parvenu*. They deposed him, replacing him by Albert, the son of Rudolph of Habsburg (1298–1308). In accordance with the tradition which was a legacy from his father, Albert was cherishing hopes of uniting the Kingdom of Bohemia with Austria, when his assassination, in 1308, led to the failure of a plan which was never again forgotten by the tenacious memory of his heirs.

For the third time a petty prince from whom it seemed that there was nothing to fear was called to the throne. Appointed through the influence of his brother, the Archbishop-Elector of Trèves, Count Henry of Luxemburg (1308–1313) belonged to the Low Countries, which, although they were comprised within the frontiers of the Empire, were now only nominally dependent on Germany. Like his neighbours of Liége, Hainaut, Brabant and Flanders, he was steeped in the civilization and the manners of France, and was also of Walloon origin, so that once he had crossed the Rhine he seemed a complete foreigner. Nevertheless, it was this foreigner, this "Welche," who restored the Imperial tradition, which his three predecessors had neglected in order to attend to their own affairs. His initiative was sufficiently explained by his origin. Since by virtue of this origin he was indifferent to German affairs he was bound to turn his attention to the affairs of the Empire. He dreamed of the glory of donning in Rome the crown which had never been worn since the reign of Frederick II, and, by reconciling the Empire with the Papacy, of winning for it by peaceful means a new and beneficent majesty.

The news of his arrival sent a thrill of hope through Italy. The annihilation of the Hohenstaufens had not restored tranquillity to the fiery cities of Lombardy and Tuscany. Under the old name of Guelfs and Ghibellines the factions still continued to wage war upon each other with a ferocity which was enhanced by the divergence of economic interests, the conflicts of the artisans and the patricians, and the mutual hatreds of the nobles. Pisa had recently surrendered to the Genoese forces, and Florence profited by her defeat, subjecting Tuscany to her democratic government. In Lombardy the majority of the cities, exhausted by their quarrels, accepted the *signoria* of a successful soldier or a podestà, and resigned themselves to tyranny for the sake of peace. The Della Torre ruled in Milan, the Della Scala in Verona, and the Este in Ferrara. In Rome, which had been abandoned by the Popes, the Colonna and the Orsini were in desperate conflict. Venice alone, under her powerful aristocracy, preserved a state of tranquillity which enabled her to devote herself with all the greater energy to the naval war which she was waging against Genoa.

Henry VII made his appearance in this world of unbridled passions and appetites as the restorer of order and peace. He had been sincerely anxious to reconcile the parties and to rally them to himself by the justness of his policy. But how could he impose justice without the aid of force? He had brought with him only three or four thousand knights, and the hope which had greeted his arrival was followed almost immediately by disappointment. Despite his intentions, he found himself obliged, if he was to obtain any support, to choose between the adversaries whom he had dreamed of pacifying. King Robert of Naples, who felt uneasy at seeing Henry's influence replacing his own in the peninsula, assumed a threatening attitude. When Henry arrived in Rome the troops of his enemies were in occupation of the greater part of the city. He could not reach St. Peter's, and had to content himself with receiving almost secretly, in the Lateran, from the hands of the cardinals appointed by the Pope, the Imperial crown, which it would perhaps have been better not to receive at all rather than receive it thus (June 1312). Of his plan for restoring the majesty of the Empire nothing was left. Without finances, and almost without an army, he was reduced to subordinating his policy to that of the Neapolitans, and soliciting the support of the King of Sicily against them. In Tuscany Florence closed her gates against him. In order to fight Florence he had to depend on Pisan support. The descent was too great after such brief and exalted illusions. Worn out by chagrin, Henry died at Buonconvento in August 1313. He was buried at Pisa; his sarcophagus is still there, under the gallery where the terrible frescoes of Orcagna represent so cruelly the vanity of human ambitions.

But he had reopened the road that led from Italy to Germany, and Louis of Bavaria, his successor, followed in his footsteps (1314–1347). He had hardly conquered Frederick of Habsburg, whom some of the electors had opposed to him, and taken him prisoner, when he took it into his head to cross the Alps. He was immediately confronted by the most desperate opposition from the Pope. The Holy See, forced by France and England to abate its claims, could not capitulate before the kings of Germany. By reviving the question of the Empire, which had been so long forgotten, they were reviving also the hateful memory of the Hohenstaufens, and there was reason to fear that they might rally around them in Italy all the enemies of the Papacy, and of the kings of Naples, its auxiliaries. War was all the more certain in view of the fact that their political power was so disproportionate to their ambitions that the Papacy, when it attacked them, was almost sure to be victorious. Already the rupture between Henry VII and Robert of Naples had embroiled Henry with Clement V, and only his premature death had prevented the outbreak of war. John XXII was resolved to surrender none of the supremacy which his great predecessors of the 12th century had won over the Empire. On ascending the pontifical throne he had solemnly declared that the Pope held from St. Peter both the spiritual and the temporal empire, and that it was his duty to watch over the latter in the absence of the Emperor. Immediately putting this theory into practice, he appointed Robert of Naples Vicar Imperial in Italy.

Encouraged by the adversaries of the Neapolitans, Louis of Bavaria believed that he was strong enough to accept battle. His excommunication and deposition, pronounced by John XXII (1324), brought over to his camp the spiritual Minorite friars, who, like him, had just been excommunicated, while Marsilius of Padua took advantage of his quarrel to launch against the Pope the *Defensor Pacis*. Bewildered, and carried away by this political and theological opposition, for which he was less the centre of gravity than the pretext, and unable to perceive that it was merely trying to use him under colour of serving him, he allowed himself to be dragged into an adventure which was to be his ruin. His coronation, in 1327, in the Capitol, by two excommunicated bishops, and four syndics of the city, who represented the people, was a sorry parody, in which reminiscences of the anarchy of the 10th century and the mystical republicanism of Arnold of Brescia were curiously blended. Having thus accepted the crown, Louis could refuse nothing, whether to the Roman people, now the victims of one of those crises of pride which made them believe themselves the masters of the world, or to the enemies of John XXII, blinded by their hatred and their dreams or illusions. He allowed a popular assembly to pronounce the deposition of the Pope, who was accused of heresy and *lèse-majesté*, while a commission of ecclesiastics and laymen appointed in his place a mendicant monk who took the name of Nicholas V. The poor man then perceived that he had been merely an actor in a revolutionary comedy. Horrified by what he had done, he sadly returned to Germany. Less than two years later the Romans were begging the Pope to grant them absolution, and Nicholas V, a rope round his neck, knelt at his feet in Avignon and implored his forgiveness.

The death of John XXII (1334) a few days after he had pronounced, in a solemn Bull, the separation of Italy from the Empire of Germany, did not in any way change the attitude of the Curia toward Louis of Bavaria. Benedict XII and Clement VI remained pitiless; they seem to have taken the harmless insult to the majesty of the Holy See more seriously than it deserved. As for Louis, who had completely lost his bearings, he wore himself out with attempts at reconciliation, which were disdainfully rejected. At one moment he seems to have cherished hopes of compelling Avignon to make peace by allying himself with Edward III against France. This was yet another illusion, and he was soon cured of it. Completely incapable of making war, he not only did not support Edward, but he presently allied himself with Philip of Valois. If Germany had been a State, this would have been the moment for acting as France and England had done under Boniface VIII, and making an end of the humiliations which the Papacy was inflicting on her king. The Electors, supported by the Diet, confined themselves to protesting against the right which the Pope had arrogated to himself of ratifying their nomination of the king; and that was all. They had seen no more in the quarrel than an opportunity of confirming the unjustified privilege which enabled them to dispose of the crown. In short, Louis of Bavaria was left to his own devices. His quarrel with the House of Luxemburg was disastrous. Forgetting their declarations of independence, the Electors, being required by Clement VI to appoint a new king, sold their votes to Charles, Margrave of Moravia, the son of the blind King John of Bohemia, and the grandson of Henry VII, who took the name of Charles IV (1346).

By a fortunate chance Henry VII was able, at the beginning of his reign, to marry his son John (the Blind) to the heiress of the Kingdom of Bohemia. The House of Luxemburg was thus transplanted from the Roman to the Slav frontier of the Empire. And there it maintained itself for more than a century. John having fallen at Crécy soon after the election of his son, Charles IV was able to unite the crowns of Germany and Bohemia. In 1355 he added to these the Imperial crown, going to Rome, in order to receive it, with a small retinue, and taking every possible precaution to remain on good terms with the Pope. It is not surprising that he was concerned before all else to augment the position of his house. To Bohemia and Moravia he added Silesia and Lusatia, and in 1372 the Mark of Brandenburg. In this way a compact power was constituted in the east of Germany, but it was not a German power. Its centre was Bohemia, where Charles introduced an administration which was modelled upon that of France.

The Golden Bull by which Charles IV had finally confirmed, in 1356, the attributions and the composition of the College of Electors, as they were to continue until the end of the 18th century,[1] had reconciled him with these kingmakers. Without paying too dearly for the honour, he induced them to appoint his son Wenceslas, during his lifetime, to the dignity of King of the Romans (1376). This was the first time since the reign of Frederick II that a son had succeeded to his father on the throne of Germany.

The reign of Wenceslas (1370–1400) was really an interregnum for Germany. Exclusively occupied with Bohemia, the king took no interest in the rest of the Empire. He neither cared to take the Imperial crown nor to intervene in the incessant quarrels of the German cities and the German princes. In 1400 the four Electors of the Rhine arrogated to themselves the right to depose him, and in this case we may perhaps regard their action as a sort of protest against a king who showed only too plainly that he was a foreigner. If it was their intention, on giving the crown to the Count Palatine Rupert, to set up a truly national sovereign in opposition to their Bohemian sovereign,

[1] The College comprised three ecclesiastical Electors: the prelates of Mayence, Trèves, and Cologne, and four lay electors: the King of Bohemia, the Count Palatine of the Rhine, the Duke of Saxony, and the Margrave of Brandenburg.

the experiment was a lamentable failure. The new king was hardly acknowledged by anyone apart from those who had given him the crown. He thought he was striking a masterly blow when he risked an expedition to Italy. The Imperial crown would have given him some prestige, and he counted on seizing Milan on his way south, for the Duke of Milan, Gian Galeazzo Visconti, was on the best of terms with the House of Luxemburg. The naïvety of this plan tells us what the policy of such a king and such electors was worth. Having no money, he calculated that as soon as he had crossed the Alps the Florentines, as the enemies of the Milanese, would kindly place their troops at his disposal. But the Florentines despised him as heartily as did the Milanese. Having reached Brescia with a few knights, he found it impossible to proceed any further. He was forced to return, covered with shame, to hide himself in the Palatinate, where he died in 1410. His death reminded the world that he had worn the crown. The Electors, who had learned something from experience, reverted to the House of Luxemburg. Wenceslas had two brothers, the Margrave John of Moravia, and Sigismond, King of Hungary. The Electors appointed both, since they had not all contrived to sell their votes to the same candidate. Thus Germany had three kings, for Wenceslas calmly continued to bear the title. Fortunately the death of John in 1416 reduced the number to two, and when Wenceslas followed him in 1419, Sigismond alone was left.

The activity of this last Luxemburger (1410–1437) offers a strange contrast to the apathy of Wenceslas. His interest in his Kingdom of Hungary, which from year to year was more seriously threatened by the Turks, inspired him with the hope of finding salvation in a Crusade against the infidels. And as a Crusade was impossible so long as the schism continued, he did his very utmost, though his zeal was a little indiscreet, to bring about the convocation of the Council of Constance and to ensure the success of its deliberations. The heir, since the death of his brother, to the Kingdom of Bohemia, the revolt of the Hussites, which prevented him from taking possession of his kingdom, was yet another motive for urging the reformation of the

Church. His title of King of the Romans was an excellent pretext for meddling in the affairs of the Papacy while attending to his own. The expeditions ordered by the Popes, and the Councils convoked for the purpose of dealing with the Hussites, were one and all unsuccessful, to the confusion of the German chivalry. At last, in 1434, after the war against the Taborites and the Utraquists, the *modus vivendi* of the Compactates having been accepted, Sigismond was able to make his entry into Prague. He died three years later, on December 9th, 1437, and his kingdoms of Bohemia and Hungary passed to his son-in-law, Albert of Austria. Thus the vast territories of the House of Luxemburg were added to the Duchies of Austria and Styria. The aim envisaged by the House of Habsburg since its establishment in the valley of the Danube was achieved. A great dynastic power, a hybrid mixture of German, Slav and Magyar countries, was constituted on the east of Germany. All the efforts of so many kings to establish the power of their families had the final result of promoting the Habsburgs to the rank of the most powerful sovereigns in Europe. Chance, of course, played its part in the fortunes of their house, as it plays its part in the destinies of every rich heritage. A miscarriage, a childless marriage, the premature death of a child would have compromised everything. Yet we must not exaggerate the influence of the unforeseen and the unexpected. Do we not find it in military operations just as often as in matrimonial arrangements? It must be acknowledged that if fortune favoured the Habsburgs, it was because they helped it to do so. From the end of the 14th century their whole policy consisted in establishing, by means of politic marriages, their claims to the crowns of Bohemia, Hungary, and even Poland. They counted on the generative power of their race, as others counted on their sword, and they had not miscalculated. If their policy had been applied to countries whose civilization was more ancient, and whose national consciousness was more highly developed, the result might of course have been different. In this connection we have only to recall the measures taken by France at the beginning of the 14th century to prevent the kings of England from claiming the crown. But neither in Hungary nor in Bohemia was the monarchy as yet so intimately wedded to the nation as to make the latter refuse to yield the crown to a foreigner. It was enough to come to an understanding with the great nobles, however much they might really hate the Germans, and to make them certain concessions, in order to be accepted. What would not have been possible in the West of Europe was possible in the East. None of the conditions that gave rise to the Hundred Years' War existed in the basin of the Danube. The extraordinary luck of the Habsburgs was therefore far less the result of chance than one might suppose. Their matrimonial policy alone does not suffice to explain it. The indispensable and primordial condition was the absence of any political spirit in the peoples who were the instruments or the victims of that policy.

Germany also, if we consider her as a whole, seems to have been just as completely devoid of this political spirit. The rapid survey of the reigns of her kings contained in the last few pages affords an irrefutable proof of this statement. If we compare the history of Germany with that of France and England during the same period, we shall see that in the latter countries the three privileged classes, clergy, nobility and bourgeoisie, were associated, either through taxation or by military service, with the actions of the king, and also that they intervened immediately in the government of the country, while the crises which were provoked by their claims or their quarrels were merely the tumultuous manifestations of an incontestable public life. Germany, on the contrary, had neither a system of taxation nor anything resembling a parliamentary organization. The Diet (*Reichstag*) was merely an assembly of prelates, princes, nobles, and representatives of the cities, whose competence was restricted to paralysing the activities of the sovereign, but which did not replace him in the government of the country, and merely weakened this government by complicating it. The Crown possessed no administration and no finances. The archaic majesty of its language and its emblems was in almost comical contrast with its actual strength. Sigismond, who for the sake of greater majesty gave the eagle of the Empire a second head, was obliged to pawn his crown, and was pursued from city to city by a flock of creditors. If Germany had been a State, the Hundred Years' War would have provided that State with an excellent opportunity of consolidating itself. Since France and England had cancelled each other out, such a State could have imposed its will upon Europe. But Germany was incapable of doing anything of the kind. In Italy she had lost her last actual outposts. The alliances of Adolphus of Nassau and Louis of Bavaria with Edward III merely added to the troubles of these two needy princes, who, having been paid for their services in advance, never rendered any. Consequently France continued to expand upon her eastern frontier without even eliciting a protest from the Emperors. The Dauphiné was acquired by France in 1349. If Charles IV, in 1365, had himself crowned at Arles in order to maintain his right to the ancient kingdom of Burgundy, this was doubtless only in order that he might sell it at a better price. For almost immediately he appointed the Dauphin Vicar of the Empire at Arles. The Franche Comté became the possession of Philip the Bold. In 1388 a French army waged war upon the Duke of Guelders, and no one protested. We have seen how the House of Burgundy extended its power in the Low Countries, absorbing Hainaut, Holland, Zeeland, Namur and Brabant, establishing its protectorate over Liége and Utrecht, and in the end actually annexing Luxemburg, the cradle of one of the Imperial houses. Philip the Good defied Sigismond. Placed by him under the ban of the Empire in 1433, he responded by addressing an insolent manifesto to the princes and cities of Germany. From every side he received the assurance of the neutrality on which he had counted. When at last, in 1437, the Emperor, driven to extremities, endeavoured to take action, he was reduced to sending Ludwig of Hesse with four hundred lances into Brabant in support of his pretended rights. The peasants of Limburg were able, unaided, to drive the Imperial agent back into Aix-la-Chapelle.

The episode is characteristic. It throws a vivid light on the true nature of the Empire: an agglomeration of princes and cities caring nothing for the sovereign unless his policy favoured their interests. Germany was not a State; it was an aggregate of local sovereignties, lay or ecclesiastical principalities, and free cities (about seventy). Moreover, the free cities hardly counted. Only a few of them—Cologne, Nuremberg, Augsburg—were strong enough to defend themselves unaided; not one of them was strong enough to pursue, as did the Italian cities, an influential policy. Their politics were little more than parochial. It is true that the German bourgeoisie had greatly developed in the course of the 14th century. But its progress profited no one save itself. The princes tried to restrict its activities, and the king did not support them. It therefore did not play in Germany the very considerable part which it played in the general development of France and England. An exception must be made in the case of the Hansa. Although there was no very effective alliance between them, the common interests of the Hansa cities united them against their enemies, who, fortunately for them, were very weak. Denmark was the most dangerous. King Valdemar was defeated in 1369, and the Baltic remained, until the beginning of the 15th century, a German lake.

In the interior of the country there was continual conflict between the princes and the cities, which, since there was no central power in the country, resulted in a state of insecurity, by which the petty nobles joyfully profited, the pillage of the merchants being one of their normal means of livelihood. Here the *Raubritter,* who elsewhere would have been a soldier or a functionary, became a professional robber.

As for the principalities, apart from Bavaria and the territories of the Houses of Luxemburg and Habsburg, none of them were very large. And they were much less stable than those of Italy, for example. They were continually being divided between the children of the princes. In the interior of the country the administration was rudimentary. If there were assemblies of the Estates, the bourgeoisie was nowhere powerful enough to counterbalance the nobility, which had the say in everything and enforced its will upon the country. A large proportion of the nobles were not the descendants of freemen. They were still numerous in the

14th century. The prince surrounded himself with them, and recruited from their ranks his confidential agents and advisers. Brute force enjoyed a predominance quite unknown elsewhere. The peasants, who from the middle of the 14th century were entirely at the mercy of the nobles, were beginning to relapse into serfdom,[2] for emigration was no longer possible, and there was not, as elsewhere, a king who might intervene for them. One of the most striking features of German life was this regression of the people into servitude under nobles of whom many were themselves of servile origin. Here and there the peasants resisted the nobles. The origin of the Swiss Confederation may be referred to such resistance: the three original cantons, Schwiz, Uri and Unterwalden, defeated Leopold of Austria at Morgahten in 1315. This was the beginning of a federation which was joined by Lucerne (1332), Zürich (1351), and Berne (1353), and which was further consolidated by the battle of Sempach, which was fought against Leopold III of Austria in 1386.

This centrifugal tendency of Germany cannot be explained merely by the weakness of the monarchy. We must allow also for the fact that the economic life of the country, down to the middle of the 15th century, was very poorly developed. There was no unity about it. On the sea-coast the Hansa ports exported the corn of Northern Germany to Flanders, and brought back the products of the Orient. The Rhine gravitated towards the Low Countries, but its importance was diminishing now that there was direct navigation between Flanders and Italy. In the South the cities maintained commercial relations with Venice, for the Danube was not a trade route below Vienna. Moreover, there was hardly any export industry apart from the metals of Bohemia and the Tyrol.

In the centre of the country there were no important cities. On the whole, the greater part of the country was still rural. It had need of the outer world, but the outer

[2] In Flanders serfdom disappeared in the 13th century. In France it was largely abolished in the 14th century.

world had no need of it. The Low Countries looked westward.

As for the seaport cities of the North, they played hardly
any part in the life of the interior. Until the middle of the
14th century the Rhine and the South were the true Germany. But with the advent of Rudolph of Habsburg there
was for a moment—as there had been, sporadically, before
his time—a tendency toward an eastward orientation. This
was very obvious in the case of Luxemburg. The Slav
countries lent themselves to political absorption. There was
no longer any colonization in these countries, but there was
a dynastic orientation toward the East, which, at the same
time, produced in the Slav peoples a corresponding orientation toward Germany.

2. The Slav States and Hungary

At the moment when the Slav peoples made their appearance in history they occupied the region extending
from the Upper Vistula and the Carpathians to the Dnieper. In the course of the 5th century, following upon the
general movement of the Germans, their western neighbours, in the direction of the Roman Empire, they advanced in their turn and occupied the territories which the
Germans had vacated. The Poles installed themselves in the
basin of the Vistula; the Wends spread from the Elbe to the
Baltic Sea; while the Czechs took possession of Bohemia
and Moravia. Others, moving toward the south-west, colonized the valley of the Danube and penetrated far into
Thrace, at the expense of the Greek Empire: these were
the Bulgars, the Serbs, the Croats, and the Slovenes. As for
those Slavs who had remained in the East, and who, thanks
to their position on the Dnieper, lay across the trade route
connecting Byzantium with the regions of the North, in the
9th century, as we have already seen, they fell under the
domination of the Scandinavian Vikings—half merchants,
half warriors—from whom they acquired their name of Russians. Kiev, where the eldest son of Rurik's dynasty established himself under the name of the Great Prince, became
the centre of a political group of secondary principalities

which extended from Novgorod to the shores of the Black Sea.

The economic organization of this country presented a character which was not to be found elsewhere in the territory of any other Barbarian people. It was essentially commercial. The Vikings, who were gathered round their princes in the fortified enclosures (*Gorod*) established along the Dnieper and its affluents, subjected the Slav population to the payment of tribute, consisting mainly of honey, wax and furs, which the hunters and bee-keepers of this forest region were able to furnish in abundance. In the spring of each year their boats assembled at Kiev and carried this merchandise to Constantinople, together with a considerable number of slaves, bringing back in return wine, textiles, and manufactured objects. When at the beginning of the 11th century the Scandinavians became Slavized, these commercial practices, together with the political exploitation of the rural population, did not disappear, but the aristocracy of *boyars*, at once military, mercantile and urban, dominated the rest of the nation. Such was the salient character of the Russian State at this period.

Being in constant touch with Byzantium, the Russians were bound before long to become Christianized. As early as the first half of the 10th century Christianity was beginning to make its way, following the course of trade, among the inhabitants of Kiev. The Princess Olga professed it openly about 955–957. However, paganism maintained itself as the dominant religion as late as the reign of her grandson Vladimir, who still encouraged the sacrifice of human beings, and to whom ecclesiastical tradition attributed, no doubt a little generously, as many as eight hundred concubines, whom it compared with those of Solomon. But after his marriage with a Greek princess the inevitable conversion took place (983), and the conversion of the prince was immediately followed by that of the *boyars*. As for the people, they were evangelized by methods whose simplicity recalls those which Charlemagne employed in converting the Saxons. The inhabitants of Kiev were baptized *en masse* in the waters of the Dnieper. The idols were overthrown, and the prince commanded that churches should be built on the sites of the pagan temples. In order to furnish recruits for the clergy, he seized the children of the leading families and entrusted their education to the Greek and Bulgar priests who had been sent from Byzantium to guide the first steps of the young Russian Church.

If external causes had not supervened to hinder it, the historical development of Russia would have brought about a progressive orientation toward Constantinople. For Russia this great city was not merely, as was Rome for the Christians of the West, the religious centre *par excellence:* it was also the great commercial market, and for both these reasons its influence was bound, in the long run, to make itself felt in all the domains of social life. We know that even in our days the ecclesiastical architecture of Russia retains the Byzantine forms which were then imposed upon it, and the *Ruskaja Pravda,* the most ancient compilation of Russian laws, is completely imbued with the spirit of Byzantine law.

But the situation of Russia exposed her to the repercussions of all the tumultuous movements of those Asiatic peoples whose territory extended, across the Great Plain, toward the mountains and the inland seas of the true Europe. The steppes on the shores of the Black Sea and in the basin of the Don and the Volga were the domain of nomadic hordes of Turki or Mongol origin, against whom the Russian principalities were perpetually forced to fight.

The victory of the Great Prince Jaroslav over the most powerful of these peoples, the Petchenegs, in 1036, dispelled the danger for some time. It recurred in a more dreadful form with the advent of the Kumans. In 1096 their Khan advanced to the very walls of Kiev; and from that time onwards the attacks of these ferocious Barbarians never ceased. By the middle of the 12th century it was becoming impossible to resist them. The region of Kiev, hitherto so flourishing, was becoming impoverished and depopulated. When the Barbarians occupied the mouths of the Dnieper there was an end of the trade with Constantinople. Gradually the country was deserted, some of the inhabitants migrating to Galicia and Volhynia, and others, more numerous, moving off in a north-easterly direction toward the upper reaches of the Volga (Sousdal).

This migration from south to north determined the future of the Russian people. Not only did it impose upon it a new manner of life, but it even modified its national character. The Slav colonists of Sousdalia mingled with the Finns, who had hitherto been the sole inhabitants of its immense forests, and from this mingling of the peoples modern Russia (Great Russia) emerged. At the same time a purely agricultural life replaced the old commercial activity. Henceforth deprived of all communication with the sea, the Russians were restricted for long centuries to a purely rural economy, which had no outlets. The neighbourhood of Constantinople had caused them to practise commerce at a time when it was still unknown in Western Europe, and the fatality of circumstance made them abandon it just when it was beginning to develop in the West. Kiev had been a great international emporium, but the towns of central Russia—like the castles of the West in the early Middle Ages—were merely the residences of the princes, their *boyars,* and the servants necessary for their maintenance. Moscow, founded in 1147, acquired more importance than its neighbours only through purely political causes, and in so far as its prince was more powerful than the other princes. Novgorod alone, which was assiduously frequented, from the beginning of the 13th century, by the merchants of the Hansa, was a centre of commercial importance, and this importance it owed entirely to the foreigner. It was a German factory in Russia rather than a Russian economic centre.

Novgorod was the only point from which the civilization of the West might have been diffused throughout Russia. Unfortunately, the rude and rapacious merchants of the Hansa were incapable of revealing any but the least attractive features of that civilization; and their contact with the inhabitants had little result beyond provoking a mutual hatred and contempt. Religious differences still further envenomed the relations whose beginnings were so unfortunate. The Greek Orthodoxy which the Russians brought from the banks of the Dnieper kept them isolated from Europe, while the civilizing influence of Byzantium, since they were now too removed from the metropolis, could no longer remedy the disastrous result of this isolation.

As a crowning misfortune, this isolation was rendered still more complete by the great Mongolian invasion of the 13th century. In 1223 Juji, the son of Jenghiz Khan, conquered the whole region occupied by the Kumans between the Don and the Volga. His son Batu, pushing further west, captured Moscow in 1234 and Kiev in 1240, and extended his power over the whole of Russia, now terrorized and half depopulated. However, the Mongols did not establish themselves beyond the Don. Their Khan contented himself with imposing his overlordship upon the Russian princes and subjecting them to tribute. Nevertheless, as long as the Empire of the "Golden Horde" retained its power, they were nothing more than the humble vassals of an Asiatic despot, and even though this did not make them become Asiatic, it was at least enough to prevent them from becoming Europeanized. The decadence of the Golden Horde after the death of Usbek (1313–1341) left them a liberty of action of which the princes of Moscow took advantage by annexing the neighbouring principalities. With Ivan III (1462–1505) this work of unification was completed. Ivan, allied with the Khan of the Crimea, made an end of what was still left of the Mongol domination. With his reign a new era of Russian history began.

As in the case of the Russians, it was the invasion of an Asiatic people, the Hungarians, which determined the destiny of the Slavs of the South and West. Before the arrival of these barbarians the Slav peoples were in immediate touch with one another, from Thrace to the shores of the Baltic Sea. If this state of things had continued it is evident that the Greek Church, which had converted the Bulgars and the Serbs as early as the 9th century, would have continued its apostolate, favoured by the community of manners and of language, amongst their brothers of Bohemia and Poland, and would have absorbed them as it absorbed the Russians in the 10th century. But the sudden and unexpected arrival of the Hungarians altered the course of history. Making their way into the valley of the Danube, they interposed themselves between the Slav peoples, dividing them into two groups, which henceforth had nothing in common. Cut off from Byzantium, and at the same time separated from the Serbs and the Bulgars, the Czechs and the Poles, like the Hungarians themselves, naturally went over to the Roman Church.

Their conversion was wholly agreeable to the religious zeal and the political interests of the German sovereign. Otto I did not fail to attach the young Slav bishoprics to the Germanic metropolis of Mayence, while he subjected the princes of Bohemia and Poland to a rather vague protectorate. His successors—embarrassed by their expeditions to Italy, and then engrossed in the War of Investitures—far from continuing his efforts, could not even safeguard their results. Prague in Bohemia, and Gnesen in Poland, became independent archbishoprics, while the dioceses established among the Wends on the right bank of the Elbe disappeared, leaving paganism a free field.

We have seen further back how the great economic revolution of the 12th century had the unexpected consequence of provoking a decline of the Slav nationality to the advantage of the Germans. The surplus rural population of Germany overflowed into the country on the right bank of the Elbe, where the Saxon knights, as they advanced, massacred the pagan natives. Under the pretext of evangelization the Teutonic Order continued this policy of massacre and repopulation into the 13th century. Prussia was Germanized by them, as Mecklenburg and the Mark of Brandenburg had been. The shores of the Baltic, which had hitherto been Slav, now became German. The Poles, who were endeavouring to reach to the Baltic across Pomerania, were cut off from the sea.

Hitherto the political constitution of Bohemia and Poland had exhibited the natural development of those tribal institutions which we find in almost identical forms among all agricultural peoples when they adopt a sedentary life. This is readily explained by the absence of that direct contact with the Roman civilization which had lifted the Germans out of barbarism. The progress of a society is all the more rapid in proportion as it is more completely subjected to external influences. In consequence of the remoteness of the Western Slavs it was long before they emerged from the narrowness and poverty of their isolated existence. Despite their local importance, we need not here dwell on manners and institutions which did not exert any influence over Europe. Princes of whom each had his entourage of noble retainers, on whom they depended more than the nobles depended on them, until one of these princes, gradually raising himself above his rivals, seized their lands and rallied their followers to himself—this, in a few words, is the essential character of the first few centuries of history both in Bohemia and in Poland. The introduction of Christianity, which was not brought into these countries by foreign conquest, did not in any way change their political condition. The religious character which it gave to the princely power did not alter the fact that this power had to reckon with a landed aristocracy from which it could not possibly liberate itself, because, if united, this was definitely the stronger. But there was nothing in these Slav States to correspond with the feudality of Western Europe. And this may be readily understood. The great vassals of the West were merely the descendants of royal officers who had profited by the king's inability to administer the State and had usurped the powers which they ought to have exercised in his name. But neither in Bohemia nor in Poland do we find, from the very beginning, any trace of that administrative character which the Roman tradition had impressed upon the West. There the prince was merely a military leader, surrounded by noble companions who assisted him in time of peace, and represented him, as *starosts* or châtelaines, in various parts of the country. They were not his servants, but his natural auxiliaries. The government was exercised by them and by the prince in common, and none of them could appropriate to himself the power which was temporarily delegated to him in his circumscription. The very insignificance of the political attributions of the prince, and the permanent control exercised over these attributions by the aristocracy, rendered impossible the formation in the Slav States of such territorial principalities as had been constituted, ever since the 10th century, in all parts of France and Germany. The power of the great

landed nobility, both in Bohemia and in Poland, was exercised from the beginning by the participation of each of
its members in the government of the whole country. This
did not lead to the subdivision of the country, for its political and national unity were preserved by the very weakness
of a central authority which was dependent on the aristocracy. It should be added that these peoples, being cut off
from the sea, had no bourgeoisie until a very late stage in
their history.

The immediate neighbourhood of Germany, and the
rights which Germany claimed over Bohemia, naturally involved the latter country in her quarrels. The Bohemian
princes took advantage of the disorders which followed the
death of Frederick Barbarossa to increase their independence. Being at war with Otto III, Philip of Swabia, in order
to secure the support of Duke Ottocar I, conferred upon
him, in 1198, the title of king. The intervention of the
kings of Bohemia in German affairs was henceforth of sufficient importance to enable these Slavs to enter the College
of Electors. It might well have seemed, after the accession
of Wenceslas II (1230–1253), that the kingdom was
destined to become Germanized. Wenceslas did everything
in his power to encourage German immigration into the
country, which was still wholly agricultural. Above all, he
encouraged the immigration of artisans and traders, who
established themselves *en masse*, during the whole of the
13th century, in the "burgs" of Bohemia, where they retained their own law and their own language. For a long
while the bourgeoisie was, in the literal sense of the word,
a foreign population in the midst of the Czechs. But this
fact made it only the more conscious of its dependence on
the monarchy, and its loyalty greatly augmented the resources, the prestige, and the strength of the dynasty. The
progress of this dynasty was made strikingly apparent under Ottocar II (1235–1238). The nobles of the Duchy of
Austria, whose duke had fallen in battle against the Hungarians, appealed to him for aid, and acknowledged him
as their seigneur. He added the Duchy of Styria to Austria,
expelling the Hungarians, and forcing the Duke of Carinthia to acknowledge him as his heir. From the Riesenge-

birge his power henceforth extended to the shores of the
Adriatic. It seemed as though the crown of Bohemia was
on the point of annexing the whole of Danubian Germany.
Encouraged by success, Ottocar, on the death of Richard
of Cornwall, offered himself as a candidate for the title of
King of the Romans. The title was conferred upon Rudolph
of Habsburg, and henceforth war between the two rivals
was inevitable. If Rudolph had been forced to rely on his
own resources he could not have coped with his adversary.
But now the Hungarians, for the first time, played the part
which they were so often to play afterwards, assisting the
Germans against the Czechs. Ottocar was defeated and
killed in 1278, at the battle of Marchfeld. The Danubian
duchies became the property of the Habsburgs, who henceforth never ceased to covet Bohemia. Ottocar's successors
no longer attempted to expand in the direction of Germany; but they cast their eyes on Hungary and Poland.
Wenceslas II (1278–1305) contrived to procure the crown
of Hungary, for a time, for his son Ladislas, and in 1300 he
obtained the crown of Poland for himself. With his son
Wenceslas III, assassinated in 1306, the ancient Slav
dynasty of the Przemislides became extinct. The throne
being vacant, the King of the Romans, Albert of Austria,
hastened to secure it for his son Rudolph. But this first
attempt to absorb the country for the benefit of the House
of Habsburg was unsuccessful. Rudolph lived only a few
months, and the Bohemian aristocracy elected as their king
the husband of the eldest daughter of Wenceslas III, Duke
Henry of Carinthia. This second German king reigned
hardly longer than his predecessor. Profiting by the discontent which he had excited, Elizabeth, the younger
daughter of Wenceslas IV, proposed to take as her husband
John the Blind, the son of Henry of Luxemburg, who had
succeeded Albert of Austria as King of the Romans. The
marriage was concluded in 1310. It gave Bohemia a Walloon dynasty, only a few years after a French dynasty had
established itself in Hungary by the accession of Robert of
Anjou.

Hitherto the German influence in Bohemia had continually increased. Its progress was checked by the advent of

the House of Luxemburg. Although John the Blind passed the greater part of his reign travelling about Europe, occupied with political intrigues or military enterprises, which ended in his meeting his death, at the age of fifty, on the field of Crécy, he did not forget to introduce into his kingdom a very large number of men from the Low Countries who, as advisers or functionaries, taught the Bohemians the improved methods of the French administration. His son Charles IV, who from 1333 was entrusted with the government of the country, continued and perfected the improvements introduced by his father. A Frenchman by education and in his tastes, and speaking the French language, this King of Bohemia, who was at the same time King of the Romans and Emperor, was nevertheless regarded by his Czech subjects as a national prince. It was probably enough that he should have shaken off the German influence without systematically opposing it. Bohemia being the centre of his power, he applied himself to making it capable of independent development. In 1348 he founded in Prague the first university of Central Europe, modelled upon that of Paris, and he delighted in adorning the city with monuments that gave it the aspect of a capital, so that its like did not exist in the whole Empire. His beneficent and intelligent administration, by encouraging the economic development of the country, resulted in the formation of a native bourgeoisie side by side with the German bourgeoisie. All this explains the popularity of his government, and the fact that his reign saw the awakening of a national sentiment which was soon to provoke a reaction against the Germanic elements which had been introduced into Bohemia by the colonization of the 13th century. This reaction found violent expression under his son Wenceslas (1378–1419), on the occasion of the Hussite explosion. John Huss has remained for the Czechs what Luther is to the Germans, a national hero. In a certain sense he is even more truly a national hero than Luther, for not all the Germans followed Luther, whereas all the Czechs followed Huss. The religious conflict which he inaugurated in Bohemia was complicated by a conflict of nationalities. The Germans represented Catholicism, and the Czechs the new heresy, and in proportion as this heresy had spread among them they persecuted the foreigners, as much because they regarded them as intruders as because they considered them infidels. The war which they had to fight in order to defend their religion diffused their hatred of Germany throughout the country. For it was from Germany that those armies of knights came which John Ziska, and then Procopius, so often cut to pieces. One can hardly avoid comparing the mentality of the Hussites with that of the French revolutionists at the end of the 18th century. Both peoples were fighting against the foreigner in defence of their ideal, and in each case the national sentiment was sublimated by the conviction that supported and inspired it.

The comparison is all the more inevitable inasmuch as Hussitism soon assumed a revolutionary form. The Taborites, as we have seen, aspired to the complete renovation, not only of the Church, but of society. Abandoned by the Utraquists, and then conquered by them, they were obliged to surrender. The "Compactat" (1434) negotiated with the Council of Basle was a somewhat ambiguous compromise, which, while it reconciled Bohemia with the Church, left her in the enjoyment of a religious autonomy which no one thought it prudent to define. However, a good proportion of the nobility, alarmed by the violence of the Taborites, had returned to Catholicism. The nobles took advantage of the circumstances to increase their domains by the addition of the confiscated ecclesiastical estates, and to impose serfdom on the rural masses.

Sigismond, the brother of Wenceslas, and his successor, was at last able to take possession of his kingdom. He had no son, and on his death in 1437 his son-in-law Albert of Austria succeeded him, both in Bohemia and in Hungary. However, he was acknowledged only by the Catholics and the Utraquists. What was left of the Taborites gave the crown to Casimir of Poland. The moment for the final union of Bohemia with the domains of the Habsburgs had not yet arrived. Albert was killed in 1439 while campaigning against the Turks, and a Czech noble, George Podebrad, who at first governed the country in the name of Ladislas, the posthumous son of the king, received the crown on the death of Ladislas in 1457. Bohemia thus became a national and independent kingdom. But this was to be only a brief interlude in its tragic history. About the same time, while German influence was declining in Bohemia, it was doing the same in Poland, but in consequence of events of a totally different character. While Bohemia was clearly outlined by the mountains that enclosed her, Poland, stretching from the Oder to the Vistula across the vast plain by which Russia is prolonged into the north of Europe, was exposed on every side except on the south, where she was protected by the Carpathians, to the aggression of her neighbours. No other people had such fluctuating frontiers. Like a garment they followed the movements of the nation; they expanded or contracted according as the nation was strong or weak, sometimes extending themselves until they enclosed all sorts of heterogeneous nationalities, sometimes shrinking until they were no longer wide enough to enclose the whole nation.

Boleslas Chrobry (the Valiant), who had taken the title of king in the 10th century, extended his influence to the Russian principalities of the Dnieper, leaving his successors only an artificial power, for it was based upon nothing but the energy of the man who had created it. Of these successors, none was able to retain it. The royal title itself disappeared at the end of the 11th century, and the dukes divided the Polish territories among themselves, amidst intestine conflicts which have no interest for the general historian, except that they explain why the Teutonic Order, in the 13th century, was able to take possession of Prussia and cut off Poland from the Baltic Sea, without encountering any resistance. However, the settlement of the Teutonic Knights was only an episode in the mighty movement of German expansion, which, at this same period, was spreading through Poland as it had spread through Bohemia. These immigrants were all the more warmly welcomed inasmuch as the country had just been ravaged by the Mongol invasion, which, overflowing from Russia, had reached Silesia, where it made a protracted halt, and began to flow backwards on receiving the news of the death of the great Khan Ogotai (1241). The Germans did not settle in great numbers except in Silesia, which from that time forward began to show signs of Germanization. Those who penetrated into the interior introduced urban life there and constituted a bourgeoisie, which, protected by privileges and provided with Magdeburg law, retained its nationality for centuries. It found itself in juxtaposition with the Jews, whom the persecution of the era of the Crusades had swept out of Germany and Hungary into Poland in the 11th and 12th centuries.

The introduction of the Bohemian dynasty of Poland under Wenceslas II and Wenceslas III (1300–1305) was followed by the restoration of the royal title. On the death of Wenceslas III the great nobles called Duke Wladislas I to the throne. His son Casimir (the Great) was to Poland much what his contemporary, Charles IV (1333–1370), was to Bohemia, and he was incontestably inspired by Charles's policy. He wished to make of Cracow what Charles had made of Prague, and following the latter's example he established a university there (1364). He endeavoured to organize a royal administration by the institution of a central court of justice, a treasurer and a chancellor, and to model his government on the Western type adopted by Bohemia. But a strong monarchy can impose itself upon a country only by trusting to the services which it renders to the people, thereby interesting the latter in its maintenance. In the 12th century the kings of France had counterbalanced the power of their great vassals by allying themselves with the bourgeoisie, but the scattered German bourgeoisies of Poland could not serve as auxiliaries of the Crown. In this purely agricultural country the nobles, in the middle of the 14th century, by reason of their power and their ascendancy, were as incompatible with monarchical government as those of the Frankish Empire had been three centuries earlier. They were not so very different from the Frankish nobles. The predominant characteristic of the nobility of the Occident was their social function, while that of the Polish nobility was their juridical character. In consequence of a much simpler historical evolution, the nobles were directly related to the freemen of the Barbaric epoch; they retained the pride of the freemen, and claimed for themselves that they alone constituted the nation. Apart from the nobles, there were only the servile peasants whom they exploited and despised. Above them there was only the king, whose authority they acknowledged on the condition of his reigning only for them and with them. The spirit which inspired the nobility, and which never ceased to inspire it, was a spirit of liberty, but a liberty of caste which was to give the Polish State, more and more definitely, until its final collapse, the paradoxical character of an aristocratic democracy.

Thus the task of which Casimir had dreamed was incapable of execution. His attempts to introduce a monarchical centralization were bound, whatever his intention, to diminish the nobility. It was so perfectly aware of this fact that it gave him the nickname of "King of the Peasants," while the wretched agrarian plebs which it dominated even to our own day has piously cherished, through the centuries, the memory of this prince, who enabled it for a moment to hope that its miseries would be ended.

With Casimir, in 1370, the dynasty of the Piastes became extinct. His successor, King Louis of Hungary, hastened to come to terms with the nobles. The concessions which he granted them constituted the first of those *Pacta Conventa* which from that time forward they so often imposed upon the Crown, and by which they gained increasing control of the destinies of the nation. However, the first use they made of these prerogatives resulted in an extraordinary increase of the Polish power.

Casimir had conquered Galicia and Volhynia, and by these conquests had extended the frontiers of the kingdom to Lithuanian territory. Since the beginning of the 14th century the Lithuanians of the Baltic shore, driven back from the sea by the Teutonic Order, had turned southwards; they had extended their power over the principalities of Western Russia, and had reached the shores of the Black Sea. They had remained pagans, but on being brought into contact with their Orthodox subjects they began to adopt their religion, and their future adhesion to the Greek Church appeared to be certain. Now, on the death of Louis of Hungary (1382), the Polish nobility, in order to escape the rule of his brother Sigismond, offered Prince Jagellon of Lithuania the hand of the king's younger daughter, Elisabeth, on condition that he accepted baptism and professed the Catholic Faith. The bargain was accepted. Jagellon became King of Poland under the name of Wladislas II, and at the same time his people adopted the religion which he had just accepted. With this the Lithuanian principality was united with the kingdom, although it retained a formal independence (1386).[3]

Since their establishment in Prussia the Teutonic Knights, on the pretext that the Lithuanians were pagans, had waged against them a war of extermination. It was now evident, however, that these Barbarians were not obstinately attached to their cult. But it was more profitable and, extraordinary though the use of such a word may seem, more enjoyable to hunt them, for the Order organized veritable man-hunts in its persecution of this people. The fame of these hunts had spread throughout the Empire, and the princes and seigneurs of the West assembled, as people now assemble at the Olympic Games, to take part in these expeditions, which were organized every winter, when the ice had rendered the marshes of the country practicable. Such a degradation of the religious spirit, and such brutality of manners, shows how completely the Order, in the course of time, had lost the spirit of Christian proselytism and heroic mysticism of an earlier day. The military monasticism created to fight Islam could preserve its traditions only by remaining faithful to its original mission, as did the Knights of St. John of Rhodes, or the Knights of Alcantara or Calatrava in Spain. The Teutonic Knights, on the contrary, like the Templars, having turned away from the East, were now distinguished only by the energy which they applied to the pursuit of purely temporal objects. Their rule, rebelling, so to speak, against the sentiments which had originally inspired it, now employed the strength which it gave them only in the search of wealth and power. Just as the Templars, since the middle of the

[3] The perpetual union of Poland and Lithuania was proclaimed in 1499.

13th century, had become a formidable financial power,
so the Teutonic Knights, having destroyed the pagans of
Prussia, now exploited the country as "consummate econo-
mists." One may say, indeed, that they were the first
"Agrarians" of Prussia. Their vast domains, administered
by *Grosschäffer*, provided grain for a considerable export
trade, for which Bruges was the market. The money derived
from this trade was invested to advantage or lent at interest.
But the Order had become merely an oligarchy of knights;
and their pride and egoism finally exasperated the population of which they considered themselves the masters. The
cities, from the end of the 14th century, and the rural nobility, endured their yoke with impatience.

The new King of Poland did not fail to profit by these
circumstances. As a Lithuanian he was passionately hostile
to the Germans. His accession rendered a war with the
Teutonic Knights inevitable. It broke out in 1409. In the
following year the Polish army inflicted on the Order a
terrible defeat at Tannenberg (July 15th, 1410). For the
Knights this was the beginning of the *débâcle*. The cities
and the nobles were not slow to rise against them. In 1454
they placed themselves under the Polish suzerainty. At last,
in 1466, the Grand Master resigned himself to surrendering East Prussia, with Danzig, Thorn, Marienburg and
Elbing, to Casimir III. The rest of Prussia retained its political autonomy, but henceforth made part of the Polish
State. No one in Germany felt any concern for this decline
of Germanic influence. The population of the country, with
the exception of the sea-board cities, became rapidly
Polonized, and the Slav nationality resumed possession of
the regions from which it had been expelled in the 13th
century. Poland henceforth possessed a wide frontier in the
shape of the Baltic coast. In the South it extended to the
Black Sea. It might have had a brilliant future but for
the fact that at this same period the Turkish advance had
put an end to the trade between the Christian countries and
Asia. Moreover, no one was concerned with the economic
development of the country. For the nobles the accession
of Jagellon had been merely an opportunity for finally consolidating their position. The new king had promised them,

amongst other privileges, immunity from taxation. Under the sceptre of its kings the Polish State was definitely becoming an aristocratic republic.

The Slavs of the South—the Croats, Slovenes, Serbs and Bulgars—presented a very different spectacle from that of the Poles and Bohemians. In consequence of their weakness, the Croats and the Slovenes soon fell under the domination of Hungary, who took care to deny them the least measure of political autonomy. The Serbs and the Bulgars, on the other hand, established to the south of the Danube on the territory of the Greek Empire, and faithful to the Greek Church, profited by the weakness of the Empire, after the reign of Justinian, to penetrate deeply into Macedonia, and even into Greece. While in the long run they became Hellenized, the Slavs of Macedonia preserved their language and their customs, as did the Germans who had occupied the north of the Empire. In the 10th century, under the Emperor Romanus Lacapenus (920–944), the Bulgars threatened Constantinople, which was forced to pay them tribute. Nicephorus Phokas (963–969), followed by John Tzimiskes and Basil II Bulgaroktonos (976–1075), reduced them to a state of dependency on the Empire. But they revolted on the eve of the Fourth Crusade, and from this revolt emerged the new Bulgar Empire, that of the Asen dynasty. Baldwin made war upon them, and perished.

As for the Serbs, under Stephen Nemanja they shook off the Byzantine domination. His son Stephen I, in 1221, assumed the title of king. His successors increased their territory to the detriment of the Empire and the Bulgars, and Stephen III Ourosch destroyed the Bulgarian power. His son Stephen IV Duschan conquered the whole of Macedonia and Albania, and even advanced to the north of the Save. He took the title of Tsar, and had himself crowned "Emperor of the Serbs and Romans" (1346). The Empire, of course, since the Latin conquest, could not continue to fight, and sought only to preserve the coasts, allowing a Serb empire to establish itself on its frontier; and this empire would probably have installed itself on the Bosphorus if the arrival of the Turks had not caused a general upheaval in the Balkans.

Driven like a wedge into the Slav mass, the Hungarians or Magyars, after long terrorizing Germany, and even Northern Italy and Eastern France by their terrible raids of horsemen, had at last settled down, owing to the victories of Henry I and Otto, in the plain of the Danube. The Church of their conquerors eventually became their own. Under Sylvester II they went over to Rome, and the erection of the archbishopric of Gran gave them a religious metropolis.

If one wished to invoke an example in order to prove the unimportance of race in historical development, such an example is certainly provided by the Hungarians.[4] By their origin, and by virtue of their language, these Finns, who were related to the Turks and the Mongols, were completely alien to the ethnographical group of the Indo-European peoples. However, they had hardly taken their place in the midst of these peoples and adopted Christianity, when, despite the nature of the blood that flowed in their veins, their cephalic index, and the linguistic characteristics of their idiom, their social life became so similar to that of their neighbours that it would be quite impossible, if one did not know the facts beforehand, to recognize them as intruders. The fact is that the physical individuality of a people is entirely subordinated to its moral existence. Still Barbarians, and without any civilization of their own, the Hungarians could have preserved their Finnish peculiarities only by retaining their religion. Having become Christians, they were bound to enter the European community, and so prove that they too possessed that pretended "faculty of assimilation" which a certain school of ethnologists claims as peculiar to the "Germanic race," though it is really a characteristic of all Barbarians. Having entered the plain of the Danube as conquerors, they subdued the Slav population of the country and reduced it to servitude. There is nothing in this procedure that can be attributed to their race. The Lombards had done exactly

---

[4] It is amusing to note that at the beginning of 1917 the Finnish Republic sent a deputation to Hungary to notify its birth to the Hungarian people, related to the people of Finland by virtue of their Finnish origin.

the same thing, in the 7th century, in Cisalpine Gaul. But being less civilized than the people they had conquered, the Lombards were rapidly Latinized by them, while the Hungarians, in contact with a subject people no more advanced than themselves, had no difficulty in preserving their nationality and remaining the dominant people. As in all agricultural nations, a nobility of magnates was quickly created. But the feudal system did not make its way into Hungary, for the same reasons that prevented its naturalization in Bohemia and Poland. When Stephen I (997–1038) had succeeded in getting rid of the princes who had hitherto shared the country between them, and had assumed, with the crown which Pope Sylvester sent him, the title of king, these magnates were necessarily associated with the king in the exercise of the monarchical power. In 1222 they exacted from King Andreas II a Golden Bull, which consecrated their political status and acknowledged their right to assemble each year at Stuhlweissenburg, together with the bishops, and also the right of rebellion in case their privileges were violated. This Golden Bull was almost contemporaneous with the Magna Carta of England. The contrast between the two texts is extremely instructive. In England the clergy and the burgesses stood behind the nobles, and the law which the Crown was compelled to accept was a truly national law. In Hungary, on the contrary, a single caste made a covenant in respect of its own interests, and in so far as it succeeded in safeguarding these interests the rest of the people was sacrificed to them.

Things would doubtless have been otherwise if Hungary had possessed a bourgeoisie. But like those other latecomers, Bohemia and Poland, Hungary was a backward country, her economy being purely agricultural. Just as in Bohemia and Poland, so the only bourgeois in Hungary, from the 12th century onwards, were the German immigrants, who remained aliens in the heart of the Hungarian nation, and were further divided from the nation by the privileges which the kings conferred upon them. It is possible that the conquest of Dalmatia, which was effected at the beginning of the 12th century, and which gave Hungary

an outlet on the Adriatic, might in the long run, thanks to
Spalato and Zara, have given rise to commercial activities
in the interior which would have resulted in the creation
of an urban population. However, this could have happened only if Hungary had lived in peace; but the fact
that the country was in contact with so many peoples upon
its various frontiers—Bohemia, Poland, Germany, the
Southern Slavs, and the Byzantine Empire, to say nothing
of Venice, jealous of retaining her control of the Adriatic—
meant that it was always at war, now on one frontier, now
on another. The eastern frontier of Hungary gave upon the
indeterminate domain of Asiatic Barbarism, and the Hungarians had either to repulse, or submit to, the Petcheneg
hordes, and later the Kumans, who came down from Southern Russia. They had, moreover, to defend themselves
against a people which consisted of Slavs and Finns, in-
termingled with the descendants of the ancient Roman
colonists of Dacia, whose Roman dialect they finally
adopted, and who were one day to be known as the Roumanians. This much-tried people was in danger of being
destroyed by the Mongol invasion. Nowhere, unless in
Russia, were the ravages of the Mongols so terrible as in
the plain of the Danube. When they had at last retired the
country had almost to be colonized afresh. King Bela IV
(1235–1270) did his best in this direction, inviting the
Italians to settle in the country and sending for more Germans, to augment the number of those who had already
settled in Transylvania, where they have remained to this
day. Buda was founded in 1245. The Italians introduced
the culture of the vine. The Roumanians made their way
into all parts of the Hungarian plain as agricultural labourers. Thirty years later Hungary had become strong enough
to support Rudolph of Habsburg against Ottocar of Bohemia, and to curb, on behalf of Germany, the menace of
Czech expansion. It was soon evident to Hungary that the
Habsburgs, now her neighbours, had included her in their
dynastic projects. When Ladislas IV died without children
Rudolph of Habsburg, disposing of the country as a fief of
the Empire, gave it to his son Albert. But since Pope Sylvester II had sent the crown to Stephen the Popes regarded

Hungary as a fief of the Holy See, and this fief was immediately claimed by Nicholas IV on behalf of Charles Martel,
the son of Charles II of Naples, and the brother-in-law of
Ladislas. In order to get rid of these foreigners the magnates
gave the crown to Andrew III, a scion of the national
dynasty; but on his death in 1301 they acknowledged the
son of Charles Martel, Charles Robert, as their king (1308–
1342). Thus the French dynasty of Anjou, which the
Papacy had established in Naples in opposition to the
Hohenstaufens, was now established in Hungary in opposition to the Habsburgs. There it held its own until 1382,
contributing largely to the "Westernization" of the country.
The greatest king of this dynasty was Louis (1342–1382),
who occupied Moldavia, abandoned by the Mongols, subdued Croatia, and forced the Venetians to surrender the
coast and the islands of the Adriatic as far as Durazzo.

His policy reveals the resource and ambition of a great
king, but it was almost megalomaniac. His brother Andrew,
the husband of Queen Joanna of Naples, having been assassinated, he undertook two expeditions against this kingdom. Besides this Italian policy, he also pursued a northern
policy, for as we have seen, he was King of Poland, so that
his influence extended from the Vistula to the Adriatic and
the Black Sea.

The contemporary of Charles IV and Casimir of Poland,
it is interesting to note that he pursued the same policy.
He founded a university at Fünfkirchen. The polished manners of the court began to diffuse themselves among the
magnates. The middle of the 14th century was an interesting period in Bohemia, Poland, and Hungary, owing to the
influence, Occidental rather than specifically French, which
had replaced the German influence of the 13th century.

But the position which Louis had made for himself had
no lasting consequences. Since he had no son, the enormous
structure which he had created was fragile in the extreme.
Poland passed under the sceptre of Jagellon. An Angevin
kinsman, Charles of Durazzo, was assassinated in 1387, and
Sigismond of Luxemburg, who had married Maria, Louis'
daughter, was finally acknowledged as king.

His was not a distinguished reign. The Turks were beginning to appear on the frontier. An Adriatic policy was henceforth impossible. The titles of "King of the Romans" and "Emperor" bestowed upon the King of Hungary were powerless to save the country. On the contrary, they involved it in the Hussite war. As we have seen, the plans of the Council were explained by the Turkish peril, but they were ineffective. On the death of Sigismond in 1437, Albert of Austria, who had married his daughter Elizabeth, inherited the crown of Hungary. He died prematurely in 1439, having had no time to assure the Habsburg rule over Hungary. And now, for a long while to come, the history of the country was to be substantially the history of the Turkish peril.

The total impression produced by the history of the Slavs and the Hungarians up to the middle of the 15th century may be summed up by saying that although they had entered into the Christian community, they had remained almost entirely outside the European community. They had never experienced that initiation into the Romanic civilization which the Germans had received from the Carolingian Empire. They had never lived, like the Germans, under that theocratic régime whose intimate alliance of the spiritual with the temporal power enabled it to propagate all that the Church had preserved of the Roman administration, law, learning and literature. The Empire of Otto, prematurely and too exclusively oriented toward Italy, had abandoned the attempt to subject the Hungarians to its influence, and the process of Westernization was effected only through the medium of their bishops and monks. But since the latter had to rely exclusively on their own resources, had no political power, and were far removed from the centres of religious life, their influence was inevitably quite superficial and was confined to the domain of religious worship and discipline. These peoples knew nothing of the domainal organization, nor of the feudal system; they played no part in the War of Investitures, nor in the Crusades. For them the only consequence of the great *épopée* was the advent of the Jews who sought refuge in their territories, having been driven across the Elbe by the followers of Christ. And when the economic life of the Occident was revived by the influence of commerce, and the bourgeoisie made its appearance everywhere between the Mediterranean and the North Sea, they were made aware of this great movement only by the sudden afflux of German colonization. Placed at a disadvantage by their old agricultural institutions, they yielded to the German pressure; retreating along the Elbe before the invaders, they allowed the latter to establish themselves among them, and to found cities which were like foreign islands in the midst of the national population. With the arrival of these newcomers, who looked down upon them but were a necessity for them, there began a period of superficial Germanization which continued until the middle of the 14th century. Then a reaction began to make itself felt, of which, almost simultaneously, Charles IV in Bohemia, Casimir I in Poland, and Louis I in Hungary were the instruments. The German penetration ceased, and in all three countries there was a sudden awakening of national energy. This was manifested, under very different forms, by the explosive outbreak of Hussitism in Bohemia, the conquest of Prussia by Poland, and Hungary's advance toward the Adriatic. It seemed as though the moment had come for the Western Slavs and the Hungarians to play an active part in European civilization. But the Turks were advancing across the Balkan peninsula, and the Slavs and Hungarians had to meet the thrust, turning back to the East in order to defend the civilization of the West instead of beginning to collaborate with it.

CHAPTER IV

Spain. Portugal. The Turks

1. *Spain and Portugal*

The Crusades had attacked Islam at its centre. The Mohammedan world surrounded Palestine on every side, and in order to maintain its position and to counterbalance the pressure of Islam on this narrow strip of coast without being driven into the sea, the West would have had to develop a vigorous offensive, which at this distance from its base, and with the resources at its disposal, was beyond its power. Once it had lost the positions which had been captured by the enthusiasm of the First Crusade it struggled in vain to reconquer them. After the reign of St. Louis, the Levant, ceasing to be a base of military operations, became and remained, until the discovery of the New World, the halfway house for trade between Europe and the East.

In Spain the respective situation of the Musulmans and the Christians was very different. There the two adversaries were far less unequally matched. They met face to face on a well-defined battlefield, and both adversaries, in the event of a reverse, could fall back and repair their losses before taking the field again. Under these conditions, that side would finally be victorious which was capable of the most long-continued aggression; that is, the poorest adversary would be victorious; in other words, the Spaniards. For it was not their faith alone that impelled them to make war. The fierce desire to possess the noble cities and the beautiful champaigns which, thanks to Musulman industry and agriculture, offered such an insolent contrast to their own rugged mountains, fanned their hatred of the infidel to a white heat. Their attack upon Islam was almost like an invasion of Barbarians, at all events in the beginning. But these Barbarians were Christians, which prevented them from merging themselves in the conquered population, as the Germans had formerly merged themselves in the Latin population of the Empire. Race had nothing to do with the matter. The Turks, in the 10th and 11th centuries, became thoroughly assimilated, despite their Mongol origin, with the Semitic civilization of the Arabs of Baghdad. There is no reason to suppose that had the Spaniards been pagans, like the Turks, at the time of their first contact with Islam, they would not, like the Turks, have been converted. The material superiority of the superior civilizations was the most potent means of religious propaganda among the pagans. But when these civilizations came into contact with the adepts of an alien and exclusive faith, their very wealth and brilliance exasperated religious hostility until it became hatred, because that wealth and brilliance seemed an impiety, an offence against the true God. And then, pillage and devastation being justified in advance, the most brutal instincts could give themselves free vent without troubling men's consciences. Duty, sentiment, and interest all combined to rally the Christians of Spain to the Holy War. It was a Holy War in the full meaning of the term, for its aim was not the conversion but the massacre or expulsion of the infidels. In the Spaniards there was no trace of that tolerance which allowed the Catholic subjects of the Musulmans, the Mozarabs, to practise their religion unmolested. Their religious exclusivism was so complete that it was not softened by offers of abjuration, and they regarded the Moriscos (baptized Musulmans) with insurmountable suspicion. It was not enough to be a Christian; a man must be an "old Christian," which really meant that he must be "of old Spanish stock"; so that nationality became the proof of orthodoxy, and national feeling, becoming confounded with faith, was imbued with its uncompromising spirit and its fervour.

We have already seen that the Moors, who after the middle of the 11th century were no longer capable of resisting the victorious Christian armies, appealed for aid to the Almoravides of Morocco. The battle of Sabacca (1086) checked the advance of the Spaniards, but did not shatter it. While for the next hundred years the war was not distinguished by any more great military actions, it was waged with untiring tenacity. The exploits of national heroes provided matter for the "romances" which, about the time when the feudal *épopée* of France found expression in the *chansons de Roland,* extolled the glory of the Cid Campeador, who met his death in 1099, the year Jerusalem was captured. While Roland became a great figure in European literature, the Cid remained a local hero. The fact is that the attention of contemporaries, attracted by the more impressive spectacle of the Crusade, overlooked the Spanish war of the 12th century, just as in 1812 it overlooked the Spanish war for the Russian campaign. Nevertheless, it was in Spain that the decline of Napoleon had its beginnings, and it was Spain that furnished the Catholicism of the Middle Ages with its only lasting victories over Islam. These victories would have been more quickly won and more decisive if the Christians had combined their efforts against the common enemy. Unfortunately the kings of Castile and Aragon, constantly at war with each other, or obliged to defend themselves against the encroachments of the nobles, made it only too easy for the enemy to recover from their blows and to avenge themselves. In 1195 the Emir Iacub Almansor won such a signal victory over Alfonso VIII of Castile at Alarcos that for a moment there seemed a danger of a general catastrophe. But the Papacy, though engrossed in the Holy War, had never lost sight of the fact that Spain constituted the right wing of Christendom in that war. Innocent III immediately intervened. He urged the faithful to take the Cross, sent money to Spain, and extended his protection to the kings of the peninsula. Pedro II of Aragon went to Rome to be crowned by the Pope, and acknowledged that his kingdom was a fief of the Holy See. For once, thanks to the exhortations of Rome, Aragon, Castile, Leon and Portugal combined their forces. In 1212 the battle of Navos de Tolosa avenged the disaster of Alarcos and shattered the Musulman resistance.

Henceforth the advance of the Christians was irresistible and definitive. Jayme II of Aragon (1213–1276) obtained a foothold in the Balearics, and in 1238 captured Valencia. Ferdinand III of Castile captured Cordova in 1236 and Seville in 1248. Meanwhile Alfonso III of Portugal annexed the Algarves and gave the kingdom the expanse which it has retained to this day. Of all its possessions in Spain, Islam retained only the territory of Granada, and even this was subject in vassalage to Castile.

As they enlarged themselves by extending southwards at the expense of the Moors, the Spanish States, so numerous in the beginning, became more compact by a process of agglomeration. The States of Asturias, Galicia and Leon (1230) were united to Castile, and Catalonia was combined with Aragon. Navarre, now ruled by a French dynasty, and too confined within her mountains to compete with her more fortunate neighbours, was restricted to a local existence. Portugal, inevitably oriented toward the West by her long seaboard and the course of her rivers, the Douro and the Tagus, turned her back upon the peninsula, which was divided between Castile and Aragon. Of these two kingdoms Castile was much the larger, but Aragon was more favourably situated, and for this reason was brought into contact with the outer world much earlier than Castile. I am not thinking here of the considerable fiefs on the north of the Pyrenees which had long been in the possession of the Aragonese dynasty. They would only have involved the kings of Aragon in wars with the kings of France, in which they would inevitably have been the losers, and Jayme II had the good sense to cede them to St. Louis in return for the French king's renunciation of his suzerainty over Catalonia (1258). What drew Aragon toward Europe and gave it, from the 14th century, a character less narrowly Spanish than that of Castile, was its situation on the shores of the Mediterranean. Owing to this situation it was encouraged to take part in that Levantine trade which was, *par excellence*, the important trade of the Middle Ages. Barcelona was not slow to follow in the track

of Venice, Pisa, and Genoa, and in the 12th century the
Catalan sailors mingled with the Italians and the Provençaux in the ports of Syria and Egypt. It was this maritime
activity, rather than the relationship of Pedro III (1276–
1285) to Manfred, that involved Aragon in the affairs of
Sicily, and in 1285 gave Spain a foothold in this kingdom,
one of the sensitive points of European politics, from which
she was afterwards to expand over the rest of Italy. Under
Pedro's successors the Mediterranean expansion of the kingdom continued. Alfonso III (1285–1291) conquered the
whole of the Balearic archipelago, which, after existing for
some time as a vassal kingdom, was annexed to the Crown
under Pedro IV (1336–1387). Alfonso IV (1327–1336)
made war upon Genoa for the possession of Corsica and
Sardinia. Under Alfonso V, in 1443, the conquest of the
Kingdom of Naples was effected. Aragon was thus a Mediterranean power. It was Aragon that opened up for Spain,
cut off from Europe by the Pyrenees, the only possible
means of communication, the highway of the Mediterranean. Think what the reign of Charles V would have been
if Sicily had not been included in his heritage!

However, not Aragon but Castile was the true Spain. It
was Castile that played the greatest and the most glorious
part in the war against the Moors, and Castile could lay
claim to the most popular of heroes, the Cid in the 11th,
and Perez de Castro in the 13th century, and the "romances" which sing their exploits are also Castilian. In
Castile the nobles were more numerous and more influential than elsewhere in Spain. It was in Castile that the
national character and the national language were formed.
Of course, the country was not entirely cut off from the
outer world. The ports on the Gulf of Gascony maintained
a fairly active coasting trade with Flanders, and in 1280
the Castilian merchants obtained a Charter of Privileges
from Bruges. But neither the trade nor the fleet of Castile would bear comparison with those of Barcelona. We
should not therefore be surprised that the kings of Castile
were not drawn, like the kings of Aragon, into the orbit
of European politics. We have already seen that when a
somewhat singular ambition had induced him to buy the

title of King of the Romans, Alfonso X (1252–1284) was unable to derive any advantage from it. The dynastic quarrels which marked the reign of Sancho IV (1284–1295), who was attacked by the sons of Fernando de la Cerda, provoked the intervention—which was, however, unsuccessful—of the King of France; and later Pedro the Cruel (1350–1369) allied himself with the Black Prince in order to cope with his rival, Henry of Trastamara, who was supported by Du Guesclin. And here we have almost the whole story of the foreign relations of Castile until Spain, having suddenly become a great power, began to overrun the world. Until the close of the 15th century the influence of Castile was rigidly circumscribed by the frontiers of the peninsula.

The activities of Castile were not confined to making war upon the Moors. In contact with Portugal on the west and Aragon on the east, the kingdom was constantly involved in conflicts with its neighbours, for which the relationship between the royal families furnished only too many occasions, perhaps in respect of the regency of an infant prince, or the legitimacy of the heir to the throne. It was these continual quarrels between the Christian States that enabled the Kingdom of Granada to survive despite its weakness. There were even occasions when it participated in, and so prolonged, the quarrels which it found so useful.

In spite of their dynastic wars, there was a striking resemblance between Castile, Aragon and Portugal, a sort of family likeness, which is very easily explained by the similarity of their histories. Except in Catalonia, to which the preponderance of Barcelona gave a special character, which impresses the observer even to this day, the same institutions and the same social groups were to be found everywhere. The nobles, who were essentially military, long preserved a haughty and arrogant attitude in respect of the monarchy, and of this attitude the right of the grandees of Spain to remain covered in the presence of the sovereign survived, under the absolute monarchy, as a harmless but significant relic. In order to resist this nobility of *ricos hombres* and *hidalgos*, the kings, from the beginning of the 13th century, depended on the support of the bourgeoisie.

In this connection their conduct was dictated by political interests, as was that of the kings of France after Louis VII. But the alliance of the cities and the Crown was far more intimate and of far longer duration in Spain than in France. Why was this? Perhaps it was on account of the greater arrogance of the nobles. What the bourgeois expected of the king was peace and security on the highways. In order to obtain these, they themselves formed leagues (*hermandades*), like the German cities, and the leagues also reinforced the judicial power of the king, for the judicial function played a very important part in the activities of these kings. Under Alfonso X the *Codigo de las siete pardidas* was compiled for Castile, and Jayme II of Aragon won fame as a legislator. King Denis of Portugal (1279–1325) was known as *el Justo*. Pedro I (1357–1367) was praised for his pitiless severity. Consequently the bourgeoisie did its utmost to support the king, as against the military nobles, in his rôle of guardian of the law and the public peace. The *hermandades* may therefore be said to have provided him with a voluntary police, which dealt with bandits and malefactors. It goes without saying that the cities, being so intimately associated with the exercise of the royal power, obtained representation in the Cortes at a very early date. From the 13th century their deputies sat beside those of the nobles and the clergy. The dynastic quarrels which troubled Spain in the 14th century afforded the Cortes an excellent opportunity of increasing their intervention in the government, and more than once they prescribed to the kings, above all in Aragon, where the cities were more influential than elsewhere, concessions not unlike those which were obtained from the princes of the Low Countries in the same period. Here, however, their influence ceased. Spain, like the other continental States, did not evolve beyond the system of political dualism, in which the prince on one hand, and the privileged orders on the other, met together and agreed upon compromises. Neither here nor elsewhere had the parliamentary system made its appearance, the collaboration of the two elements of the nation in the English manner. As elsewhere, questions of taxation played their part in the constitutional struggles of the 14th century. That essentially Castilian tax, the *alcabala*—a tax on sales and purchases—was granted for the first time to Alfonso XI (1312–1350) by Burgos, on the occasion of an expedition against Algeciras. Subsequently it was gradually introduced throughout the country.

Dynastic quarrels and political disputes kept the Spanish kingdoms so fully occupied that during the 14th century and the greater part of the 15th they did little in the way of resuming the war against the Moors of Granada. On the other hand they developed their commerce and added to their wealth. Sheep began to cover the countryside, and in the trade with the North of Europe Spanish began to compete with English wool. The exports of wool to the Low Countries were considerably increased, and sheep-farming began to give Castile its characteristic aspect and to enrich the nobility. There was also an increasing trade with the North in iron from Bilbao, olive oil, oranges and pomegranates. Bruges was the central market for this trade; and in the first half of the 15th century the Spanish nation was almost as strongly represented in that city as the Hansa. This economic orientation toward the North must not be overlooked; indeed, we can hardly avoid regarding it as a preparation for the dynastic alliance which in 1494 was to bind the Low Countries to Castile.

But at the same time, on the Atlantic coast of Portugal another kind of expansion was beginning, and this was to change the future of the world. Opposite the Algarves lay the coast of Morocco, and religious zeal inspired the Portuguese to make war upon Islam. Henry the Navigator (1394–1460), the son of King John I, in whom curiosity was blended with the spirit of Christian propaganda, devoted his life to equipping maritime expeditions which inaugurated the great era of discovery. In 1415 he took part in his father's expedition against Ceuta and in the capture of that city. What lay beyond? What unknown world was in hiding beyond Cape Bojador, past which no ship had ever sailed? Navigation was now sufficiently advanced to venture upon the high seas. In 1419 a ship despatched by Henry discovered the Madeira Islands, and another, in 1431, the Azores. In 1434 Cape Bojador was passed. Before his death in 1460 Henry was able to receive tidings of the discovery of the Cape Verde Islands and the coast of Senegambia. The path to the southern world lay open. This Atlantic Ocean, which had hitherto seemed the end of the world, was about to become the highway leading to a new world.

Thus, in the middle of the 15th century, even before the marriage of Ferdinand and Isabella, which was to effect the permanent union of Castile and Aragon, Spain had won a position in the world whose future possibilities no one could as yet foresee, but which prepared her for the part which she was about to play. Through Barcelona and Sicily she was involved in the affairs of the Mediterranean; she was in contact with the North of Europe through the trade of the seaports of Gascony; and she had just ventured forth across the Atlantic. Her power, still divided, was not yet very considerable, but no other State, not even Venice, had undergone such expansion. And if we reflect that the Spanish people had been tempered by the wars against Islam, that it had the profoundest confidence in itself, and that it was both a military and a sea-going people, we shall have no difficulty in realizing the strength of this new factor which was about to play its part in the life of Europe.

2. *The Turks*

The only result of the foundation of the Latin Empire improvised in Constantinople by the Fourth Crusade was to hasten the decomposition of the Byzantine State. Venetian and Genoese factories had been established on most of the islands of the Ionian Sea, and upon the coast, while Greece was divided into feudal principalities—the Duchy of Athens, the Duchy of Achaia. The Bulgars and the Serbs had occupied Thrace and Macedonia. Hardly anything was left of the European possessions of the Empire, apart from Constantinople, Salonica, Adrianople and Philippopolis, when Michael VII Palaeologus, in 1261, re-established the Greek rule. On the other side of the Bosphorus, however, in Asia Minor, which the Latins had not yet penetrated, the

Empire still possessed Western Anatolia with Broussa, Nicaea, and Nicomedia.

This Empire was obviously destined to fall asunder. Exploited by Venice and Genoa, it had lost all economic viability and was no longer capable of providing for the enormous expenditure necessitated by its defence. Trade and industry, as they declined, had made way for the preponderance of the great landowners, a preponderance not unlike that which they had enjoyed in the West after the fall of the Empire. As matters stood in the reign of Michael VIII (1261–1282) it seemed inevitable that the Empire would shortly be subjected to a triple dismemberment. In Sicily Charles of Anjou coveted Greece, and was evidently making preparations for its conquest; the Serbs, who were increasing their possessions in the north, made no secret of their ambition to capture Constantinople; and lastly, there were the Turks in Asia Minor. The catastrophe of the Sicilian Vespers, for which the intrigues of Michael VIII were to some extent responsible, put the Angevins out of the running. They were obliged to turn back from the East in order to face their Aragonese rivals. From the European standpoint this was a great misfortune. The formation in the south of Italy of a State powerful enough to subject Greece to its influence would have been the best of safeguards against the Turkish advance. For it was obvious that the Slavs of the Balkans could not hold the Turks in check unaided. Since in any case the Greek Empire was no longer capable of defending itself, the essential thing was to ensure that it should not be forcibly detached from the European and Christian communities. But the policy of a State is rarely concerned with anything beyond its immediate and actual interests. Michael VIII regarded the disaster which had befallen Charles of Anjou as a triumph for Byzantium.

From the 10th century the Turks, Barbarians of Finnish origin, had been for the Caliphate of Baghdad very much what the Germans, six hundred years earlier, had been for the Roman Empire. They had invaded it, and naturally were immediately converted to its religion. The brilliant civilization of Islam was too fragile to endure contact with these rude neophytes. The Turks derived nothing from this civilization beyond a few purely external characteristics. They remained, in its midst, essentially peasants and soldiers, but the less polished they were the more eagerly they received the new faith, and the zeal which inspired them against the infidels necessarily helped to nourish their military spirit. The great Mongol invasion of the 13th century, which so brutally devastated Hither Asia, drove them into the mountains of Armenia. But they soon descended from the mountains, under the leadership of Omman, and moved westwards into Asia Minor, which was easily wrested from the feeble grasp of the successors of Michael Palaeologus. Broussa (1326), Nicomedia, and Nicaea (1330) fell into the hands of the invader. Nothing was left of the Empire's Asiatic possessions, and its impotence still further aggravated the political intrigues amidst which it was floundering. After the death of Andronicus III (1341) the Grand Domestic Cantacuzene, taking advantage of the minority of John V, assumed the purple, and in order to hold his own against the Bulgars and Venetians whom the court had called to its assistance he negotiated with the Turks, allowing them to cross the Bosphorus. The conquest of Europe followed immediately upon the conquest of Asia. Murad I captured Adrianople in 1352 and Philippopolis in 1363, defeated the Serbs in 1371, drove them back into Macedonia, and entered Sofia in 1381. Imprisoned within the walls of Constantinople, the Greeks left the defence of Thrace to the Slavs. In 1387 the Serbs were victorious in Bosnia, but two years later they were defeated in the bloody battle of Kossovo (June 15th, 1389), in which both their prince, Lazar, and the victorious Sultan were slain. The Slav resistance appeared to be shattered. Bajazet (1389–1403), the son of Murad, subdued Bosnia, Wallachia, Bulgaria, Macedonia, and Thessaly. The whole Balkan peninsula, as far as the Danube, was now merely an annex of the Musulman world. The Cross was no longer seen save on the domes of Constantinople and Salonica, and in the mountains of Albania. The frontiers of Hungary, and with them those of the Latin Church, were threatened. The desperate appeals of the Palaeologi were heard at last.

Boniface I preached the Crusade. Sigismond of Luxemburg called the Hungarians and the Germans to arms. In France the Duke of Burgundy, Philip the Bold, doubtless as much to enhance the prestige of his house as in any spirit of Christian enthusiasm, sent his son Jean (the Fearless) at the head of a brilliant army of knights to fight the infidel. All these efforts were defeated at Nicopolis by the impetuosity and the unfamiliar tactics of the Turks (September 12th, 1396). It seemed as though Constantinople's hour had nearly come. It was delayed for fifty years by the unexpected incidence of a fresh Mongol invasion.

Once again, and happily for the last time, following in the trail of Attila and Jenghiz Khan, a Barbarian of genius, Tamerlane, had just released a torrent of yellow hordes. His conquests had been as overwhelming as those of the terrible destroyers to whom he was a worthy successor. He had pushed westward as far as the Volga, had subdued Persia and Armenia by terrorism, and had finally conquered that cradle of so many successive civilizations, Mesopotamia, which has never since recovered from the devastation that he wreaked upon it. The Turkish Empire was menaced. Bajazet had just laid siege to Constantinople; he raised the siege in order to hasten to the defence of Asia Minor. The two Barbarians met in 1402 at Angora, and the man whom the Europeans had been powerless to check was vanquished by the Mongols (July 20th, 1402). But Tamerlane's career was as brief as his rise had been sudden. After his death (1405) the peoples bowed under the Mongol yoke raised their heads amidst the ruins of their civilization. Sulieman, the son of Bajazet (1402–1410), succeeded in reorganizing the débris of Turkey-in-Asia. This would have been the moment for the Christians to take the offensive. But the Emperor Manuel contented himself with a treaty which gave him Salonica and a few of the islands, and arranged a marriage between one of his nieces and the Sultan. The tribute demanded from the Greeks and the Serbs was abolished. The world was pleased to think that the peril was averted, as though a defeat could ever subdue a barbarian people for longer than the time needed to replace the warriors who had fallen on the field of battle. There was only one possible means of stopping the Turks, and that was to absorb them into Western civilization; but since they professed Islam, this was simply unthinkable. Consequently the catastrophe which had been averted for the moment was soon more imminent than ever. Murad II (1421–1451) reappeared before the walls of Constantinople and recaptured Salonica; and despite the heroism of George Castriotis (Scanderberg) in Albania, and Hunyadi Janos on the Hungarian frontiers, the Turkish domination, after the battle of Varna (1444), was reestablished throughout the Balkan peninsula.

This time the fate of Constantinople was inevitable. What help could be anticipated from Europe, where France and England were exhausted by the Hundred Years' War, Germany was troubled by Hussitism, and the Church was a prey to the disputes of the Pope and the Council? The union of the Greek and Latin Churches, which the Emperor Manuel had allowed Eugenius VI to proclaim in 1439, had attracted little attention in the West, and its only result was to exasperate the Byzantine populace and the Orthodox clergy, who were ready to turn Turk rather than Papist. In the Low Countries, it was true, Duke Philip the Good spoke of organizing a Crusade, but he made no move, and even if he had set out for the East! . . . No mere military expedition, however powerful, could have saved Constantinople. In dealing with an enemy like the Turk, who was always able to bring up fresh reserves from Asia, and to carry on the war without excessive expenditure, thanks to the robust energies of a whole nation of warriors, what was really needed was a powerful and permanent military base on the shores of the Bosphorus, in the islands, and on the Danube. What State, under the political and economic conditions of the time, could have organized such a base, and borne the expense of it, and provided for its upkeep? Uncivilized though they were, the Turks were at least the equals of the Westerners in the military arts. They had warships, artillery and an incomparable cavalry, and theirs was the brute impetuosity and heroic fanaticism of a primitive people. Moreover, the States which should have been readiest to oppose them, whether or not they would have proved more powerful, either would not or could not move against them. The Venetians thought only of safeguarding their factories. Dismembered Germany was incapable of any effort. She left the Hungarians to their own devices, and what could they do beyond defending their own frontiers? As for the Serbs and the Bulgars, they were exhausted. When in 1452 Mahomet II laid siege to Constantinople, no one came to the help of the city. Its fall was inevitable. And we must not blame Europe for its failure to intervene. The necessary effort would have been too great. And this Europe realized. From the moment when the Byzantine Empire had failed to defend Asia Minor against the Turks Constantinople was lost. It is therefore not surprising that the West turned a deaf ear to Aeneas Sylvius (Pius II) and Nicholas V. For the West realized that it must resign itself to the inevitable. Honour at least was saved. Constantine XI was a worthy last representative of the long series of Emperors who derived directly from the Roman Emperors whose title they continued to bear. On the day of the final assault, May 29th, 1453, he fell fighting against the enemy. On the morrow, amidst scenes of pillage and massacre, the victor entered the Basilica of St. Sophia, and transformed it into a mosque; a Barbarian's unconscious act of homage to the superior civilization over which he had triumphed.

BOOK THREE

The Renaissance and the
Reformation

Introduction

The period extending from the beginning of the 14th century to the middle of the 15th offers the spectacle of a disturbed and tormented society, struggling against the tradition which oppressed it, and which it could not contrive to shake off. The barrier which the past opposed to the thrust of the future held firm; it appeared to be still intact, and yet, undermined by invisible flaws, it suddenly gave way, and the energies which it had contained poured through the breach and gave the historic landscape an entirely new aspect.

Before the Renaissance, the intellectual history of Europe was merely a chapter of the history of the Church. There was so little secular thought that even those who contended against the Church were entirely dominated by it, and thought only of transforming it. They were not free-thinkers but heretics. With the Renaissance the supremacy of the Church in the domain of thought was questioned. The cleric no longer had the monopoly of learning. Spiritual life, in its turn, became secularized; philosophy ceased to be the servant of theology, and art, like literature, emancipated itself from the tutelage which had been imposed upon it ever since the 8th century. The ascetic ideal was replaced by a purely human ideal, and of this ideal the highest expression was to be found in antiquity. The humanist replaced the cleric, as virtue (*virtus*) replaced piety. Of course, although we can say, truthfully enough, that the Renaissance replaced the Christian by the man, it was not anti-religious. Were there not many Popes amongst its most enthusiastic promoters? But it is perfectly true to say that it was anti-clerical. Not only for the Italian humanists, but also for Christians as convinced as Erasmus or Thomas More, the claim of the theologian to domineer over learning and letters, and even morality, was as ridiculous as it was harmful. They dreamed of reconciling religion with the world. They were tolerant, not unduly dogmatic, and extremely hostile to the secular studies which Scholasticism had superimposed upon the Bible. They were interested above all in moral questions. Their programme, which we find in *Miles Christianus* and the *Utopia,* is that of a broad, rational Christianity, entirely devoid of mysticism, which would make the Church, not the Bride of Christ and the source of salvation, but an institution for moralization and education in the highest sense of the word. They felt very strongly that if the Church was to be this it must be reformed. But they were optimists, and they hoped that it would be possible to induce it, by gentle pressure, to enter upon the new path.

We may say, then, that the Renaissance stated the religious problem in its own way. But it went no further than sketching the moderate, prudent and aristocratic solution which it proposed. The Reformation, on the other hand, attacked the problem with passion, violence and intolerance, but also with profound faith, and the passionate longing to attain to God and to salvation which was destined to conquer and subjugate men's souls. There was nothing in common between it and the Renaissance. It was properly speaking the antithesis of the Renaissance. It replaced the human being by the Christian; it derided and humiliated the power of reason, even when it condemned and repudiated dogmatism. Luther was much more akin to the Middle Ages than to the humanists, his contemporaries. Indeed, he horrified the majority of the humanists. Erasmus and More very soon turned aside from this revolutionary, whose brutality and radicalism were as disturbing to their intelligent opportunism as they were repugnant to their good taste and moderation. They divined the tragedy which was about to commence, and they shuddered at it, understanding that it meant the end of their hopes of reconciliation.

Yet it was not Lutheranism that provoked the catastrophe of the wars of religion. After a first popular effervescence, marked by the rising of the German peasants and the insurrection of the Anabaptists, it submitted with docility to the control of the princes. It abandoned the Church to the secular power so completely that when Charles V decided to take action against it he had to fight the princes, and the conflict that followed was far more political than religious. As for Rome, surprised by the success of a movement in which she had seen, at first, no more than a monkish dispute; wholly engrossed in temporal interests, and having allowed the Catholic masses to become lukewarm in their faith, she could do nothing more effective, at first, to stem the rising flood of heresy than to launch her impotent anathemata. The kingdoms of the North adopted the new confession. Henry VIII, in England, founded a State Church which was half schismatic and half heretical, but above all, the National Church to which the followers of Wycliffe had already aspired. All this was effected without any great disturbance; there were a few sentences of banishment, and a certain amount of torture was inflicted, but there was no civil war; less blood was shed, incomparably less, than by the war of the Albigenses or the Inquisition.

But then Calvin made his appearance, and with him the hitherto comparatively peaceful course which the Reformation had followed under the control of the State was suddenly modified. An austere, exclusive, intolerant religion claimed the right to impose itself upon the government, and to force it, even by rebellion, to obey the Word of God. Calvinism was no longer satisfied with the national existence which had hitherto contented Protestantism. The Calvinist propaganda aspired to conquer the world. The faith which it inspired in its "elect" urged them to political action, and this action was the beginning of the tragic epoch of the wars of religion.

The indispensable condition of the success of the Renaissance, and also that of the Reformation, was the decline of the Catholic Church, which, as we have seen, had been constantly accelerated since the beginning of the 14th century. This alone had rendered possible the enfranchisement of thought and the renewal of faith. European society was too vigorous to remain tied by the fetters that bound it to the past. And it was not only in the domain of faith and of thought that a movement of renewal had been manifested since the middle of the 15th century. It had been perceptible everywhere. While the thinkers were shaking off the yoke of Scholasticism, and while the artists were freeing themselves from the restrictions of the Gothic style, the industrialists, capitalists and politicians were protesting and rebelling in their turn against the restrictive system of the trade corporations, against the economic limitations, the traditions and prejudices that impeded the free expansion of their activities. Everything was undergoing transformation, the economic world no less than the intellectual; the birth of modern capitalism was almost contemporaneous with the appearance of the first scientific works, and it collaborated with science in the discovery of the East Indies and America. The constitutions of the States felt the influence of the ideas, necessities, appetites and ambitions which were affecting the community as a whole. Indeed, we should do wrong to restrict the application of the word "Renaissance" to the new orientation of thought and art; it should be extended to the whole field of human activity, as revealed in its manifold aspects from the middle of the 15th century. If at the same time we reflect that this exuberant life was poured into the veins of a Europe in which a new State, Burgundy, had just been created, while Spain had lately acquired the rank of a "great power," and the arrival of the Turks had resulted in a formidable Eastern problem, we shall appreciate the enormous magnitude and the absorbing interest of the spectacle of European history at the moment when, about 1450, it suddenly quickened its pace, affording a conspicuous contrast, in its vigorous decisiveness and its lucid enthusiasm, to the painful and groping confusion of the preceding period.

CHAPTER I

The Transformation of Social Life from the
Middle of the Fifteenth Century

1. *Italy and Italian Influence*

The Renaissance, in the more general sense of the term, does not appear to have been a more specifically Italian phenomenon than the expansion of urban life had been at the close of the 11th century. Neither the Renaissance nor the new form of urban life could have become so rapidly diffused had not the conditions favourable to its success existed to the north of the Alps. But it is true that these conditions, in each case, were of earlier occurrence in Italy, and more favourable than anywhere else. Just as Florence took precedence of all the cities of the Middle Ages, so the Italian Renaissance manifested a variety and originality and vigour unknown elsewhere, and to which it owed its astonishing influence.

The fact is that the traditional authorities which dominated both social and intellectual life declined or disappeared far earlier in Italy than in the rest of Europe. And this was largely a consequence of the extraordinary development of urban life. Just at first the nobles inhabiting the cities were involved in incessant conflicts with the bourgeoisie, but gradually, insensibly, they began to engage in commerce, so that the very clear line of demarcation which elsewhere divided the noble from the non-noble was slowly effaced, the descendants of knights and the offspring of enriched merchants intermingling in a community of manners and interests, independently of birth. The social status became more important than the juridical status; moreover, in the course of the 14th century the Italian nobility abandoned the profession of arms, thereby losing the *raison d'être* of its constitution as a distinct and privileged class. War became a profession which was left to specialists, the *condottieri,* men of the most various origins, the majority being successful *parvenus;* men in whom there was no trace of the old feudal loyalty. And while the noble was divesting himself of his specific class characteristics a similar transformation was proceeding in the ranks of the wealthy bourgeoisie. The progress of economic organization, the development of commercial society, and the improvement of instruments of credit had the consequence, from the very first, of requiring in the banker or the man of affairs an intellectual ability and culture which were not found in the same degree among the merchants of the North, and far less than the latter was he "subdued to what he worked in." While giving due attention to his business, he allowed himself some hours of leisure, so that he was able to distract himself by intellectual interests, embellish his house with works of art, and acquire a refinement which made him singularly unlike the "patricians" of Germany, Flanders or France. And so, recruited at once from the nobility and the bourgeoisie, a sort of mundane aristocracy came into existence, comprising all those who lived the same kind of life, enjoyed the same degree of education, had the same tastes, and indulged in the same pleasures; and this kind of aristocracy had not its like in any other country. The old society was disintegrating. New groups were in process of formation, no longer determined by convention and prejudice, but coming into existence freely, by virtue of affinities; and in these groups one may say that the spirit of class was replaced by the spirit of humanity.

The development of capitalism involved still further consequences.[1] We should note, as a quite extraordinary

[1] Here I should need my books and my notes before I could say anything definite.

phenomenon, the effective principality of the Medici in Florence, which had no other origin than their wealth.

Florence presented every possible kind of political and social problem, every imaginable contrast of fortune, and was ready to test every possible device of the political spirit to which she had given birth. Florence is the only European city that could be compared with Athens; and like Athens, Florence was in every sense of the word a State which had to deal with as many foreign as domestic problems. It is not surprising that the first political theorists worthy of the name, Machiavelli (1469–1527) and Guicciardini (1483–1540), should have been born upon this fertile soil. Their political judgement was no longer subject to any doctrinal influence. They were as independent of theological conceptions as of the juridical constructions which had hitherto influenced political ideas. Urban life was overflowing the narrow frontiers of the Middle Ages and becoming civic life.[2]

The spectacle of the other Italian cities exhibits with the same completeness the breaking away from political traditions. There, as the result of intestine rivalries, they finally placed themselves in the hands of tyrants, all *parvenus*, who exercised, without any legitimate title, relying only on force, a government against which there was hardly any other recourse but assassination. Aeneas Sylvius (Pope Pius II) says: "In our Italy, amorous of change, where nothing endures, and where no ancient lordship exists, varlets may readily aspire to become kings." These tyrants, who got the Emperors to give them titles which had no legitimate basis, like the Visconti of Milan, established a monarchical power which had nothing in common with that of the kings, or even of the ultramontane princes. One could not imagine a Joan of Arc in Italy! In her place, the sovereigns made use of people of whom they could never be sure, so that it was best to contrive their disappearance as soon as they became

[2] Cf. on the contrary, the passage in which Commines describes the bourgeois of the Flemish cities: "Ce n'estoient que bestes et gens de villes, la plupart." Cf. also the Gantois, who, under Charles V, could find nothing better to do but return to their constitution of the 14th century.

powerful. Their principle was the *raison d'État*. They stood outside all traditions, and they were bound by nothing; neither by suzerainty, nor sworn charters, nor customs, nor privileges of any kind; still less by any religious or juridical ideals. Like the old Roman Emperors, they could permit themselves everything. There were among them monsters like Giovanni Maria Visconti (1412), who fed his dogs on human flesh, or Gian Galeazzo Sforza, whom Commines describes: "the builder of the Certosa of Pavia, a great and evil tyrant, but honourable." (Book VII, Chap. VII.) The absence of any political unity in Italy, which Machiavelli regretted so bitterly, was doubtless the condition of her breaking with the past. Never having been squeezed into a single State, Italy was then able to become, in respect of the rest of Europe, something of what ancient Greece was for Rome. If the policy of Frederick II had succeeded in unifying Italy, Florence would have been impossible.[3]

The overthrow of social and political traditions was accompanied by the decadence of manners and morals. Completely dominated by the Church, the morality of the Middle Ages had been essentially ascetic. This morality saw human perfection in renunciation. It regarded the secular life as something secondary and inferior; its ideal was the monk, and the laymen themselves accepted this ideal. Hence the extraordinary number of pious foundations— monasteries, convents and hospitals—which princes, nobles and bourgeois vied with one another in establishing. Those who did not live within the cloister sought to atone for their inferiority by founding cloisters, and to assure their salvation by acquiring some portion of their merits. Hence the veneration paid, not to the secular priests, but to the monastic clergy; so that princes gave orders that they should be buried in the robe of the Minorite friar, while merchants and bankers required their executors to make restitution of property wrongly obtained. How often the conscience of such men must have been tormented in the hour of death! For actually, in accordance with the strict theological pre-

[3] We must also remember that although the Italian States— such as Milan or Florence—were small, their influence was none the less universal, thanks to their political situation.

cept, all commercial profit, all successful speculation, all bargaining was to be condemned as proceeding from the sin of avarice; the doctrine of the just price restricted profit to the minimum necessary for the maintenance of the vendor and his family. One must read compilations like those of Caesar von Heisterbach (1180–1240) or Thomas de Cantimpré (1201–1263) to obtain an exact idea of the mentality of the 13th century with regard to commerce. It could hardly imagine the merchant's strongbox without picturing the devil squatting on the lid. From first to last, the Church never ceased to enlarge upon this text of St. Jerome: *Homo mercator vix aut nunquam potest Deo placere.*

Asceticism was so intimately allied with the pessimistic conception of life which lay at the root of mediaeval Christianity that the two cannot be separated. Under the shock of a powerful moral stimulus the ascetic would sometimes resume its empire, a fact which explains the prodigious success of Savonarola in the wealthy, luxurious and libertine Florence of the end of the 15th century, and the *autos da fé* of jewels, ornaments, musical instruments, books, and works of art—miserable mundane vanities—which were provoked by his sermons. But this was only a momentary blaze, fanned from the dying embers. Life was henceforth too exacting, too absorbing, too intensely interesting for even the noblest minds to feel at ease within a conception of things that condemned them. As for the others, they let life have its way with them, and they did so all the more readily inasmuch as the majority of the clergy set them the example. For the clergy allowed itself to be carried away with the tide. The pontifical court indulged in the most dazzling luxury, and nothing could have been less edifying than the conduct of the secular priests. The monks themselves, in the shaken and tormented Church of the 15th century, and perhaps the monks above all, contributed to the decline of faith. Not that their morals justified the attacks, the sarcasm, and the disdain which the literature of the period lavished upon them. The cloister was still the asylum of many pure and noble souls. But on the whole, the monasteries no longer fulfilled their mission,

because they were no longer adapted to the needs and requirements of the moment. The scholastic and mystical education of the monks rendered them so ignorant of the ideas
prevailing in the world that they were powerless to influence them. The lettered aristocracy regarded them as the
representatives of a bygone period; they pitied them, and
it is but a short step from pity to contempt. The monks
themselves were conscious of this, and resigned themselves
to exercising only a popular apostolate, which degraded
them, because they had not wished to undertake it. Moreover, they were now recruited only from the ranks of the
people and the lower middle class, and of their new con-
frères many entered the cloister merely in order to live in
security under the protection of the monastic rule. Thus,
the prestige so long enjoyed by the Franciscans and the
Dominicans was a thing of the past. Educated laymen
spoke of them now only in a jesting tone, and the pious
tales which were formerly told of them were replaced by
ribald anecdotes. Before the monks could recover their influence in the world a new order had to make its appearance, that of the Jesuits, in which asceticism mastered the
new intellectual culture in order to combat its effects. But
it must not be supposed that the men of the 15th century
had lost their respect for sanctity. They were very far
from having done so; and in proof of this, it is enough to
cite their veneration for the Carthusians. Did not a tyrant
like Gian Galeazzo Sforza surround the Cortosa of Pavia
with the most magnificent architectural setting, as a venerated relic might be encrusted with jewels? But the Carthusians were purely contemplative monks, who took no
part in the life of the world, leaving to its own devices the
society which admired them, and which they could not
hope to influence otherwise than by prayer.

While the Renaissance had liberated itself from the ascetic morality of the Middle Ages, it did not replace this
by any other morality. The strongest and noblest souls imposed upon themselves an ideal of virtue and honour; for
others glory was the dominant motive; but the majority
seem to have obeyed no other rules than those of personal
interest, or they allowed themselves to be led by their tastes

and their passions. The loosening of the conjugal tie, and the frequency of assassinations, poisonings, and crimes of every kind and in every class of society, are incontestable evidence of a moral crisis. And yet, in the midst of this disorder, we see the beginnings of a sense of individual liberty, of human dignity, of the beauty of energy, and of the responsibility of the private man before his own conscience. Shall we go too far if we credit the Renaissance with having realized, more or less definitely, that morality should not consist of a mere code of precepts, and that it cannot be complete without the free adhesion of the personality? This, no doubt, is an aristocratic conception; in the sense, at least, that it is given to few to attain to it. But was not the whole achievement of the Renaissance aristocratic? Was it not characterized above all by the formation of an intellectual élite?—in which it was completely opposed to the Middle Ages, when a priestly caste possessed the monopoly of learning and knowledge. And was it not to this intellectual élite that it owed its most striking feature, which—above all in Italy—gave it its final and proper physiognomy—the return to antiquity?

We know that in its first acceptation the very word "Renaissance" means simply the re-birth of antiquity. And yet if we employ it only in this sense we shall strangely restrict its scope. The change in the ideas, the manners and the morals of the 15th century was not, as we have seen, a consequence of the study of the classic authors. It proceeded naturally from the social life of Italy. If the literature of antiquity had had the power of provoking it, the Renaissance would have occurred as early as the reign of Charlemagne. For after all, the majority of the Latin authors were known and studied then; they were constantly copied and re-copied until nearly the end of the 12th century, and their influence can readily be detected in the style of many of the chroniclers. Virgil above all was held in the greatest honour by the clerks of the Middle Ages, and so great was the respect which he enjoyed that he was regarded as a precursor of Christianity. Dante was accompanied by him in the other world, and the homage which he pays him in the "Divine Comedy"—*tu duca, tu signore e tu maestro*—is more enthusiastic, more sincere and eloquent than all the panegyrics of the humanist in honour of the Mantuan poet. Nevertheless, between the Aeneid and the "Divine Comedy" there is a gulf. Dante did not understand Virgil, and could not have understood him; he was too profound, too exalted a Christian and a mystic. What the Middle Ages was able to feel and appreciate in the thought of antiquity was neither the form nor the spirit, but a few sentences, a few anecdotes, a few "moralities," understood in a symbolic sense. And what is true of literature is even truer of the art of antiquity. The unknown masters who built the Romanic and Gothic Cathedrals had before their eyes a great number of ancient monuments, and they lived in their midst without seeing them. Their conception of beauty was exclusive, as is that of all sincere and vital schools. Their incomprehension of classic art is comparable only to the incomprehension of the art of the Middle Ages itself after the triumph of the Renaissance. As a matter of fact, the influence exercised by antiquity over the Renaissance may be compared with the influence exercised by the Middle Ages over Romanticism. Without a preliminary orientation of thought and feeling, neither the Renaissance, at the close of the 14th century, nor Romanticism, at the beginning of the 19th century, would have found so many and such fervent adepts. For a long time men had observed the works of art of these periods without really seeing them; had read the books, without understanding them. For neither these works of art nor these books had impressed themselves on men's minds by virtue of their intrinsic qualities. People came to them, admired them, and understood them, or thought to understand them, when the bandage fell from their eyes, when the authority which had governed their minds had ceased to impress them. Just as unless the classical, rationalistic and cosmopolitan ideals of the 16th century had been abandoned, the Romantics would not have been filled with enthusiasm for the Middle Ages, so, unless the men of the Renaissance had been enfranchised from theological and ecclesiastical tradition, they would not have found in antiquity a new source of knowledge and beauty.

However, it must be admitted without question that the influence of antiquity was incomparably more profound and more fruitful in the epoch of the Renaissance than the influence of the Middle Ages in the epoch of Romanticism. The Middle Ages, in fact, gave the Romantics only their picturesqueness and their local colour. Antiquity, on the other hand, offered secular thought, at the moment of its awakening, a treasury of science and the humanities, embellished with all the prestige of form. At the very moment when the Church was ceasing to satisfy the needs of the intellect, it happened, by an extraordinary piece of good fortune, that an incomparable art and literature became available, which did satisfy them. Men deserted the cathedral to find themselves before the open doors of the temple of antiquity.

It is not surprising that the cult of antiquity had its beginnings in Italy. It had never quite died out there. Rome was still a living memory. Consider, for example, Arnold of Brescia. Petrarch regarded all other peoples as Barbarians. As soon as men's eyes were opened and able to see the beauty of antiquity, they felt that they had found something that was akin to them. They began to describe the art of the Middle Ages as *gotico*. The art of Greece had come to them from Byzantium.

It is impossible here to give even a rapid sketch of the Italian humanism of the 15th century. In spite of its exuberance and its overweening presumption, it has none the less exerted a most enduring influence on modern thought. To begin with, it made Latin—not the scholastic Latin of the universities and the jurists, but a classic Latin, correct and elegant—the international language of all educated people, down to our own day. It thus created, for the benefit of laymen, a uniform culture, externally very like that of which the clergy had hitherto retained the monopoly. In so doing it completed the constitution of that intellectual aristocracy which social evolution had created in the heart of the nation. But it did more than this: at the same time it imposed an aristocratic influence on the development of all modern literatures. Writers whose taste was formed by the study of the classics transferred to their national languages the ideal of beauty which they discovered in the classics. Writing became an art which, although it was inspired by antiquity, was not enslaved to it, but preserved a liberty of its own, just as the sculpture and architecture of the Renaissance treated their Greek and Roman models with a peculiar freedom. Men assimilated the forms and the ideas of antiquity, but did not allow themselves to be dominated by them. Their minds were sufficiently enfranchised to retain their independence; they did not abdicate their individuality, their originality. When they wrote in Latin they wrote imitations, or, if you will, *pastiches* of the ancients. But as soon as they began to write in their national tongue they sought to rival the ancients, and imitation gave way to emulation. Their admiration of antiquity, and its lessons, served to stimulate and refine their creative genius rather than to stifle it. This is as true of Donatello, Andrea del Sarto, Bramante and Raphael as it was of Ariosto, Tasso, Guicciardini or Machiavelli.

These last two names remind us that while the literature in the national tongue acquired a greater beauty, it also became more intellectually comprehensive and profound. For a long while, of course, Latin still remained the language of science. But it no longer had the monopoly of science. The modern languages were now sufficiently rich and flexible to lend themselves to the expression of the most abstruse ideas, and those who made use of them were sure of finding readers among that intellectual aristocracy who had become aware of the need of thought. A universal curiosity was abroad. Hardly anything was known of the philosophy of the ancients, apart from Aristotle, and he was discredited by the portrait which the Scholastics had drawn of him. Platonism was therefore welcomed with all the greater enthusiasm. The Greek literature which Byzantine refugees had revealed to Italy, even before the Turkish capture of Constantinople, opened up new intellectual horizons. Already a few pioneers dreamed of going even further, and ventured into the domain of Hebraic studies and Oriental philology. Lastly, the exact sciences began their glorious careers. Physics, astronomy and mathematics flourished in that springtime of modern thought which gave the Italy of the 15th century its incomparable charm. It must not be forgotten that Copernicus studied at Padua and Bologna, and that the scientific labours of Toscanelli and Luca Paccioli contributed largely to the discovery of the New World.

2. *The Renaissance in the Rest of Europe*

The Renaissance of the North was very far from being a mere imitation of that of Italy. If it had been no more than this, it would have been a somewhat superficial and comparatively restricted phenomenon. No: the essential fact is that at the moment when the North gave welcome to the Italian Renaissance it was passing, quite independently of Italy, through a crisis of social and economic transformation. For the North the middle of the 15th century was the beginning of a period of renewal, a time of profound travail, which, though it did not alter its intimate constitution as violently as the revival of commerce had done in the 12th century, and as the discovery of steam power was to do in the 19th century, nevertheless shook the whole fabric of that constitution and gave it the form which it was to retain more or less until the end of the *ancien régime*. And we must thoroughly realize the obscure travail that was stirring from 1450 to about 1550 if we are to understand the Renaissance and the Reformation. Not by any means because this travail was the cause of the Renaissance and the Reformation, but because it explains the manner in which they acted, and the force which they set in motion, both for resistance and for attack.

The great novelty which appeared at this time was capitalism. It would not be true to say that it was making its first appearance. It had already undergone considerable development in the 12th and 13th centuries, and the urban patricians were the heirs of the enriched merchants of that epoch. Two causes had checked this first expansion. In the first place, the irresistible competition of Italian capital, which, from the end of the 12th century, had everywhere monopolized the traffic in money. And secondly, the organization of the trade corporations favoured the *petite bourgeoisie*. The free economic expansion of the earlier period was followed—as we shall have occasion to show in a later chapter—by a period of rigid regulation.

From that time, capitalism, to the north of the Alps, although it had not entirely disappeared, was hindered, supervised, restricted. It could operate only by evading the regulations, and it had little vitality, being crushed by Italian competition. The ecclesiastical and civil laws with regard to lending money at interest were also not without effect. In short, the patricians were transformed into a class of *rentiers* who no longer engaged in business. It has even been said that the great merchant by profession did not exist in the Middle Ages. This is false if the statement is accepted in a general sense; but it is true enough if we restrict it to the 14th century. The only persons who still engaged in affairs of any magnitude were those who had interests in the Italian companies, and the brokers. There was no such thing as a great commercial house or a great bank to the north of the Alps. Even in Flanders the capital which fed the cloth industry and furnished it with wool was almost exclusively Italian.

But this situation began to undergo transformation as early as the first half of the 15th century. A new class of capitalists began to make its appearance almost everywhere in Flanders, France, and England, and in those cities of Southern Germany which maintained commercial relations with Venice. It consisted of new men; it was not in any sense the continuation of the old patriciate. It was a group of adventurers, of *parvenus,* like all those groups that made their appearance during each economic transformation. They did not work with old, accumulated capital. This they acquired only at a later stage. Like the *mercatores* of the 12th century, and the inventors and industrialists of the late 18th and the 19th centuries, these pioneers bought, as their sole investment, their energy and their intelligence or cunning.

Their device, the device of the conquistadors of wealth, was: liberty. It was liberty that their predecessors of the 12th century had demanded—enfranchisement from the shackles of the agricultural and feudal system, which prevented the expansion of commerce. The liberty that the new men demanded was that which would enfranchise them from the urban regulation of the monopolies enjoyed by the trade corporations, the restrictions imposed upon sale and purchase, the control of the markets, the fixing of wages by the law, the official apprenticeship, and the privileges which, in every city, reserved commerce for the burgesses and reduced the stranger to the status of a pariah. What they claimed was the common right to engage in industry and commerce, which must be rescued from municipal exclusivism, and disencumbered of those privileges which were doubtless indispensable when industry and commerce were in their infancy, but which were now preventing their development. What they wanted was "natural liberty," liberty without qualifications, not a restrictive liberty as understood by the bourgeois, which was as incompatible with the "general liberty" as the "liberty" of the nobles had been with that of the villeins. They wanted the cities to be accessible to all, so that all could share in their commerce; so that they would no longer exist merely for their own burgesses. But they also wanted the power to industrialize the countryside, to draw upon that great reservoir of labour, to employ hands that were accustomed to guide the plough, and by their aid, thanks to the low tariff of wages, to compete with the trade guilds of the cities: and all the more victoriously, inasmuch as, not being subject to their regulations, they could manufacture, at their own pace, as much as they wished, employ such methods as were convenient or useful, follow the changes of the fashion, market their products where they chose, and conclude such contracts as suited them.

These adventurers—for they were just as truly adventurers as the *mercatores* of the 12th century—were favoured by the political changes no less than by the inability of the cities to maintain their privileges in the midst of a progressive civilization. The princes, who required more and more money as the cost of wars increased, had need of them. It was more convenient to make use of these men of business than to parley with the States-General for taxes. Hitherto the men of affairs at the courts of Philip the Fair and Edward III had been Italians. But now the native man of affairs was beginning to replace the Italian. In Austria the Fuggers obtained the right to exploit the silver mines of the Tyrol, Bohemia and Hungary, thereby laying the foundations of their fortune outside the cities. In France, the story of Jacques Cœur (1466) is particularly interesting. Beginning with nothing, he joined a consortium, one of whose members was a bankrupt merchant, which leased the privilege of minting money from Charles VII. This was a profitable business. All the master-minters were robbers who considered that the profits which they made in minting money were as legitimate as the profits which our modern bankers make by the issue of Government loans. In 1432, having learned the ins and outs of the trade in metals, Cœur began to export silver to the East and import gold, which he disposed of in France at an enormous profit. From this time forward we see him constantly increasing his business interests. He leased the Crown mines in Lyonnais and Beaujolais, in which he employed German miners. He became "argentier," which made him purveyor to the court, to which he advanced considerable sums of money at from 12 to 50 per cent interest. Nevertheless, he continued to increase his business interests, acting either on his own account or in association with other capitalists. It was estimated that he had no less than three hundred factories, extending from Famagusta to Bruges, and into England. He was accused of ruining "honest merchants," presumably by speculation and forestalling. His career had nothing in common with that of these "honest merchants," who were faithful to the traditions of the Middle Ages. He built himself a palace at Bourges, and houses in Paris, Tours, and Montpellier. He was ennobled, and became a councillor to the king. At a rough estimate, his fortune, at the moment of his fall in 1451, was equivalent to more than twenty-two millions of our francs.

These new capitalists did not appear in consequence of an extension of the market, since the outlets for goods had not multiplied, nor had the population increased, but in consequence of the unaccustomed necessities which arose in the course of the formation of new States.

If Jacques Cœur was a kind of 15th-century Rothschild,

he was not the only one. He was merely the most illustrious specimen of a group of new men who were beginning to replace Italians like the Rapondi, who fulfilled the same function at the court of Philip the Good. In the Low Countries, a little later, the Laurins also enriched themselves in the service of the princes. The hotel of Jean Laurin, seigneur of Watervliet at Malines, was so luxurious that the Governess, Margaret of Austria, bought it in 1507. In 1506 Jerome Laurin built the town of Philippine in his Philippus Polder. He too, owing to his office as treasurer, rose from "very great poverty, not possessing the value of a denier, to the possession of an income of 10,000 marks." Just as intelligence, three hundred years earlier, amidst the lethargy of the agricultural and feudal system, had created the first accumulations of capital in the hands of the burgesses, so now, in a society of ampler structure, it served as the instrument of the *parvenus*, who, discovering new outlets, and profiting by the favour of the prince, escaped the net with which the cities thought to have enmeshed commerce and industry to their own advantage. The cities could not contend on equal terms against these newcomers, who had their agents everywhere, forestalling and monopolizing, and supporting the new political powers. By means of their capital new industries were established in the countryside. We have already mentioned the mining industry. And a "new" textile industry had been established in Flanders, at Hondschoot and Armentières, despite the opposition of the cities, which vainly insisted on their privileges. The same thing happened in England, where new manufacturing centres were established. For example, the making of tapestries became a rural industry. And a rural industry was a capitalist industry. A completely novel mode of production made its appearance. The supervision which the trade guilds imposed upon the workers and the market was replaced by liberty. The peasant turned weaver contracted with a "master," but his wage and his labour were not subject to regulation. The masters themselves worked in conjunction with a contractor or wholesaler, from whom they received the raw material, and who disposed of their products. The small workshop survived, but it became degraded, so to speak; it lost its independence by subordinating itself to a new system—the system of manufacture. The urban industry, encompassed by its privileges, like a rampart raised against capital, managed to survive by producing for the local market. Its guilds and corporations continued to exist until the end of the *ancien régime*. Elsewhere, apart from a few special and artistic industries, it was compelled to abandon the struggle. The whole of the new industrial development, from the 15th century onwards, was opposed to it and outside it. The urban cloth industry of Flanders, the great export industry of the Middle Ages, lapsed into decadence after the middle of the 14th century. Owing to its excessive prices and its conservatism, it could not cope with the competition of the new English cloth trade and the rural weaving industry. The linen industry which replaced it until the age of factories was entirely rural.

Naturally, the organization of commerce, like that of industry, was stimulated by the pressure of capitalism, and by liberty. All the restrictions with which it had been surrounded—markets, brokers, the obligation to transact business only through the medium of the burgesses—were for commerce merely so many obstacles that hindered its progress. The example of Bruges is characteristic. As early as the middle of the 15th century its cosmopolitan customers were beginning to desert it for the young port of Antwerp. Here business was not burdened by tradition; commerce was able to organize itself from the very outset in accordance with the new spirit. This was a city which was adapted to future needs; for economic history shows us clearly how new needs were accompanied by a displacement of social classes and business centres. In England the "merchant adventurers" made their appearance, while the Dutch merchant fleet began to replace that of the Hansa. At the moment when this development had already made considerable progress an unlimited field of enterprise was opened by the discovery of the New World. This so completely transformed the surface of the globe that it seemed almost like a planetary catastrophe. The only thing that we can compare with it, as having had analogous results, although much less in degree, was the expansion of Islam. This too transformed the surface of the globe, changed populations and languages, and acclimatized new civilizations under alien skies; it also, in some degree, orientalized the Occident. But this was a small thing in comparison with the stupendous transformation which made the Atlantic an inland sea; the discovery of the Pacific, the propagation of Christianity beyond the equator, the diffusion of Spanish and Portuguese, and presently of French and English, throughout America, the transformation of so many peoples, the hybridization of some, the annihilation of others, and the appearance of so many new products, which modified the conditions of life: tea, coffee, and tobacco, which conquered the markets of Europe, the introduction of cotton, and of our domestic animals, in America; and lastly, the gigantic achievements which were to open new highways for world traffic—Suez, Panama. Of course, all this did not happen all at once, and the immortal mariners who "saw new stars emerging from the waves" neither desired nor could have divined the future that they were opening up for Europe. The economic motive had very little to do with their designs. The Europe of the 15th century was not overpopulated; it had no need of colonies, and Portugal in particular, who inaugurated the new discoveries, was not conscious of the least need of extending her commerce. There was nothing of the mercantile prince about Henry the Navigator. He was actuated by scientific curiosity and the desire to propagate the Faith. They were purely spiritual aspirations that gave rise to the discovery of the lands of gold and spices. These expeditions are in no way comparable with those of the ancient Phoenicians. But it must be admitted that without the development attained by Mediterranean navigation at the beginning of the 15th century these discoveries would have been impossible. It was the Mediterranean that furnished the ships and their captains. As in the case of the Crusades, moreover, there were exciting factors: the old tales of the Indies, memories of the journeys of De Plano Carpini and Marco Polo, and all the rumours of the Levantine port.

This is not the place to retell this wonderful story. It will suffice to recall the principal dates: the Madeira Islands were discovered in 1419 and the Azores in 1431, and the Cape Verde Islands and the coast of Senegambia some little time before the death of Henry the Navigator (1460), who lived long enough to hear of their discovery. After these first groping ventures progress was accelerated. In 1482 Diego Cam sailed as far as the mouths of the Congo; in 1486 Bartolomeo Diaz reached the Cape of Good Hope, and saw the Indian Ocean lie open before him. In 1497 Vasco da Gama ventured upon that ocean, reaching Calicut in 1498. The Cape had justified the name which King John II had given it. At last the marvellous Indies had been attained; the Western caravels, after a protracted voyage upon desert seas and along wild coasts, came into contact with the dhows of the Arabs, and reached at last the source of that stream of wealth of which Europe had hitherto known only the Levantine outfall.

The Portuguese were the first pioneers to sail the unknown seas. They proceeded slowly, keeping at first within sight of the coast, and then, making enquiries as they advanced, they rounded the Cape, touched at Zanzibar, and set sail for the East; in short, their plan consisted in rounding the Cape, and circumnavigating Africa, so as to get to the further side of Syria and Egypt, for they knew that beyond these they would find the Indies. Thanks to their patience and energy, the thing was done. They had sufficient indications to guide them. Relying on a mass of empirical data, they felt that each fresh advance brought them nearer to their goal. All that the Portuguese needed, in order to succeed, was certain technical improvements; that is to say, vessels large and seaworthy and handy enough to keep the sea for some months at a time.

The voyages of Christopher Columbus, on the other hand, would have been inconceivable without the science of the Renaissance. Had he reposed a less heroic confidence in the works of Toscanelli and the Italian geographers of the 15th century, how could he ever have brought himself to sail straight across the Atlantic, hoping to arrive at the Indies by encircling the globe? His plans were too audacious for the Portuguese court, but the Spaniards allowed themselves to be persuaded. On August 3rd, 1492, the caravels disappeared below the horizon; on October 12th they reached the Antilles. There was still more than half the circumference of the earth between them and the Indies! The world was much larger than Toscanelli had supposed; all his calculations were erroneous, but, as so often happens, the very errors of science were fruitful, and in this case they led to the discovery of America. The subsequent voyages of Columbus (1492–1502) and the voyage of his compatriot Sebastian Cabot, who had entered the service of Henry VII of England, revealed the stupendous nature of the discovery, by reaching the American mainland: Columbus discovering the Orinoco and the Isthmus of Panama, and Cabot the coast of Labrador. In 1500 Cabral, blown out of his course, touched another point of the immense coastline, in Brazil. It was not until 1513 that the Pacific Ocean was seen from the heights of the Isthmus of Panama. In 1520 Magellan doubled Cabo Deseado, set out across the wilderness of this vast new ocean, and discovered the Philippines. His companions returned to Spain by way of the Moluccas and the Indian Ocean. The voyage round the world had been accomplished for the first time.

From the first years of the 16th century the consequences of these marvellous discoveries were manifested in the economic life of Europe. The first of these consequences was that the headquarters of the Oriental trade was removed from the Italian ports of the Mediterranean to the shores of the Atlantic Ocean. The spices which the caravans brought to the ports of the Levant, whence they were carried by the trading vessels of Genoa and Venice, could not long compete, either in quantity or in price, with those which the Portuguese and Spanish ships brought direct from the equatorial countries in which they were produced. Italy, which had hitherto been the intermediary between Europe and the long mysterious Indies, found that the springs of her prosperity were drying up, and the drought was a prolonged one. Until the day when the piercing of the Suez Canal (1869) made it the highway to the Indian Ocean, the Mediterranean lost the great commercial importance which it had enjoyed without interruption since the dawn of civilization. But neither Spain nor

Portugal took its place; neither Cadiz nor Lisbon was the heir of Venice and Genoa. The commercial hegemony which these ports had hitherto enjoyed fell to the lot of Antwerp.

There were two obvious reasons for this. To begin with, the international importance of a seaport depends on both its import and its export trade. It is not enough that ships should bring merchandise to the port; they must also be able to obtain wares in exchange. Venice and Genoa in the south, like Bruges in the north, had fulfilled these conditions during the Middle Ages; Venice and Genoa thanks to the industries of the Italian cities, and Bruges thanks to those of the cities of the Low Countries. Moreover, by reason of their geographical situation they were in touch with the interior of Europe, whose roads were centred upon them, providing ready access for the products of the hinterland. The situation of the Iberian ports was not so favourable from either point of view. Their position, on the shores of an outlying peninsula, and the undeveloped state of the national industries, made it impossible for them to attract a considerable import trade. Lastly, the manner in which the trade in spices and precious metals was carried on in Portugal and Spain prevented the establishment of powerful commercial houses. The Crown, as the possessor of the overseas factories and colonies, excluded foreigners from them, and reserved for itself, as a monopoly, the greater part of the import trade. Its agents were entrusted with the sale of the imported products, and in order that they might sell them more promptly and more readily the Crown took good care not to exclude those very foreigners who were forbidden access to the country where the merchandise was produced. Accordingly, from the beginning of the 16th century the capitalist merchants of Antwerp maintained at Cadiz, and above all in Lisbon, factors who were entrusted with the purchase of the precious wares. Consequently the seaport on the Scheldt became the great international emporium for spices. Only there did they become the objects of commercial transactions and enter into circulation. As we have already seen, the economic importance of Antwerp antedated the period of discoveries.

But the afflux of the wealth of the Indies and the New World was the beginning of a period of extraordinary prosperity, which soon exceeded that of Venice in the days of her greatest splendour. Never has any other port, at any period, enjoyed such world-wide importance, because none has ever been so open to all comers, and, in the full sense of the word, so cosmopolitan. Antwerp remained faithful to the liberty which had made her fairs so successful in the 15th century. She attracted and welcomed capitalists from all parts of Europe, and as their numbers increased so did their opportunities of making their fortune. Germans, Englishmen, Frenchmen, Portuguese, Spaniards and Italians, all hurried thither. And there was not a single great bank or commercial house without its representatives in Antwerp. The greatest financial power of the 16th century, the Fuggers, had their headquarters at Augsburg, but it was their Antwerp branch that made the most enormous profits. This rendezvous of contractors, merchants, sailors and adventurers became the centre of the commercial world. One can hardly imagine a more striking and more complete contrast with the economic organization of the Middle Ages. In Venice the foreigners could buy only from Venetians; in Bruges they had to employ a broker who was a burgess of the city. But no such restrictions were in force in Antwerp. There was no supervision, no control: foreigners did business with other foreigners as freely as with the burgesses and the natives of the country at their daily meetings. Buyers and sellers sought one another and came to terms without intermediaries. Prices were fixed, and credits were opened by the commercial companies, and speculation claimed its first victims. From the year 1531 all this commercial activity was concentrated under the galleries of a special building constructed at the expense of the city, the Bourse, the forerunner and model of the future Exchanges of London and Amsterdam.

The great wars of the beginning of the 16th century gave a fresh impetus to the spirit of capitalism. Charles V especially, whose immense States provided him with resources which were singularly inadequate in proportion to his power, was an extraordinary client for the financiers. Without the development of capitalism it may be said that his reign, which set so many armies on the march and launched so many fleets, would have been impossible. However, the profits of the bankers were fully comparable to the services which they rendered him. The prosperity of the Low Countries was largely responsible for maintaining the Emperor's credit, enabling him to reimburse his creditors, despite the fact that he had to pay from 12 to 50 per cent interest. The Fuggers owed a great part of their fortune to the advances which they made to him. However, the readiness with which princes were able to borrow, and the tempting profits within reach of the bankers, soon resulted in their exceeding the limits of prudence. The bankruptcies of Philip II in 1575 and 1596 put an end to the alliance of private capitalism and monarchical policy.

At this moment, however, another source of gain offered itself to the insatiable financiers. About 1550 the silver mines of Peru and Mexico began to furnish Spain with ingots which presently found their way all over Europe in the form of silver coins. This inundation of precious metals reduced the purchasing power of the currency, the result being a general rise of prices. Trade, and especially industry, received a powerful stimulus, and had yet one more motive for enfranchising themselves from the insupportable control of the guilds and corporations. Manufacture—that is, the form of production in which the artisan worked under his own roof, and was paid and given orders by a contractor—became, from the middle of the 16th century, the typical form of industrial organization; and so it remained until the appearance of the modern factory, of which, however, some precocious examples might already be found here and there.

Remarkable as the development of capitalism may have been, we must not exaggerate its scope. It was superimposed on the old economic organization of the privileged cities, but it did not abolish this organization. The *petite bourgeoisie* continued to live in the shelter of the trade corporations and to supply the local market. Bakers, butchers, cabinetmakers, shoemakers, etc., remained faithful, until the end of the *ancien régime,* to the protectionism which reserved for them the exploitation of their municipal clientèle. In no case did the governments think it wise or prudent to make them amenable to the common law. They were well aware of the faults of the system, which became increasingly apparent as time went on: routine methods, high prices, and the increasing restriction of each trade to a small number of masters; but their fear of democracy persuaded them to tolerate these defects as the best means of keeping the "compagnons" in a docile mood. They contented themselves with gradually suppressing the obstacles which the municipal regulations offered to the development of trade and the circulation of wealth: markets, commissions, etc. Above all they began to abolish the political privileges of the guilds, and to keep a tight hand, or at least a close watch, over the urban administrations, and despite the resistance which was offered in France during the disorders of the League, and again, to some extent, in the 18th century, they were everywhere successful. The cities could have retained their political and economic autonomy intact only by retaining their military strength. But what could their guilds and corporations do against regular armies, and what could their ancient walls avail against artillery? Only where the State was powerless, as in Germany, did they hold their own. Elsewhere they submitted. The few attempts at resistance, such as that of the Liégeois against the Dukes of Burgundy, the people of Gand against Charles V and the people of La Rochelle against Francis I, showed that their claims were inspired only by a past which was indeed the past. The democratic policy which the *petite bourgeoisie* had so ardently supported in the 14th century was henceforth a lost cause. Just as capitalism was supreme in the domain of wholesale trade, so the State was supreme in the domain of politics.

Under the influence of the new conditions which were transforming social life the conception of the bourgeoisie was transformed in its turn. The political and juridical characteristics which had given it its special position in the society of the Middle Ages, beside the clergy and the *noblesse*, were gradually becoming less marked. From the beginning of the 16th century the bourgeoisie had become

essentially a class of men living by exploitation or by the
revenues of their wealth. The mere manual worker, according to current ideas, had ceased to belong to the bourgeoisie. It now rejected the artisans in whom its strength had
formerly resided. It began to affect definitely plutocratic
manners, which distinguished it from the *petite bourgeoisie*
and brought it nearer to the noblesse. In each country, of
course, it developed its special features, and it is impossible
to frame a description of the bourgeoisie which would be
equally applicable to the Low Countries, to France, and to
England. It is enough to say that henceforth wealth was
everywhere the sign *par excellence* of the bourgeoisie. The
bourgeois of the Middle Ages was privileged by law; the
modern bourgeois is privileged by virtue of his economic
situation. But there is yet another difference between the
two. In the Middle Ages the bourgeois depended on his city
for his livelihood, and existed for his city; the commune of
which he was a member was the indispensable guarantee
of his person and his interests; his mode of life and his
ideas alike were dominated by the municipal group to
which he belonged. But after the Middle Ages these conditions disappeared. For the modern bourgeois the city is
merely a place of residence and a business centre; it is no
longer the centre of his affections, his ideas and his interests. The sources of his wealth are widely dispersed, no
longer contained within the municipal boundaries. If he is
a manufacturer his factories may be in the country; if he is
a merchant his correspondents and his merchandise are distributed over distant ports and markets; if he lives on his
dividends his money may be invested in distant countries,
in loans, or in commercial or industrial enterprises of every
kind. His livelihood is now dependent upon a multiplicity
of conjunctures; it is implicated in the existence of the nation as a whole, and its relations to foreign nations. He has
to know what is happening in all parts of the world. Hence
the development of the post, and presently, of the Press,
whose object, in the beginning, was merely to bring within
reach of all the news which until then had been translated
only by private correspondence.

Economic liberty, indissolubly bound up with the development of capitalism, immediately imposed its consequences upon the world of workers. While the corporative legislation of the Middle Ages did not prevent the master artisan from lording it over the countryside, it did set a limit to his exploitation of the latter. The regulations of the guilds determined the worker's rights, safeguarded his wages, and guaranteed him against too glaring abuses; they often granted him aid in case of sickness or old age, and sometimes they even allowed him a certain degree of intervention in the nomination or control of the heads of the trade corporation. Moreover, the *compagnonnages* or trade unions which had been constituted since the 15th century, comprising the journeymen of a particular trade, not only of one city, but of a whole group of cities, or even a whole country, created a system of mutual aid which might be regarded as a rudimentary labour organization. But there was no trace of all this in the new system of manufacture. Here, in conformity with the "common law," the employer and the employee entered into contracts directly, without the interposition of any authority or association. The one sold his labour, the other bought it, and the price depended only on their "free will." This means that it was actually imposed upon the weaker by the stronger. Completely unorganized, whether in the city or the country, the workers of the new industries had to submit to the law of the capitalist. Since the workers elaborated the raw material supplied by the capitalists under their own roof, they were particularly liable to exploitation, thanks to the regulations of all kinds which the capitalist was able to impose upon them. And in fact, from the beginning of the 16th century there is abundant evidence of the wretchedness of their conditions, and of their discontent. The rise of prices in the middle of the century exasperated them still further, and contributed largely to the success of the semi-social, semi-religious propaganda of the Anabaptists. As for the government, it did nothing for them, ignoring them as long as they did not trouble the public peace. While a pioneer like Thomas More had dreamed, in his *Utopia* (1563), of labour legislation of a communistic type, the State and the public authorities, whether then or for centuries after, did not envisage what we to-day should call the labour question except as a matter concerning the police. Hence their intervention, after the end of the 15th century, against the abuses of mendicity, and, a little later, their reforms in the domain of charity.

Here again we have striking evidence of the degree in which social changes had weakened the influence of the Church. The magnificent impulse of Christian charity which the Church had inspired in the Middle Ages no longer corresponded with the needs or the spirit of the age. The numberless charitable foundations which the Church had encouraged and inspired confined themselves, in accordance with its mystical ideal, to succouring the poor; to maintaining them in that state of life without seeking to help them to emerge from it. The poor man had his definite place in society, and very pious souls even regarded him with a certain veneration, which is sufficiently explained by the ascetic spirit of the period. But as this ascetic spirit declined, the halo of sanctity which surrounded the mendicant faded. People began to regard him as a vagabond, dangerous to the public peace, professional loafer. On the other hand, the increasingly rigid regulations of the urban guilds, which condemned great numbers of men to unemployment, and the demobilization of bands of mercenaries, which left these old soldiers without a profession, so multiplied the numbers of wandering men who had no other resources than alms, that towards the beginning of the 15th century they had become a veritable social plague. The authorities therefore began to persecute them mercilessly, in the hope of compelling at least the able-bodied among them to work. The first administrative regulations directed against mendicity authorized it only in the case of children, the aged, and the infirm, and sought to prevent others from begging by the threat of corporal punishment. This, of course, was only a palliative. It was well understood, from the beginning of the 16th century, that it would be necessary to attack the root of the evil and abolish mendicity by removing its cause. Hence, for example, the reforms introduced at Ypres in 1525, under the influence of Vivès, which, by concentrating the resources of all the charitable establishments of the city, appointing visitors to the poor, and sending children in receipt of charity to school, or apprenticing them to a trade, sought to abolish pauperism by enabling the poor man to earn his living. From this time forward attempts of the same kind were made in all parts of Europe. It is interesting to note that they were especially numerous and effective where the development of capitalism and manufactures enabled the charitable societies to find situations for their charges. The example of Holland, and above all of England, is particularly significant in this respect. The English laws of 1551 and 1562 relating to the employment of the poor were the precursors of the famous *Act for the relief of the poor* of 1601, which was so admirably adapted to the needs of modern industry that in its essential features it has survived to this day.

The contribution of the new society to the problem of social legislation was, however, confined to the organization of charity. Society contented itself with compelling the poor man to work; it did not attempt, as the cities of the Middle Ages would have done, to regulate the work itself. Until the 19th century it subjected labour to no restrictions, and this fact is eloquent of the capitalistic character which was henceforth the essential feature of the economic world.

It is therefore not surprising that from the second half of the 15th century, contemporaneously with free industry, and increasing with its expansion, a proletariat made its appearance whose history has yet to be written. It is true that there existed in the Middle Ages, in the workers engaged in the cloth industry of Flanders and Florence, a class of wage-earners whose condition was very nearly that of the proletariat. It differed from the latter, however, in respect of the organization imposed upon it by the corporative system. Once he was excluded from this system, the modern proletarian was completely at the mercy of his employer. He had no redress against the employer; the public authorities gave him no assistance, since they abstained from intervention, and he had not even the help which spontaneous association might have furnished, for the workers were forbidden to form associations. Moreover, they were too wretched and too uneducated to organize themselves, and the authorities which refused to intervene on their behalf protected the employer, and were very ready to intervene in his interests if the workers, driven to extremities, declared a strike. Moreover, it must not be forgotten that the home industry, the general form of industrial organization until the end of the 18th century, was as favourable to the exploitation of the workers as it was unfavourable to any mutual co-operation and understanding. However, we must not exaggerate the importance of the proletariat, or that of unrestricted industry, during the three centuries that began about 1450. Despite its definitely capitalistic form and its continual progress, manufacture, even in those countries in which it was most advanced, still played only a limited part in the activities of the nation. The urban industry of the guilds and corporations, which, side by side with free manufacture, continued to supply the majority of the cities, very greatly hindered its progress. It was far less important than commerce, and above all, than agriculture, which everywhere remained the essential branch of production.

But in the domain of agriculture itself, what a revolution! Here too the advance of capitalism was profoundly felt. In some countries it had the effect of enfranchising the peasant, while in others it forced him back into a state of servitude far completer, and above all, much harsher than that of the Middle Ages. The explanation of these contradictory consequences is not far to seek. In those countries which were economically the most advanced, like Italy and the Low Countries, the landowners, like the manufacturers (and for the same reasons), were inclined systematically to favour free labour.

Just as the trade corporations hampered the expansion of industrial capitalism, so the old hereditary ties which bound the peasant to the soil, and gave him rights over it, hampered the capitalism of the landowner. In the 14th century the seigneurs had hoped to increase their revenues by accentuating their rights over the villeins. They now saw that they had been following the wrong course. However strictly they were demanded and collected, the rights of *corvée, champart* (field rent paid in kind), *formariage* (dues payable when serfs married who belonged to different lords), etc., etc., never furnished more than an inconsiderable revenue, quite out of proportion to the value of the soil, which was increasing, thanks to the progress of commerce and the greater circulation of produce. The true means of benefiting by this plus value was by free farming, or the direct exploitation of the soil by means of free labourers, working for a wage. Thus, as early as the beginning of the 15th century we see that in Italy what was left of the ancient servitude was replaced by personal liberty. As early as 1415 a Florentine statute decreed the obligatory suppression of serfdom, of personal services in lieu of quit-rent, of the attachment of the man to the glebe, of all kinds of corvées, of all juridical conditions incompatible with personal liberty, and of all feudal or judicial subordination of the individual to the profit of another. In the Low Countries, from 1515 onwards, the prince issued a number of edicts whose purpose was to enfranchise both the man and the soil. In 1531 seigneurs were forbidden to demand of their tenants "gratuitous gifts, services, days of labour," etc., under penalty of twofold repayment and arbitrary punishment. In 1520 the establishment of new tithes was prohibited, and all seigneurial rights which had existed for less than forty years were abolished. Everywhere free farming was substituted for the ancient feudal and hereditary tenures. The enfranchisement of the peasants was in reality the enfranchisement of the landowner, who, having henceforth to deal with free men who were not attached to his land, could dispose of the latter by means of simple revocable contracts, whose brief duration enabled him to modify them in accordance with the increasing rent of the land. Here again, of course, we must not exaggerate the consequences of this innovation. Capitalism did not cause the disappearance of personal servitude in the rural districts, any more than it suppressed the trade corporations in the cities. Not until the French Revolution were both abolished by proclamation. But just as the trade corporations ceased to develop, and merely vegetated, after the 16th century, so what was left of serfdom was merely an archaism, a survival, a relic of a bygone epoch, which still obtained on the estates of a few abbeys or in the depths of the provinces. Wherever the new mode of life had penetrated it disappeared, being swept away as an inconvenient obstacle to progress.

Further, as serfdom disappeared, and in the same degree, the technical methods of agriculture were improved and modernized. In the 15th century the cultivation of rice was introduced in the Lombard plain; the rearing of silkworms became general in the Midi in the reign of Louis XI. In Flanders the method of triennial rotation of crops was abandoned. Fallow land was sown with clover, so that it no longer lay idle. Moreover, the general development of commerce impelled the landowners to specialize in production. Spain and England sacrificed the cultivation of cereals to sheep-farming, with a view to exporting the wool. It was the flocks of sheep that gradually made Castile the stony, treeless desert which it has become, and it was owing to sheep-farming that pastures began to cover a larger and larger area of the English soil, where the sheep replaced the peasant and his plough. From the reign of Henry VI onwards Parliament was continually passing Enclosure Acts, which authorized the conversion of arable soil into pasturage, driving the evicted tenants into the ranks of the proletariat, from which the manufacturers recruited their workers.

While in Western Europe the evolution of capitalism tended to make the peasant a farmer or a worker for wages, in Germany it created a new form of serfdom. The essential cause of this phenomenon, which is at first sight so surprising, must be sought in the omnipotence and brutality of the nobles, whom the territorial princes did not dare to oppose. As soon as the colonization of the Slav territories beyond the Elbe had ceased, which was towards the end of the 13th century, the nobles took advantage of the distress caused by the excess of population in order to oppress the rural class. If agriculture had been further advanced, or if industry had been more extensively developed, the peasant might have discovered new resources on the spot. But the feeble economic development of Germany delivered him, defenceless, into the hands of his seigneurs. And since then the situation had grown worse and worse. To the west of the Elbe the change had no particular consequences beyond a recrudescence of *corvées*, prestations, and arbitrary measures of every kind. But beyond the river, in Brandenburg, Prussia, Silesia, Austria, Bohemia, and Hungary, the most merciless advantage was taken of it. The descendants of the free colonists of the 13th century were systematically deprived of their land and reduced to the condition of personal serfs (*Leibeigene*). The wholesale exploitation of estates absorbed their holdings and reduced them to a servile condition which so closely approximated to that of slavery that it was permissible to sell the person of the serf independently of the soil. From the middle of the 16th century the whole of the region to the east of the Elbe and the Sudeten mountains became covered with *Rittergüter* exploited by *Junkers*, who may be compared, as regards the degree of humanity displayed in their treatment of their white slaves, with the planters of the West Indies. The negro in the New World, and the German peasant in the Old World, were the most typical victims of modern capitalism, and they both had to wait until the 19th century for their enfranchisement. This is a fact which must never be forgotten when considering the modern history of Germany and Austria. The enslavement of the peasant to his noble master explains many things.

The expansion of capitalism and the development of commerce and industry were followed by a general increase of population, analogous to that which characterized the 12th and 13th centuries. This must be attributed to the new fields which industry had opened to labour, and to the progress of trade, which put an end to those alimentary crises that had caused such cruel suffering as late as the 14th century. There were still periods of dearth, but there were no more famines. It is unfortunately impossible to estimate with any exactness the population of Europe in the 15th century. It would seem, however, that there may have been something like forty inhabitants per square kilometre in the two regions that were then most densely populated: Italy and the Low Countries. France, about 1550, seems to have had a population of something like 18,000,000. At the same date the commercial metropolis of the West, Antwerp, which had then reached its apogee, did not contain more than 100,000 inhabitants.

In respect of its social composition this population exhibited contrasts which were far more accentuated than those of the Middle Ages. The total amount of wealth had increased, but this increase was distributed in a very unequal manner. Practically no one profited by it excepting the great landowners, the nobles, the Church, the wholesale merchants, and the manufacturers. That middle class which was composed of small independent producers, which was so widely distributed in the 13th century, and whose turbulence gave the 14th century its tumultuous character, was visibly declining. In the cities a superannuated protectionist legislation enabled it to hold its own without progressing; in the rural districts it was ousted by the wholesale exploitation of the soil, free farming, or serfdom. On the other hand, the juridical demarcation of the classes was less rigid than of old. If the noblesse of the modern era seems in many respects to have been even prouder and more arrogant than that of the Middle Ages, that is because it felt the need of maintaining the social distinction, in respect of the "nouveaux riches," which the similarity of fortune, education, and interests might easily have led the latter to overlook. However, nothing could have been easier than for the new men to obtain letters patent which would enable them to enter into the ranks of the noblesse, and share in the prestige which it owed to tradition, but which was maintained by its wealth. Aristocracy and plutocracy—these, in the last resort, are perhaps the two words which best characterize the social transformation which was accomplished at the time of the Renaissance.

3. Ideas and Manners

There was, it seems, a rather striking difference between the intellectual evolution of Italy during the Renaissance and that of the countries lying to the north of the Alps. In Italy the new orientation of ideas, manners, and artistic feeling began at the very moment when the economic develop-

ment of the nation had reached its apogee. It was not contemporary with this development, but subsequent to it, and
while the intellectual movement continued to progress
the economic development was already beginning to decline. This intellectual development was the fine flower of
the entire civilization that preceded it; the product of
thought and beauty succeeding to the product of force. This
development was not unlike that of ancient Greece in the
days of Pericles: Athens in the 4th century, and Florence in
the middle of the 15th century, shone with a glory which
was no longer commensurate with their real strength; the
dazzling radiance which they shed upon the world, before
they made way for more vigorous successors, had the
splendour but also the ephemeral quality of a sunset. At
the very moment when the genius of Machiavelli, Guicciardini, Raphael and Leonardo da Vinci was in flower, the
discovery of the New World was diverting the current of
European life from the Mediterranean.

The case was very different to the north of the Alps.
Here the Renaissance was not a sunset but a sunrise. It
meant the beginning, in every sense, and in every domain
of social activity, of a new life, of which the economic
phenomena that we have just been considering reveal only
one aspect, and of which we have now to consider the
moral physiognomy. The historian, unfortunately, is obliged
to exhibit piecemeal matters that were parts of a concerted
whole. But it must not be believed that capitalism provoked
the renaissance of thought which was contemporaneous
with it. The one and the other were different symptoms of
the same crisis of growth. And it is curious to note that in
each case the crisis was divided into two corresponding periods. What the discovery of the New World was for capitalism, the Italian Renaissance was for the intellectual
movement. In its beginnings this intellectual movement was
independent of the Renaissance, but the rapidity of its advance and the extent of its influence were explained by its
submission to the guidance of the Renaissance.

To be sure, the symptoms of a new orientation of men's
minds in the countries to the north of the Alps, about the
middle of the 15th century, were not as yet very numerous

nor very striking. Scholasticism in science, Gothic style in the arts, and the traditional forms in the literature of the vulgar tongue, were still incontestably predominant. The mysticism of the 14th century still survived, and in the *Imitation* it found its most complete expression. The great Flemish or Walloon painters of the Low Countries, Van Eyck, De la Pasture, Memling, etc., merely continued, by their genius, a long-established school. When the stupendous invention of printing made its appearance, about 1450, no one foresaw its future. Gutenberg himself had no idea of the future importance of the Press. All he had in view was to provide the clergy and students with cheaper manuscripts. His standpoint was that of the mere industrialist, and the humanists of Italy were at first disdainful of a discovery which in their opinion detracted from the charm and majesty of intellectual masterpieces by the cheapness and mechanical character of its products. Thus, even in the most lasting and most remarkable achievements of the period, in its most beautiful and most influential innovations, we do not find that it was opposed to the past. And yet, although it is very evident that it was largely a continuation of the past, it is none the less true that it did in some degree diverge from it. As in Italy, and before the influence of Italy had made itself felt, life was beginning to escape from the custody of tradition; here, as in Italy, the ascetic morality of the Middle Ages was beginning to lose its authority. The relaxation of morals in the 15th century, and the predominance of temporal interests, were no less striking in Northern Europe than in Italy. And they were most perceptible in countries whose civilization was most advanced. The Low Countries, under the Dukes of Burgundy, between France and England, the one exhausted by war and the other a prey to civil discord, were enjoying a period of peace and prosperity, and they afforded a spectacle which presented curious analogies with that of Italy. One might have observed at the court, in the society of the great nobles, and among the government officials and the capitalists, whether landowners or merchants, a kind of life whose principal features were precisely those which are commonly attributed to the early Renaissance in Tuscany and Lombardy: a general relaxation of morality, a love of luxury and social festivities, a demand for elegance and comfort in private dwellings, a pronounced taste for fine clothing, and for the nobler pleasures of art, and the general diffusion of education and good breeding. Here, very obviously, we see that the aristocracy of birth, like the aristocracy of wealth, was living a social life of a kind that no longer had anything in common with the conventional *cortesia* of the Middle Ages. Philip the Good and Charles the Bold patronized artists, surrounded themselves with painters and musicians, and founded a library whose splendour is attested by the remnants which have survived to this day. In 1465 the Sieur de la Grunthuse built in Bruges a spacious hotel, the handsome, roomy and comfortable habitation of a *grand seigneur* who was at the same time a passionate lover of books, and the patron of Colard Mansion, who had just introduced the art of printing to Bruges. The chancellor Rolin and the treasurer Bladelin commissioned pictures by Van Eyck and De la Pasture. And it is enough to recall the adorable landscapes which assuredly contributed to the success of the Belgian school of painting in the 15th century in order to realize that the discovery of Nature at this period was by no means a purely Italian discovery. The same may be said of the discovery of the individual. The individual portrait was painted as truthfully and conscientiously by the brush of Van Eyck and De la Pasture as by the pen of Chastellain and Commines. And in the work of these last two, I believe, we may see the beginnings of the modern Press; already seeking, in the case of the former, to embellish itself, though clumsily enough as yet, with the prestige of style, and nourished, by the latter, with thought so vigorous that almost the only pendant to his *Mémoires* is *The Prince* of Machiavelli.

This worldliness of manners and of thought in and about the court of Burgundy was also to be observed, though in a less degree, in France and England. Is it not a striking fact that the first mistress of the King of France whose name has been recorded by history was Agnes Sorel? It must not be supposed, of course, that the kings of the Middle Ages had no mistresses. Edward I gave a fief for the purpose of *custodiendi Domino Regi sex damisellas scil. meretrices ad usum Domini Regis.* But in the case of Agnes the king's favourite showed herself in public, and had become something more than a *meretrix.* I admit that this was hardly a symptom of an improvement in morals, but it is a proof that their relaxation was accompanied by their refinement. In England the Duke of Gloucester (the husband of Jacqueline) caused a scandal by the gallantry of his manners, but he also earned the admiration of scholars for the library which he bequeathed to Bedford. We see here the beginning of a kind of "gallantry" which was the very antithesis of the "courtesy" of the Middle Ages; but we must not forget the court's increasing taste for luxury, which to some extent explained the accumulations of such fortunes as that of Jacques Cœur. We should note, moreover, that the private hotels—the Hotel Grunthuse at Bruges, the Hotel Cœur at Bourges, the Hotel Bourgtheroulde at Rouen—were all of the 15th century, and there had been no such buildings previously. No doubt the love of luxury contributed to the spread of that venality which was so strikingly apparent in the political life of the day, as we may learn from Commines. But this luxury, as we may judge from the paintings of the time, was not purely material. It valued art and literature. I believe the 15th century may be regarded as the period when laymen began to read. It is interesting to ask what they read. What was the nature of the literature in the vulgar tongue? What were the first books to be printed? When Caxton established his printing-press in London, his customers, who consisted for the most part of noblemen, but included also a city haberdasher, asked him to produce translations from the French and Latin. He himself translated the Aeneid. His principal purpose was to provide reading for noblemen. Naturally, antiquity furnished only part of the reading-matter of that time. People read everything, eagerly, and without exercising much choice. The old heroic literature was metamorphosed into simple romances. People read, wholesale, moralities, the *Golden Legend, The Dictes of the philosophres, The Fayttes of Chyualrye,* etc. The printing-press did not create the taste for reading, for that already existed, but it hastened its diffusion. Would it be too much to say that the aristocracy had begun to read again for the first time since the age of Charlemagne? But the great difference between the 15th century and the age of Charlemagne and the Middle Ages was that the culture which the men of the 15th century acquired by reading was purely secular. The Church had no part in it. Very visibly, the world was beginning to take an interest in the things of the intellect. Edward IV was interested in Caxton's translation of Cicero, and the translation of the *Odre de Chevalerie* was dedicated to Richard III. In France, Louis XI accorded his patronage to the first printer. The Dukes of Burgundy, Margaret of York, Earl Rivers, Margaret Duchess of Somerset, and many others, were munificent patrons.

We cannot doubt that in all these people there was an insatiable thirst for learning: an awakening—unconscious, I believe, but none the less an awakening—of curiosity, eager to see beyond the two narrow frontiers within which the traditions of caste and religion had hitherto imprisoned it. In the 14th century Maerlant thought it proper that laymen should be given only works by the clergy. And now people were turning away from such works. All this secular literature was produced outside the Church. It was, however, fertile rather than elegant. Only the rhetoricians were concerned with the art of writing.

I think we must say that the essential feature of this period was the fact that a public was coming into being for literature as well as for art. The artists who worked for this public were great artists. The writers, on the other hand, were nearly all third-rate. And this, I think, can be explained, as far as literary mysteries can ever be explained. The fact is that all the traditional types of literature were dead. There was only a desiccated literature, as at the close of the 18th century; the literature which was a survival. Could it have renewed itself without help? Who can say? In any case, the impulse came from without; potent and irresistible, it came from Italy. It was an overwhelming influence, and even art bowed to the fashion and proceeded to become Italianate. It was a phenomenon like that of Romanticism at the beginning of the 19th century.

The Renaissance began to make itself felt at the end of the 15th century; in all the arts at first, excepting music; and in the arts its influence was essentially Italian, and not classic; just as the invasion of Gothic art in Europe had been essentially French. But here we should note a symptomatic effect. Gothic art was propagated outside France by the Church. The Italian art of the Renaissance, on the contrary, was propagated through the profane arts, and the Church was the last stronghold that it penetrated. Those who patronized it were the kings and the great nobles. Francis I sent for Leonardo da Vinci to come to his court. Guillaume de Clèves and Margaret of Austria made it the fashion in the Low Countries. Were not the first buildings of the new style in France the châteaux of the Loire? In short, the new orientation of taste was wholly profane and worldly in its origin.

It was otherwise with the intellectual influence of the Renaissance, which could make itself felt only through the medium of Latin, and which, unlike the artistic influence, was classical rather than Italian. The "New Learning," as the English called it, was a direct return to antiquity, provoked, of course, by the example of the humanists, but not subordinated to them. It is true that there had been humanists in the North, and especially poets, like Pierre Gilles and the author of the *Basia*, Jean Second, while the *Certamen poeticum Haftianum* of Amsterdam was in the direct line of descent. Longolius of Malines belonged to the same school. But not so the great writers: neither Roechlin in Germany, nor Colet and More in England, nor the greatest of all, Erasmus. The literature of antiquity influenced them less by its form than by enfranchising their thought. It enfranchised it from the scholastic tradition, not only by means of the classic tongue, which they immediately adopted, but by the new standpoint which it gave them. The *Miles Christianus* of Erasmus might be described as their programme. And what do we find in it? The secular spirit! By no means the anti-religious spirit; on the contrary. But religion is envisaged as an exhortation to morality, addressed to the honest man. The ideal is no longer asceticism, but the life of the citizen, with all its duties.

This had been considered as something accessory, to be regarded almost with tolerance; now it became the essential thing. Hence the aggressive sarcasms of Erasmus, the insults addressed by Ulrich von Hutten to the monks and *magistri nostri* (*Epistolae obscurorum virorum*, 1515). But hence, also, a whole plan of reforms, with a view to the future, and especially pedagogic reforms, which would replace the schools of the clergy by new schools, in which children should be educated in the cult of *belles lettres*, and in which "politesse" would have its place in a training which was to prepare the pupil not for the cloister, but for life. The *Adagia* of Erasmus, which appeared in 1500, exercised a pedagogical influence comparable only to that of Rousseau's *Émile*. For the first time, in the Renaissance, it was seen that the function of the school was to impart intellectual culture. One may say that the whole organization of education to this day is based on the conception of education evolved by these northern humanists. For them, the object of education was the free development of the personality. Hence, of course, the attacks upon the methods and the asceticism of the Church, which had their logical and final consequence in the "fais ce que vouldras" of the Abbey of Thélème. More, like Erasmus, was opposed to monasticism, asceticism, the celibacy of priests, and the worship of relics; and both, if the truth be told, tended to transform Christianity into a *philosophia evangelica*. But they went further: they wished to change not only the ecclesiastical tradition, but the entire social tradition, and if we can compare the *Adagia* to *Émile*, we can also compare the *Moriae encomium* (The Praise of Folly) and the *Utopia* to the *Contrat social*. It is true that in the North the spirit of the Renaissance was revolutionary, but it was purely theoretical, and it contented itself with verbal onslaughts, of which the *Gargantua* of Rabelais may be regarded as the synthesis. It made war upon the Church. It spared the State, hoping that the progress of enlightenment would win acceptation for its opinions.

In return, all the social authorities made much of the humanist, just as they made much of the philosophers before the French Revolution. No doubt they saw nothing more dangerous than a *jeu d'esprit* in the *Utopia*, in which More showed them a society founded on religious toleration, with universal education, community of goods, and compulsory labour. Perhaps they were chiefly impressed by the attacks upon the monks and the Scholastics. It was these attacks that were responsible for the prodigious success of the *Moriae encomium* (1509), the most widely read book of its time. And this is not surprising. Did not More, like Erasmus, proclaim the superiority of the secular life over that of the cloister? In their optimism they believed that the world might be changed. Vivès wanted the *Utopia* to be placed in the hands of schoolboys, together with the *Colloquia*. If governments, and even popes and kings, applauded these books, as did all the high officials also, it was because they were careful to avoid political discussion. Their attitude was precisely that of Voltaire. In order that enlightenment should triumph, they had need of a strong government, an authority superior to the parties, more powerful than the Church. Like all intellectuals, they were, though they did not confess it, in favour of the "intelligent despot." The revolution of which they dreamed was to be carried out from above, because they expected that it would be the work essentially of science and reason. No doubt they wanted to extend its benefits to all men, but it must begin at the top, and as for the means by which it was to be brought about, they relied on the social aristocracy, hoping for the final constitution of an intellectual aristocracy. In 1517 Jerome Busleyden, acting on the advice of Erasmus, founded at Louvain the "College of the Three Tongues," whose purpose was to apply, through the knowledge of the three current languages (Latin, Greek and Hebrew), the philological method to the Holy Scriptures, independently of all positive theology. A little later Francis I installed and endowed the Collège de France in Paris. Wolsey, with the same object, founded the "Cardinal College"—later Christ Church—at Oxford. Henry VIII was as great a patron of the Hellenists and the innovators as was Francis I in France. When in 1514 the quarrel broke out between Roechlin and the University of Cologne, in respect of the opinion expressed by Rome concerning the sacred books of the Jews, the Emperor, the Cardinal-Bishop of Gurk, the Elector of Saxony, the Duke of Bavaria, and the Margrave of Baden all supported Roechlin, and the Pope, when he bade Cologne be silent, made no secret of his own sympathies. In vain did the Dominicans protest and raise outcries of heresy; they were merely treated with disdain. It seemed as though the immense fabric of Scholasticism was on the point of being overthrown, as so many Gothic castles had been overthrown, and rebuilt in a contemporary style. Only in Spain was it holding its own; the Renaissance affected only its form, but left the Catholic spirit untouched.

Everywhere else, during the twenty years which elapsed between the end of the 15th century and the appearance of Protestantism,[4] it seemed as though a new world was on the point of birth. All that was strong and youthful and vigorous revolted against the past. Never, perhaps, have the social authorities so unanimously supported an intellectual movement. It seemed as though there were no conservatives left among them. All were moving and straining in the same direction: authority, society, fashion, the politicians, the women, the artists, the humanists. There was a boundless confidence abroad, a feverish joy. The mind was liberated from authority, was free to wander under the heavens; the monopoly of knowledge was abolished, and it was now the possession of the whole community. And the knowledge that was derived from antiquity was all the more seductive, inasmuch as it went hand in hand with beauty, and was, so to speak, almost identical with beauty.

This species of Roman patriotism, which did something to contribute to the success of the Renaissance in Italy, did not exist in the North. There antiquity was regarded more objectively, valued for its own sake, as the source of beauty and wisdom. Possibly, if it inspired less affection, it was regarded with all the more respect. And men were more conscious of its liberating force, for Scholasticism had never enjoyed the same predominance in Italy as beyond the Alps. In France, England and Germany it was far more

[4] Luther exposed his theses in 1517.

aggressive than in Italy. In adopting the Latin of the classics as their language, the humanists of the South were bent merely on continuing the work of the ancients; those of the North were eager to indicate, by its adoption, their break with *magistri nostri*. The barbarous style for which they quite wrongly reproached the Latin of the universities and the Scholastics—forgetting that it was an artificial and scientific language, perfectly adapted to its purpose—seemed to them eloquent of the barbarity, crudity, and absurdity of the ideas which it expressed. However, they did not undertake to attack the philosophy of the Middle Ages; they were content to despise it. For them, everything had to be reconstructed. Theology must be reconstructed, beginning with the study of the sacred texts. The great achievement of Erasmus was a Greek edition of the New Testament with Latin translation and paraphrase. As for morality, based on a Christian foundation, it must be remodelled and adapted to the necessities of secular life.

When we speak of the rationalism of the Renaissance, we must realize that it did not proceed beyond the limits of common sense. The liberty of thought which it claimed for man stopped short of the great religious and philosophical problems. Its standpoint was purely human and terrestrial. It did not attack the problems of destiny and the origin of the world; in this connection it accepted the Christian ideas. Its philosophy did not venture beyond the domain of practical morality and politics, and the commonplaces of the ancients on these subjects were accepted as the final utterance of wisdom. It was quite ready to admit the existence of mysterious and demoniacal powers beyond the limits of the visible world. It is interesting to note that this rationalism coincided with a recrudescence of magical practices, and it uttered no protests against the increasing frequency of the abominable trials for witchcraft, which must never be forgotten if we are to form an accurate notion of the mentality of the new era.

What this rationalism brought with it, then, was not free thought in the actual sense of the word, but what might be described as an intellectual and moral liberalism. Now liberalism is synonymous with individualism, and assuredly one of the most definite consequences of the Renaissance was that it substituted for the social conception of the Middle Ages, according to which the world was a hierarchy of perfectly distinct classes, each having its own function and rights and duties, the idea that worth and esteem are purely personal things, appertaining to every man, by virtue not of his rank, but of his merit. It is interesting to observe that in this connection the Renaissance placed on earth what the Church had reserved for heaven. For while the Church admitted and approved of inequality, the result of mundane relations, it made salvation depend only on personal merit, so that the individual, whatever rank he might have occupied here below, would assume, in the face of Divine justice, and in the eternal life, the rank of which he was worthy. This difference is perhaps deserving of remark, for is it not a striking proof of the essentially secular and mundane inspiration that animated the Renaissance?

But let us at once admit that the liberalism of the Renaissance was an aristocratic liberalism. By no means did it proclaim the rights of man, but only, in the words of Rabelais, the rights of men who were "free, well born, well educated, and conversant with honest company." In short, its ideal was the *vir bonus dicendi peritus* of antiquity; that is, the "honnête homme," the "gentleman" of the modern era. It regarded the privileges of birth as absurd, but it insisted, all the more vigorously, on the privileges of intellectual culture. In this its point of view approximated pretty closely to that of antiquity. Regarded in this sense, Rousseau's declaration that the arts and letters were destructive of equality is a protest against society as envisaged by the Renaissance. The opposition between the freeman and the slave was replaced by the opposition between the literate and the illiterate. The Renaissance felt nothing but disdain for "mechanic trades," and the prejudice in favour of the liberal professions, which survives to this day, dates from the Renaissance. This prejudice was doubtless largely responsible for the indifference to the lot of the lower classes which characterizes the modern era. Moral ideas have surely played as much part in this as the economic interests of landowners and capitalists.

Taking a bird's-eye view, it is obvious that society, as it evolved, after the beginning of the 16th century, under the influence of the Renaissance, presents a less imposing spectacle than the society of the Middle Ages, governed, instructed, and inspired by the Church, with its hierarchy of classes, sharing between them the work of society, subordinating the individual to the community of which he was a member, and inspiring one and all with the same religious faith and the same Christian ideal. But what had happened? The incessant wear and tear of life had undermined the foundations of the majestic edifice; since the end of the 14th century it had been foundering on every side, and the Renaissance merely accelerated the inevitable ruin. The organic unity which was lacking in the modern world would, however, be compensated for by the prodigious animation provoked and maintained by the enfranchisement of thought and action. In order to arrive at a just appreciation of the Renaissance, we must remember that for three hundred years the art and literature of every people have been evolving in the direction which it struck out for itself. If we work back against the current of evolution we come at last to the Renaissance. One might liken our civilization to a river which became navigable only from the point where the affluent of antiquity mingled its waters with the stream. Of course, the river has its source at a much remoter point, but its upper reaches are accessible only with difficulty; to explore them, to become familiar with their aspect, so that we can understand them, requires a considerable effort. Barely a century has elapsed since the Middle Ages ceased to be regarded with disdain. But in spite of the reaction which has occurred in their favour, they are so remote from us that we cannot blend them with our own life in a really intimate fashion. More often than not, Neo-Gothicism[5] is merely the form affected by ideas and tendencies which are in reality extremely mod-

---

[5] The allusion here is to the "Neo-Gothic" architecture which flourished, especially in Belgium, before the war.

ern. The Renaissance, on the contrary, still surrounds us on every hand. It was only yesterday that Renaissance furniture began to disappear from our houses. Despite the admirable vigour of contemporary art, our governments continue to maintain their "Écoles de Rome," their "travelling scholarships," while our Athenaeums, Lyceums and Gymnasiums are merely the continuation of the Latin schools of the 16th century. From the Renaissance, too, dates the development of the sciences; for a long while they exerted no influence upon human history, accumulating the new knowledge in silence, until, at the end of the 18th century, the spate of discoveries, increasing our knowledge of Nature, led to a second renaissance of thought, and thanks to the progress of technique, multiplied a hundredfold the output of human effort.

Nevertheless, the influence of the Renaissance upon civilization was by no means so efficacious as its early years might have led man to expect. Another force, even more powerful—the religious Reformation—began to clash with it at the very moment when it was beginning to trace the direction of intellectual progress, and it was their twofold action, sometimes combined, but more often opposed, that determined the destinies of the modern world.

CHAPTER II

The Reformation

1. *Lutheranism*

The victory of the Pope over the Councils had enabled the Church to retain its monarchical constitution, but it could not and it did not restore to the Holy See the European hegemony which it had lost since the pontificate of Boniface VIII. In vain did Pius II solemnly remind the Catholic princes (1460) of their subordination to the sovereign pontiff; the princes were so well aware of the emptiness of this pretension that they did not even think it worth while to protest against it. Though Pius obtained from Louis XI the withdrawal of the Pragmatic Sanction, this merely gratified his vanity. The monarch, whose complaisance was rewarded with the title of "Most Christian King," was happy to be rid of the guarantees with which the Pragmatic Sanction encompassed the episcopal elections, and hastened to profit by their disappearance by exercising a stricter control over the clergy of France. In England, Spain, and the Burgundian States—in short, wherever the monarchy was powerful—Rome was unable to prevent it from disposing as it pleased of the highest ecclesiastical dignities, and contented herself with the marks of deference which the monarchy lavished upon her on the condition that it was allowed to do as it chose. The prestige of Rome was so definitely on the downgrade that her exhortations to arm against the Turks were almost disregarded. No doubt the deplorable impotence which Europe displayed in the face of these Barbarians was explained mainly by the rivalries, jealousies, and divergent interests of the States; nevertheless, we are bound to regard it as in some degree the result of their indifference toward the head of the Church. At the summons of Urban II Christendom had risen with enthusiasm against the Musulmans of Syria, who were not threatening it; to the appeal of Pius II, despite the imminence of the danger, it remained indifferent; unmoved, it saw the successor of Peter reduced to "taking the Cross" himself, and dying of grief and fatigue at Ancona on embarking for the Holy War (1463); when the Venetian fleet, with which he was to have sailed, hastened to turn back when the news of his death became known.

Henceforth, the Papacy was a political power only in Italy, and even there it was greatly inferior to Venice, the King of Naples, the Medici, and the Sforza. In order to maintain itself at all it was obliged to divert, to the profit of its temporal power, a good part of the resources which it derived from Christendom; so that its spiritual primacy over the Catholic world seemed often to be subordinated to its territorial interests. The prince often seemed to take precedence of the Pope in the person of the sovereign pontiff, the more so as the tiara was now conferred only upon Italians: Adrian VI (1521–1523) was to be the last of the ultramontane Popes. By thus Italianizing itself the Papacy escaped in some degree from the interference of the great powers, but it also became more alien to them, since it was imbued with a national character which assorted ill with its oecumenical mission. It is not surprising that under such circumstances nepotism should have made the most alarming progress in the bosom of the Curia. Each Pope profited by his elevation to assure the future of his family, and of his policy, by introducing, without regard for their capacity or their morals, the greatest possible number of his kinsmen into the Sacred College. Already the cardinals of Avignon had caused distress to the many pious souls. But what can we say of those of the 15th century! Even in the world of the Renaissance, accustomed to the extreme licence of court life, their appointment was regarded as a scandal. We have to go back to the 10th century, to the days of Theodore, Marosia, and John XII, to find a spectacle of moral anarchy comparable with that which was offered by Rome under the pontificate of Alexander VI (1492–1503), and even by the pontificates of Julius II and Leo X. Again, the brutality of the feudal system afforded some excuse for the 10th century which could not be adduced in favour of the end of the 15th century. Imagine what an impression a believer must have carried away from the capital of the Christian world at a time (1490) when there were 6,800 courtesans in Rome, when the Popes and cardinals consorted publicly with their mistresses, acknowledged their bastards, and enriched them at the cost of the Church! It was really too much that a Borgia should have been able to sit on the throne of St. Peter. There is an only too painful contrast between what the Papacy should have been and what it actually was; and one would have liked to find more religious sincerity in the patrons of Bramante, Raphael, and Michelangelo. Wonderful though the achievements of the Renaissance may have been in Rome, there was something repulsive about it; the splendour which it conferred upon the metropolis of the Catholic world made it too sadly unlike the Rome of the great mediaeval Popes. The successors of Innocent III and Boniface VIII were so steeped in the new spirit that they no longer respected the tradition to which they owed what ascendancy they still retained over the world. It almost seems as though for them the Church was no more than a means of asserting their personal eminence, and that it was to their greater glory, rather than to that of Christ, that so many monuments were erected, so many works of art produced.

The Church fulfilled its religious mission hardly better than the Papacy. Discontented or discouraged by the defeat of the Councils, it fell into a state of apathy, tolerant of abuses, and of the laxity which their persistence seemed to justify. The higher clergy, almost entirely recruited from among the protégés of the Curia or the courts of the princes, were complete worldlings. Many bishops received the order of priesthood, if they received it at all, only when they took possession of their sees, and it was evidently a mere formality; as regards the majority, their morals made it plain that it caused them little inconvenience. Some, in accordance with the tastes of the day, took pleasure in posing as humanists, and gained a reputation as patrons of the arts. Others, interested in politics, spent more time at court than in their dioceses. Nearly all lived a full and joyous life, hunting, drinking and otherwise diverting themselves. Naturally, the Chapters were no better. As a general thing their prebends were reserved for the younger sons of influential families, many of whom did not take orders, did not wear clerical costume, hardly ever officiated, and publicly kept concubines. The incumbents of parishes generally contented themselves with collecting the revenues of their cure, which was administered by an assistant, who was paid a salary that barely enabled him to live. Despised by his parishioners on account of his poverty, he was obliged to make money in any way he could, overcharging for his services in respect of births, marriages and deaths. As for the monasteries, their decadence was all the more deplorable, inasmuch as more zeal, austerity and learning might have been expected of them. It may fairly be said that at the beginning of the 16th century they were all vegetating in routine and mechanical obedience to their rule. Those truly pious souls who still sought refuge in the monasteries found themselves ill at ease in the midst of companions who were completely without ideals, and asked of the cloister nothing but a quiet, comfortable and secure existence. Only the Dominicans still displayed a certain activity. But since Scholasticism had done its work, there was nothing left for them but their inquisitorial duties, and for lack of heresies to cope with they devoted themselves to the study of demonology. In 1487 two of them published, at Strasbourg, the *Malleus Maleficarum*, an abominable treatise on the crimes of witches.

Such a clergy was bound to shock public opinion. The contrast was too striking between its conduct and the consideration which it demanded, the privileges which it enjoyed, and the revenues at its disposal. The aristocracy despised it for its vulgarity and ignorance, while the bourgeoisie was scandalized by its financial or judicial immunities. The governments were already beginning to take measures against the multiplication of estates subject to mortmain, and the intervention of ecclesiastical tribunals in civil causes.

However, the faith was still intact. Since the 12th century, it would really seem that there had never been so few heretics as during the fifty years that preceded the outbreak of Protestantism. Wycliffism in England and Hussitism in Bohemia were almost extinct. And this in itself is a proof of the religious lukewarmness of the age. No one deserted the Church, or dreamed of doing so; but religion had become little more than a habit, a rule of life for those who observed the letter rather than the spirit. Hence the success of the indulgences, of which the Papacy, always short of money, was continually authorizing new emissions on all sorts of pretexts. Those who bought them forgot, of course, that contrition was indispensable to their efficacy, and believed that they were simply taking out an insurance against the risks of the future life. Naturally, this did not apply to all. There were still ardent and religious souls for whom faith was a vital necessity. But they, more often than not, sought satisfaction outside the Church, in some form of individual mysticism.

And yet at the beginning of the 16th century mysticism was far less widespread than in the middle of the previous century. The general tendency of thought was too completely opposed to it. As the influence of the Renaissance became more widely diffused, the choicer spirits envisaged religion less as an introduction to the future life than as a moral doctrine. The ideal of humanity conceived by Erasmus, More, and Vivès was completely pervaded by Christianity, but by a Christianity which was adapted, so to speak, to the necessities of earthly existence. Hence their antipathy to asceticism and the traditional theology. They had very little regard for dogma, and virtue seemed to them the supreme form of piety. For the rest, though they vigorously attacked the monks and did not conceal their disdain for the Scholastic morality, they were careful not to attack the Church. They were Catholics of a rather troublesome character, but they were Catholics; the higher clergy, the European courts, and the Pope himself did not conceal their sympathy for them. They hoped, without sensationalism, without a crisis, merely by the influence of intellectual progress, common sense, and learning, and thanks to the support of the social authorities, to bring about a religious reformation full of moderation, breadth, and tolerance.

This pleasing dream lasted only for a moment. It was, as a matter of fact, impossible of realization, for the anti-ascetic Christianity of the humanist had nothing in common with that of the Church, and there would inevitably have been a rupture between the two if time had permitted. The theologians who made common cause against Erasmus saw this plainly enough, and if the Pope compelled them to keep silence it was because the Church was so infatuated with the Renaissance that it could not immediately perceive the danger. The higher clergy paid court to the Erasmians much as the French nobility paid court to the "philosophers" at the end of the 18th century. The former no more expected a religious revolution than the latter anticipated a political revolution. There was nothing, indeed, that could have enabled anyone to foresee the sudden explosion of Lutheranism. Of course, since the lamentable end of the Council of Basle, Germany had been seething with a sullen dissatisfaction with the Papacy. This had been accused of disposing, as of sovereign right, of the highest ecclesiastical dignities, and its accusers never reflected that this was a direct consequence, not of any ill-will to the German nation, but of the anarchical constitution of the Empire, which excluded any possibility of subjecting the Church, as in France, England or Spain, to the power of the State. The humanists, for their part, aggravated this bad feeling. It infuriated them that the Italians should speak of the Northern peoples as barbarians, and in their vanity they boasted, in classical Latin, of their descent from those Germans who had once victoriously called a halt to the ambition of Rome. In their writings, and above all in those of Ulrich von Hutten, we find for the first time, expressed with some naïvety, an opposition of Germanism and Romanism at which we should be tempted to smile if the political passions of the 19th century had not exploited it with such blind fury, to the detriment of civilization. These declamations did not go beyond a small clan of scholars, but they none the less contributed in their way to the maintenance of an anti-Roman mentality. Moreover, had not the Emperors of the Middle Ages found in the Popes their constant adversaries? Whether in its pagan or in its Catholic form, Rome was thus regarded as the perpetual enemy of the German people.

To these complaints of wounded vanity the bourgeoisie added more concrete grievances. As everywhere, it was impatient of the immunities of the clergy, and showed itself rather brutally anti-clerical when any incident provided it with a pretext. But nowhere was there any manifestation of the need of religious reform. Men were accustomed to tradition, and they accepted it. It would be incorrect to suppose that Germany was devoured by a spiritual thirst which the Church was no longer able to assuage—that it felt itself cabined and confined in Catholicism, and was seeking to unite itself more intimately with God. It is only too easy to point to a religious opposition between the Germanic and the Latin soul. Reality shows us nothing of the kind. Although Protestantism was born in Germany, and while the form which it first assumed, and its early progress, can only be explained by the German environment in which it was born, this is no proof whatever of its alleged Germanic character. It would be only too easy to oppose the Frenchman, Calvin, to the German Luther. The Reformation was a religious phenomenon; it was not a national phenomenon, and although it is true that it was most widely diffused among those peoples that spoke the Germanic tongues, this was not because it found in these countries minds which were specially qualified to understand it, but because it was there favoured by political and social conditions which it did not encounter elsewhere.

Luther belonged to the number of those who, in all countries and in all ages, are troubled in the most secret places of their hearts by religious problems which are more readily felt than defined. Born in 1483, the son of a miner of Eisleben (in Saxony), he, like so many other sons of the people, after distinguishing himself at school, was destined by his father for the jurist's career. He had been studying in the University of Erfurt since 1501, when in 1505, terrified by the idea of death, which had nearly taken him during a thunderstorm, he renounced his career and assumed the robe of a monk in an Augustinian monastery. Like so many others, he failed to find spiritual peace in the ascetic life, and in 1508 he was relieved at being chosen by the general of the order to fill a chair in the faculty of theology in the University of Wittenberg. There, in 1517, his famous thesis against the sale of indulgences made him suddenly emerge from his obscurity, and inaugurated the Reformation.

Had Luther already decided to break with the Church? It is difficult to say. But his fiery and obstinate temper, excited by contradiction, soon drove him to extremes. Moreover, he was encouraged by public opinion. The protests of the Diet of Augsburg in 1518 against the exactions of the pontifical fiscality must have fortified his resolution. He had confidence in himself, he was by nature a fighter, and he was supported, in the contest, by the fire of the orator and the pen of the pamphleteer. Like Wycliffe and Huss, he wanted to address the nation, and it was in the national tongue that he wrote. Nothing could have been better calculated to rouse and win his fellow-countrymen than his humorous, passionate, angry style. Moreover, the printing-press of his little University of Wittenberg sent his mighty words all over Germany. Almost as soon as the quarrel began the sound of it filled the country. For the first time a religious question was debated in the hearing of the people, was brought within its competence and submitted to its judgement. The *Letter to the German Nobles*, and the little treatises entitled *The Babylonian Captivity of the Church* and *The Liberty of the Christian*, all published in 1520, were, so to speak, propagandist pamphlets, and their success was prodigious. Until then, the doctrine of the adversaries of the Church had been spread by preaching and apostleship. Lutheranism was propagated by means of letterpress, and in the rapidity of its diffusion we see the first manifestation of the power of the Press.

As Luther fought his battle his thought became more

definite and bolder. The debate concerning indulgences transformed itself almost immediately into an attack upon the Papacy, and then an attack upon the whole traditional organization of the Church. In 1518 the question was merely whether an appeal should be made from the Pope to the Council. But no later than the following year the Papacy was proclaimed an institution of purely human origin; the Council itself was said to be capable of error, and Scripture alone was infallible. In 1520 the decisive step was taken: the Christian was justified by his faith, not by his works; faith in Christ made every Christian a priest; the Mass, and all the sacraments excepting Baptism, the Eucharist, and Penitence, were rejected; the clergy had no privileges that were not possessed by lay society; both were subject to the power of the secular sword, whose authority was extended to the Church as well as to the State.

Luther was merely advancing still further upon the path which had been trodden before his time by Wycliffe and John Huss. His theology was a continuation of the dissident theology of the Middle Ages; his ancestors were the great heretics of the 14th century; he was absolutely untouched by the spirit of the Renaissance. His doctrine of justification by faith was related to the doctrines of the mystics, and although, like the humanists, though for very different motives, he condemned celibacy and the ascetic life, he was in absolute opposition to them in his complete sacrifice of free will and reason to faith.

However, the humanists did not fail to applaud his sensational début. They applauded him discreetly, it is true, like people who were anxious not to compromise themselves. They were a little disquieted by so much violence, but delighted with the smashing blows rained upon the monks and the Scholastics; after all this uproar men would listen more willingly to their moderation and their wisdom. Wherever the spirit of humanism prevailed Lutheranism, in its beginnings, was regarded with sympathy: in the Low Countries, at the court of Margaret of Austria, and in France, at the court of Francis I. And as for Germany, there the new movement was received not only with sympathy but with enthusiasm. The bourgeoisie of the free cities of the South especially, more turbulent and more active than those of the North, gave their immediate support to the new movement. But to tell the truth, the religious ideas of the reformer were understood only by a very small number of genuinely pious souls. The enthusiasm of the masses was excited mainly by the attacks upon the clergy and upon Rome. The doctrine of justification by faith was beyond their comprehension, and so far no one was thinking of a dogmatic rupture with the Church, but the masses were profoundly moved by the fiery attacks upon the traffic in holy things, and in the sacraments, upon the abuses of the monastic life, and finally, upon the arrogance of the priests who proclaimed that they were the Church, whereas the Church belonged to all Christians. Already numbers of monks were deserting the cloisters; and priests, preaching from the pulpit, proclaimed their adhesion to the movement. People were beginning to read and interpret the Bible. They were filled with naïve indignation against the clergy who had so long deceived them by concealing from them the true religion contained in the Holy Book. Among the nobles there was a party which was inspired with no less ardour. The knights who gathered about Ulrich von Hutten and Franz von Sickingen were moved alike by German patriotism and by hatred of Rome, and they hoped vaguely for a regeneration of the Empire, both political and religious. Meanwhile, the princes were pondering the situation. What seductive prospects were offered by the hope of secularizing the ecclesiastical estates! How much more attractive was the Word of God, how much more seductive the task of helping the cause of the Gospel to triumph, if the good work was going to facilitate the most profitable of business transactions! To tell the truth, among the very great majority of its first adherents Lutheranism was far more a revolt against the Papacy than a genuine religious awakening.

Its progress was greatly facilitated by the fact that the Church had no defenders. Neither the people nor the princes came to its aid. For its own part, it displayed an amazing apathy. It is true that a few theologians conducted polemics against Luther, but the Church made no attempt to influence the masses who, after so long obeying it, had suddenly turned against it. It was as though it doubted its own strength, and its impotence, in the midst of such a conflict, naturally increased the audacity of its adversaries. Luther had no hesitation in burning the Bull that condemned him in the Wittenberg market-place (December 10th, 1520).

The Emperor Maximilian died on January 12th, 1519, at the very moment when the crisis was about to assume its gravest aspect. But this did not in any way influence the decision of the Electors. In choosing between Francis I and Charles V it was not the religious question, but simply the question of money that made them vote for the latter.

There was no doubt as to what the new Emperor's attitude would be in respect of the Reformation. Even if he had felt any sympathy for it, his policy would have prevented him from showing it. His power was founded above all upon Spain, and was it likely that the King of Spain would compound with heresy? Moreover, how could Charles have dreamed of embroiling himself with the Papacy at the very moment when its support was indispensable if he was to hold his own against the French invasion of Italy? His most obvious interests, and his personal convictions, combined to make him the defender of the Church. It was not that he was wilfully blind to the abuses of the Church; he called most urgently for a general Council, and he most vigorously opposed the temporal pretensions of the Papacy. But being as true a Catholic as he was a conservative, he held the traditional belief that the Church was the condition and the very foundation of social order, and that its maintenance was as indispensable to the salvation of men's souls as it was to the existence of all terrestrial authority.

If Germany had been a State, the destinies of the Reformation would have been singularly compromised under the government of a prince who held such opinions. In France, or in England, it must immediately have surrendered to the Crown, or have fought it. The Protestant historians have mistakenly deplored the lack of political unity in Germany at the beginning of the 16th century; it was the weakness of the monarchical power, and the backward and particularistic character of its institutions that saved Lutheranism, or at all events assured it of its rapid and easy diffusion, compared with the formidable conflicts in which Calvinism, in more advanced and powerful States, was involved from its very beginnings.

Almost immediately after his election as Emperor, Charles hastened to submit the religious problem to the Diet convoked at Worms in the month of April 1521. Luther, summoned before the assembly, a great part of which was favourable to him, and to whose doors he advanced amidst the acclamations of the crowd, had no reason to fear the fate of John Huss at the Council of Constance. He refused to retract, and he was allowed to leave the city unmolested (April 17th, 1521). A few weeks later (May 8th) an Imperial edict pronounced the ban of the Empire upon him and his adherents. But no one was under any illusion as to the actual importance of this measure. The Empire had no means of enforcing it, and as a matter of fact, it was nowhere executed. It did not hinder the diffusion of the ideas which it condemned any more than it imperilled the security of those who continued to spread them.

Charles had to resign himself to this defeat. Being at war with Francis I, he could not possibly have provoked, in Germany, a religious conflict which would have doubled the chances of his adversary. But what he could not do in the Empire he could do in the Low Countries, and there he hastened to organize the repression of heresy with pitiless severity. As early as 1520 he had promulgated a first "bill" against heresy, and in the following year he ordained that the Edict of Worms should be strictly observed. This was only the prelude to what he had in mind. What he had wished to do was to introduce the Spanish Inquisition into his Burgundian provinces, and although he abandoned this project, in submission to the unanimous opposition of his councillors, he nevertheless organized in those provinces a system of repression as exactly modelled upon the Spanish Holy Office as was possible without rousing public opinion. In 1522 he entrusted a member of the Council of Brabant with the prosecution of heretics. The protests of the Pope against this lay inquisition, which was instituted merely by the State, led him to abandon it in the following year. In 1524 apostolic institutors—who, however, were appointed by the government—functioned in its place. And further, until the end of his reign, a series of more and more violent and merciless "bills" were promulgated, which even went to the length of compelling the lay courts to prosecute and sentence to death persons who, not being theologians, had discussed questions of faith, or who, being acquainted with heretics, did not denounce them.

The effect of this religious persecution was similar to that of all its predecessors. It aroused a truly heroic spirit in the noblest and sincerest souls. It was reserved for the Low Countries to furnish the Reformation with its first martyrs. On July 1st, 1523, two Augustinians of Antwerp, Henri Voes and Jan van Essen, were burned alive in the great market-place of Brussels. Luther celebrated them in one of his most beautiful canticles, and in the following year Erasmus declared "that their death had made many Lutherans."

One may ask oneself what would have become of Lutheranism in Germany if men had been able to profess it only at the peril of their lives. We may be sure, at all events, that its propagation would have been very greatly delayed, and that the rapidity of its diffusion is explained more than anything by the very few risks which the innovators incurred. Nothing could have been less heroic than its history, and it is reasonable to believe that the compliance which the Lutheran Church was to manifest subsequently in its dealings with temporal authority would not have been so pronounced if it had been compelled, in the beginning, to sacrifice the blood of its faithful to its faith. As a matter of fact, before very long, far from having to resist the princes, it was to place itself under their protection.

For centuries the Church had been so completely interblended with society that whenever the former had been attacked the foundations of the latter had been shaken. The heresy of the Albigenses in the 12th century had given rise to communistic aspirations. Wycliffe, without intending it, had contributed to the Agrarian rebellion of 1381, and we know that Hussitism was closely implicated with all sorts of social claims. The Lutheran propaganda was to prove no exception to the rule. Of course, from the temporal standpoint, no one could have been more conservative than Luther. Very different from the humanists, and much less modern, he accepted the traditionally established order of things; he was a revolutionary only in religious matters, and his furious attacks upon the authority of Rome were in strange contrast with his docility in respect of the secular authorities. But when it reached the heart of the masses his propaganda was bound, before long, to awaken the confused emotions born of extreme poverty; a formidable force, which, once unleashed, escapes all guidance, obeying only itself.

It will be remembered that since the end of the 14th century the condition of the German peasants had been continually deteriorating. The capitalistic tendencies of the following century had still further favoured the exploitation to which the brutal and merciless nobles subjected them. In the German art and literature of the 16th century the *Bauer* was treated with extraordinary disdain. He was apparently regarded merely as a disgusting or ridiculous brute; where he was concerned, anything was permissible. And as a matter of fact, the nobles did really behave as though anything were permissible in dealing with these unhappy creatures: the re-establishment of serfdom, the multiplication of *corvées*, the confiscation of communal property, the diminution of holdings, the increase of all sorts of prestations in kind, the arrogation of the right of dispensing justice, and demands for services of every nature. Against the feudal *Burg* which oppressed them the poor people of each *seigneurie* were quite defenceless. They had accepted their fate, and had resigned themselves, when the religious agitation which was troubling the cities began to make itself felt among them. Religion was the most ancient and the most sacred of habits, the necessary form, the very foundation of existence, and they saw it attacked with impunity, derided and defied. Their dread of and respect for the clergy disappeared. How then should they continue to dread and respect their lords? The abuses of which the Church was accused were much less obvious to them than the injustice which they had to suffer at the hands of the nobles. And in proportion as this agitation spread among them they drew closer together in their common anger. Their weakness had been the consequence of their isolation. Moved by the same passions, they became conscious of their strength, and in 1528 the first riots suddenly revealed the magnitude of a peril which no one had foreseen because it had been so utterly disdained.

The movement rapidly spread through the whole of Southern Germany, from Luxemburg to the mountains of Bohemia. And here and there the rebels were actually joined by the people of the cities. Their demands, which were advanced in the "Twelve Articles of the Peasants," were far more social than religious. They called for a return to the Gospel, but above all they demanded liberty, liberty as they understood it, which meant the liberty to enjoy the free use of forest and field, and to rid themselves of the illegal *corvées* and the arbitrary tyranny of the landlords. Their bands broke loose in all directions, and the terror which they excited paralysed all resistance. To the brutality under which they had so long suffered they responded by brutality. Castles and monasteries were given to the flames. The terror was so general, the outbreak so sudden, that counts, princes, and Electors humbled themselves to the extent of negotiating with the insurgent masses and agreeing to the "Twelve Articles." But already these seemed insufficient to hopes excited and passions fired by success. Once more the old dreams of a mystical communism, which had lingered amongst the people ever since the Middle Ages, had taken possession of their minds. Thomas Münzer, in Thuringia, excited the fanaticism of the peasants by the promise of a world of love and justice, in conformity with the Divine will, whose realization demanded the massacre of the unrighteous. The effect of such preaching upon simple and violent souls was to transform the agrarian revolt into a sort of mystical Terror. Its excesses hastened the organization of a resistance which had at first been delayed by the suddenness of its initial successes, but which was, of course, inevitable. The nobles united their forces against those of the peasants. The peasants accepted battle, and on May 15th, 1526, they were cut to pieces at Frankenhausen. The conquerors were pitiless in proportion to the terror they had suffered. Their hatred took a long revenge upon the people who had dared to defy them. The yoke imposed upon the peasants was heavier than ever, and henceforth they were to bear it with docile resignation, until the beginning of the 19th century.

The crisis of Anabaptism was even greater proof of the religious confusion into which the too sudden disappearance of ecclesiastical authority had plunged the soul of the people. Accepting Luther's preaching literally, the first Anabaptists, who before 1525 had made their appearance in Switzerland, claimed that not only their faith, but society itself must be reformed in accordance with Holy Scripture. Since the Bible contained the Word of God they must conform to it strictly in all things. What need was there of Church or State? Obedience to the Word of God should suffice to save men's souls as well as to regulate their mutual relations. Inevitably, the old heresies of the Middle Ages contributed their doctrines to the interpretation of the Scriptures. The popular form of Manichaeism, based on the opposition of flesh and spirit, had never completely disappeared since the days of the Albigenses. Now it was revived, mingled with the apocalyptic visions and the mystical tendencies which had become so widespread since the 14th century. The righteous believed that they were called upon to create a new world, in which all things would be fraternally held in common, wives as well as property. This notion found very ready acceptance in the lower classes of the urban populations, among the journeymen of the guilds and the wage-earning workers in the nascent capitalistic industries. Spreading by contagion among the manual workers, it soon reached the Low Countries, where industry, more intensive than elsewhere, had prepared a most fertile soil for such a movement. It is not surprising that its adepts were savagely prosecuted by the public authorities. Catholics and Lutherans vied with one another in their ferocious suppression of this revolutionary heresy. However, persecution merely aggravated the peril. Utopian though it had been in the beginning, Anabaptism now became a doctrine of hatred and conflict. The poor looked to it not only for deliverance, but for vengeance. Many of them seem to have been actually hallucinated, and as ready to die for their faith as they were to sacrifice, without mercy, the rest of their world. About 1530 a sort of mystico-social delirium seems to have seized upon Holland. Nearly all the lower classes of the cities became a prey to it. In some of the cities it is estimated that two-thirds of the inhabitants were infected, and the massacre, the summary condemnation, the drownings, and the outlawry of all those who adhered to the sect were powerless to arrest its progress. It was from Amsterdam and its suburbs that those prophets came, in 1534, who, taking advantage of the fact that the city of Münster had rebelled against its bishop, went thither to establish the "Kingdom of God." At no other moment of history, perhaps, has there been a more striking example of the lengths to which the masses may be driven by passion, religious illusion, and the hope of realizing social justice. For twelve months, blockaded by the troops of the neighbouring princes, Protestants and Catholics, the Anabaptists of Münster organized, in a sort of insanity, their "New Jerusalem." Polygamy and communism were instituted and practised by the whole population. For a moment a mystical and socialistic Utopia became a reality. The city was taken by storm on June 24th, 1535, and this access of collective madness was quenched in blood. Not until our own days were the iron cages brought down from the tower of the cathedral in which the charred bones of the prophet John of Leyden and the Burgomaster Knipperdalling had so long swung in the wind. The capture of Münster put an end to the violent crisis of Anabaptism, but it did not abolish it. Until almost the close of the 16th century its revolutionary ferment continued to work in the hearts of the people, as did the ferment of Catharism after the great persecution of the 13th century. But among the majority of its adherents it reverted to the evangelical simplicity of its beginnings, and it is in this form that it has been perpetuated down to our own days in the heart of the Protestant world of Europe and America.

The Peasant War, and the tragedy of Anabaptism, resulted in turning the humanists and the Erasmians away from Luther; horrified by so much violence, they moved in the direction of the Church. Luther was no less dismayed. He violently attacked the rebels and pitilessly applauded their defeat. This was the end of the popular tendencies which he had revealed in the beginning. It seemed to him that the only means of saving the Reformation was to place it under the protection and control of the princes. Knowing them as he did, he was aware that they were generally lukewarm in their religion. With the exception of the Dukes of Bavaria, who were as firmly Catholic as the Habsburgs, they were inclined to make their faith conform to their interests. We do not find in any one of them the least trace of idealism, the slightest evidence of any sincere and disinterested conviction. Doubtless they were dissatisfied with the Church, but doubtless also they would not have broken with it if this rupture had not afforded them the opportunity of secularizing its property and confiscating its revenues; and by proclaiming themselves, in their own principalities, the heads of their territorial Churches, they acquired a twofold authority and influence over their subjects. Such were the wholly mundane considerations which determined the conduct of these defenders of the new faith. Of all religious confessions, Lutheranism is the only one which, instead of exhorting its protectors to sacrifice their life and their fortune to it, offered itself to them as a profitable business transaction.

The Elector of Saxony and the Landgrave of Hesse first trod the path which others were soon to follow. In 1525 the Grand Master of the Teutonic Knights, Albert of Brandenburg, supported the Reformation so that he might secularize the Order and transform it, to his own advantage, into a lay principality. The Dukes of Anhalt, Luneburg, and Friesland, and the Margraves of Brandenburg and Bayreuth, also declared for the Gospel. After its beginnings in the heart of the bourgeoisie in the South of Germany, Lutheranism thus became, through the adhesion of the princes, the religion of the North. For the confession of the princes determined that of their subjects, just as formerly, during the Great Schism, it had determined their obedience to the Pope of Rome or the Pope of Avignon. The question of conscience was therefore treated as a question of discipline. One would hardly have expected this of a religion that proclaimed justification by faith and saw a priest in every Christian. There is surely a contradiction here, which can only be explained by the necessity, of which Luther was becoming more and more conscious, of safeguarding the future of his followers by the protection of the temporal power. As for the people, they allowed their religion to be imposed upon them by the temporal authority with a docility which sufficiently proves the truth of the old literary cliché concerning Germanic individualism. The most sacred convictions of the individual were at stake, yet there was no rebellion, no resistance. The German Catholics seem to have adopted Lutheranism in obedience to the commands of their princes as readily as the Franks of the 5th century renounced their gods when Clovis was baptized. We must conclude, no doubt, that their faith was not very fervent, but another reason for their attitude may be found in the complete stagnation of political life in Germany. No one dreamed of contesting the rights of the princes. The people were accustomed to obeying their commands; and nowhere in Germany were their prerogatives restricted by privileges, as in the Low Countries or in Spain. They were therefore allowed, without protest, to put themselves in the place of the bishops, appoint superintendents of the clergy, suppress the ecclesiastical foundations, close the monasteries, secularize their properties, and organize the schools: in short each of them, in his own principality, replaced the universal Church, subject to the Pope, by a territorial Church (*Landeskirche*) subject to the secular power.

Yet the Edict of Worms was not abrogated: Luther and his adherents were still under the ban of the Empire, and in the Low Countries Charles V was promulgating more and more sanguinary "bills" against them. But his war against Francis I kept him out of Germany and compelled him to bide his time. His brother Ferdinand, to whom he had ceded the hereditary domains of the House of Habsburg, and who represented him in his absence, was himself too occupied by the attacks of the Turks in the valley of the Danube, and the difficulty of getting the Hungarians to recognize him as the successor of their king Louis, who had perished in the battle of Mohacz (1526), to think of impeding the progress of the Reformation. It was therefore the French and the Turks who gave the ideal of the Reformation the time it needed to consolidate its position. In 1526 the Diet of Spire decreed that pending the arrival of the Emperor all could claim freedom of action in the matters judged by the Edict of Worms. When three years later Charles attempted to make it revoke this decision, five princes and certain of the cities immediately formulated a protest, and from that time onwards the partisans of the new faith were known by the name of Protestants.

It was not until 1530, at the Diet which Charles had convoked at Augsburg after his coronation, that the inevitable break occurred. The theological debate, in the course of which Melanchthon read aloud the "Augsburg confession," could only have the result of confirming each party in its own belief. It was too late to hope for a reconciliation which might have been possible ten years earlier. The Protestant princes quitted the assembly, of which the majority, encouraged by the Emperor, solemnly ratified the Edict of Worms, condemned all religious innovations, and ordained a general return to the Church.

Thereupon the Protestant princes made their preparations for a conflict which they judged inevitable. In 1531 they formed a confederation at Smalkalde, in association with a certain number of the cities. They were not unaware that the Emperor, still involved in the war with France, would give way if their attitude were sufficiently firm. In the following year, indeed, he proclaimed the Nuremberg Peace of Religion, forbidding any religious war until a Council, or the impending Diet, had assembled. This confession of impotence naturally increased the confidence of the Protestants. Philip of Hesse, the most turbulent among them, profited by the situation to do his utmost to undermine the power of the House of Habsburg. Supported by the subsidies of the King of France, he restored the Duke of Wurttemberg to the possession of his Duchy, which Ferdinand had united with Austria, and Protestantism was immediately introduced into the Duchy (1534). A little later the last lay prince in Northern Germany who had remained faithful to Catholicism was expelled from his domains (1542). Already the Archbishop of Cologne had expressed his intention of going over to the Reformation. The archbishoprics of Magdeburg and Halberstadt were secularized.

At last, having concluded peace with France at Crespy (1544), Charles V was able to attend to affairs in Germany. The Pope had decided to assemble a General Council, and thus to absolve himself from his Nuremberg engagements. The moment had come to attack the League of Smalkalde.

If in the case of the Protestant princes the interests of the faith had taken precedence over their personal interests, all would now have united in order to meet the attack upon them. But it proved that nothing was easier than to secure the neutrality or even the co-operation of many of them against their co-religionists by promises of aggrandisement. The Lutheran Maurice of Saxony won particular distinction as the ally of the Catholic sovereign in this war upon the Lutherans. The Spanish bands of the Duke of Alva did the rest. The battle of Muhlberg annihilated the League of Smalkalde (April 24th, 1547). The Electorate of Johann Friedrich of Saxony was given to Maurice. Philip of Hesse made his submission. In the same year Charles made the Diet of Augsburg accept an interim, which, pending the decision of the Council, established the religious position of the reformed estates.

It was not the triumph of Catholicism, it was the triumph of the Emperor that terrified the vanquished. They were much more afraid of falling under the yoke of Charles, and losing their princely autonomy, than of once more submitting to the jurisdiction of Rome. Maurice of Saxony, who was no more anxious than they were to see the Habsburgs supreme in the Empire, went over to their side. They were even more deficient in national than in religious idealism. Germans and Lutherans though they were, they did not hesitate to buy the aid of the Catholic King of France, Henri II, by surrendering to him a part of that which anywhere else than in the Empire would have been called the

Fatherland, or at least, the State. By the Treaty of Chambord (1552) they recognized his right to annex the three Western bishoprics of Metz, Toul and Verdun. Pretending to fear that Charles would impose "the Spanish servitude" upon them, they saluted Henri with the name of "the Protector of German liberty." As a matter of fact, of course, they regarded him only as the protector of their political particularism, which was so conveniently accentuated by their religious particularism.

Once again, then, Lutheranism was saved by France. Charles, obliged to hasten to the Lorraine frontier, left it in possession of the field, and never, until his abdication, had he an opportunity of returning to the attack. As Catholic as himself, his brother and successor Ferdinand, still menaced by the Turks in Hungary, hastened to pacify Germany. The Peace of Religion concluded by the Diet of Augsburg on September 25th, 1555, settled the problem. It acknowledged the *jus reformandi* of the princes—that is to say, their right to embrace the Reformation—whether they had already done so, or whether they wished to do so in the future. Subjects were required to profess the religion of their princes, except that they were allowed to emigrate after selling their possessions. An exception was established in favour of the ecclesiastical principalities, which were in any case to remain Catholic. There the prince's change of confession could only result in his abdication.

Thus conceived, the Peace of Augsburg appeared to be much less a peace of religion than a mere political compromise. It would have been impossible to show more absolute disrespect for liberty of conscience. By it the religion of the people was left to the arbitrary decision of the prince, as though it had been a mere matter of internal administration. The privilege of a free profession of belief was admitted only in the case of crowned heads; the masses had no privilege but that of obedience. This, of course, must be regarded as a consequence of the principle of the State religion, which, hitherto applied to the advantage of the Church alone, was now extended to Lutheranism. Intolerance was just as great on either side, and the new religion was no more inclined than the old to suffer dissidence in its midst. However, the Peace of Augsburg introduced no innovations. The state of affairs which it ratified was that which already existed in fact, as we have seen, in all the Reformed principalities.

But with the Peace, *de facto* became *de jure;* Protestantism obtained its place in the sun, and its future was assured. The majestic unity of Christendom was officially shattered. The Church, because it had not reformed itself with sufficient promptitude, had to watch the erection of a rival Church. Hitherto it had mercilessly crushed heresy, and henceforth it would be forced to suffer its presence. The fact was that the secular power, ceasing to fight for the Church, had itself gone over to the heretics. Not only did it recognize heresy as the religious truth, but it even profited by the heretics' need of its protection in order to impose upon it an ecclesiastical organization of which it was the master. With Lutheranism, in fact, it was a State Church that made its appearance, rather than a State religion. The State which appointed, trained and supervised the clergy was henceforth to benefit by the tremendous power which they exercised over men's souls. Through the clergy it would obtain that control over education which had hitherto evaded it. From the 17th century onwards it would make education compulsory, and its functions would be extended—we can divine with what benefit to itself—to the formation and control of ideas.

Obedience to the prince was inculcated as effectively by the pastors as obedience to the Pope by the Jesuits. The civil power benefited by the progress of the new faith in proportion as it gained empire over men's minds. Discipline, respect for authority, and belief in power were among the characteristics which were finally transmitted to modern Germany. In the last resort, it was the new faith that rendered possible such a State as Prussia: that is, a State in which the virtues of the subject, the official, and the soldier coincide, but where we shall look in vain for the virtues of the citizen.

2. *The Spread of the Reformation. Calvinism*

It would perhaps be impossible to find an example better calculated to enable us to appreciate at its exact value the rôle of the historic "hero" than that of Luther. However great a part he played in assuring the success of the Reformation, that success was chiefly due to the moral and political situation of Germany at the beginning of the 16th century. It was because the times had changed that the dispute with regard to indulgences almost immediately assumed the form of a religious revolution. Fifty years earlier the same man, with the same conviction, the same fire, the same eloquence, would have interested, at the very most, a few theologians in his own province, and history would have passed over him in silence, as it must have passed over so many of his precursors. And further, it may readily be shown that the fundamental ideas of Lutheranism itself were not really individual to Luther. In the Low Countries Wessel Gansfort, who died ignored in 1489, and whose works were not published until 1522, had already formulated the majority of these ideas; and we find them again in France among the members of the little circle that gathered, about 1515, round Lefèvre of Étaples. They were waiting, so to speak, on the threshold of the Church for the right moment to invade it. Luther brought his ideas into the foreground and then directed their development. He was a great moral "leader," but we know that leaders, though they are indispensable to revolutions, are not their authors.

Moreover, it is in the nature of revolutions to be contagious, and this was to prove no exception to the rule. However, the form which was so early assumed by Lutheranism in Germany, owing to its intimate alliance with the princes, was to prevent it, once it had inaugurated the Reformation, from directing the destiny of the latter, and retaining control over it. Wittenberg, which had seemed for a moment as though it would become the common centre of the followers of the Gospel, very soon disappointed their hopes. Closely subjected to the secular power, the *Landes-*

kirchen lacked the liberty of procedure and the independ-ence which would have been necessary for an effective external propaganda. They were too completely adapted to the political environment of Germany to possess the power of adapting themselves to other environments. Their nationalism, so to speak, made it impossible beforehand that they should exercise a universal influence. The only con-quest of Lutheranism was that of the Scandinavian coun-tries, and it was victorious there because the kings declared for it. In Sweden Gustavus Vasa, by agreement with the nobles, who coveted the ecclesiastical estates, imposed it on the people in 1527. The Catholic insurrections, which were fairly numerous until 1543, were severely repressed, and their only result was to consolidate the royal power, and to give the country a strong monarchical constitution which before long enabled it to intervene in the affairs of Europe. In Denmark Christian II (1503–1523) favoured the Reformation in order to enhance his authority by im-posing it on the Church. The nobles and the bourgeois of Copenhagen rallied to it, the former out of interest, and the latter because they were hostile to the clergy. Under Christian III, in 1536, the reformed faith was proclaimed the State religion. Norway and Iceland, then dependencies of Denmark, had hitherto preserved their autonomy. The king took advantage of the resistance which they offered to the Danish Church in order to deprive them of this autonomy. Lutheranism was imposed upon them by force. The Icelandic bishop Jan Areson died on the scaffold.

Lutheranism, then, was triumphant only where the princes or the kings supported it. Religious conviction had little to do with its propagation. In the beginning its really sincere and disinterested adepts appear to have been very few. Promulgated by authority and accepted in obedience, it progressed, if one may say so, by annexation. Conversion came afterwards, and slowly, just as a conquered people is slowly assimilated to the conquering nation.

The harmony between the monarchical government and Lutheranism was so complete that the Reformation, even among the German-speaking peoples, turned away from Lutheranism when it was not supported by the government. It is interesting to note that the democratic cantons of Switzerland, under the influence of Zwingli, gave themselves an independent religious constitution to which, in the beginning, a number of the free cities of Southern Germany adhered.

It is only too evident that in those countries whose princes remained faithful to Rome the Church had nothing to fear from the Lutherans. Respecting the sovereign power, they never for a moment thought of resisting it, nor even of disobeying it. They observed the stipulations of the "bills" promulgated against them, and abstained from preaching the faith in public; the only propaganda which they permitted themselves was that of martyrdom. It was soon realized that they were not very dangerous, and even in the Low Countries the Inquisition of Charles V, so ferocious in its treatment of the Anabaptists, prosecuted the Lutherans with a certain laxity.

It appears certain, however, that the religious disturbances in Germany were not without influence in respect of England's break with the Papacy. But this influence was only indirect, acting, if one may say so, as an encouragement to measures which in themselves had no relation to Lutheranism. Henry VIII, who prided himself on his theology, regarded Luther as a mere heretic, and attacked him in his *Assertio septem sacramentorum,* which earned him the title of "Defender of the Faith," conferred upon him by Leo X. He persecuted Tyndale, and placed an interdict on his translation of the Bible. The motives of his opposition to Rome, and of the constitution of the Anglican Church, were entirely external to the domain of faith. Neither Henry nor—above all—the English people felt the least inclination to reject the traditional beliefs of Catholicism. To attribute Henry's behaviour simply to his passion for Anne Boleyn is to confuse the occasion of events with their cause. The Pope's opposition to the king's divorce from Catherine of Aragon certainly induced him to have himself proclaimed by the assembly of the clergy "the chief protector of the church and clergy of England" (1531), in order that he might obtain the dissolution of his marriage (1533). But there matters might have stopped, and if they had done so England's situation, in respect of Rome, would certainly not have been irremediably compromised. The elevation of Thomas More to the post of Chancellor, after the condemnation of Cardinal Wolsey (1530), proves that the government had no thought of turning away from Catholicism. Parliament, which supported the king's cause with all its might, wished to profit by the situation and establish a national Church. But no one was dreaming of a schism, much less of a heresy. On accepting the post of Chancellor, More no doubt intended to lead the English Church, without commotion or violence, toward those moderate reforms of which the humanists had dreamed. Like Erasmus, he wished to preserve the traditional faith while purifying it. If he looked to the government to help him in this task, it was on the sole condition that it should act from motives as purely religious and disinterested as his own. But the government was then in the hands of a man who was devoting all his energies and his genius to making England an absolute monarchy. Formed in the school of the Italian politicians, Thomas Cromwell's only conception of the State was one in which the Crown was omnipotent. For him, as for Machiavelli, the Church was merely a factor of politics, but a factor whose importance was proportionate to its influence over men's minds. To place it at the service of the prince was therefore to invest him with a power and ascendancy which he derived from its sacred character. In 1534, profiting by the obedience of Parliament and its hostility to the court of Rome, he caused it to pass the "Act of Supremacy," acknowledging the king as the sole and supreme earthly head of the Church of England, with all the honours, jurisdictions, authorities, immunities, profits and advantages pertaining to this dignity, and with full power to examine, redress, repress, reform and amend all errors, heresies, abuses, disorders and enormities which might be or were capable of being legally reformed by any spiritual authority or jurisdiction. In the following year the king appointed Cromwell his vicar-general in ecclesiastical affairs. The English Church was thus laid prostrate at the foot of the throne, and henceforth the sovereign who sat upon this throne occupied, for that Church, the place which had been filled by the Pope. This was schism, but it was not yet heresy; yet it was not long before the schism gave rise to heresy.

It had not taken Cromwell long to make the Church a mere instrument of the monarchy. The Chapters were required to raise to the episcopate only persons indicated by the king. What is more, preachers were even required to obtain a royal licence. At the same time, all the monasteries were subjected to a "visit," the result of which was a foregone conclusion. The all-powerful minister had resolved to confiscate their property, partly for the benefit of the Crown, and partly for that of the nobles, in order that the lords and gentlemen of the country might henceforth be unanimous in favour of maintaining the new ecclesiastical constitution, just as the purchasers of national properties in the France of the Revolution were in favour of the maintenance of the Revolutionary régime. Since the nobles were predominant in Parliament, it was not difficult to secure the passage of the Acts which from 1536 to 1545 decreed the suppression of all the monastic communities in the country. The "Articles of Religion" which the assembly of the clergy accepted without protest in 1536 cut the last tie which, by community of faith, still bound the English Church to the Catholic Church. As the bases of dogma they accepted only the Bible and the three first Oecumenical Councils ("the Bible and the Three Creeds"), retaining as sacraments only Baptism, Penitence and the Eucharist. No modification was introduced either in the ritual or in the organization of the hierarchy. A position was adopted which was half-way between Protestantism and Catholicism, and apparently very like that toward which the humanists had wished insensibly to lead the Papacy.

Yet the best and most celebrated of these humanists, Thomas More, had resigned his position as Chancellor as early as 1532, and two years later his head had fallen on the scaffold. The most pious and enlightened spirits among those who aspired to reform the Church were revolted by the violence which was imposed upon it. The government appeared to them, and actually was, a moral despotism imposed by terror. Cromwell's police carried on a veritable inquisition, and victims, chosen for the sake of example among the most illustrious men in the country, were pitilessly sacrificed to the end envisaged by the terrible minister. In vain did the nobles of the North rebel in the name of Catholicism and liberty; their efforts resulted merely in the sacrifice of fresh victims.

The severity displayed against the Catholics was in singular contrast to the fluctuations of the king in questions of dogma. After 1536, alarmed by the manifestations of a not very numerous group of Protestants, he obviously sought to return to tradition, and the six Articles which were submitted for the approval of the clergy in 1539 marked a fairly definite revulsion in the direction of the Catholic faith. The sensational fall and death of Cromwell in 1540 were explained in part by his attempts to draw England into an alliance with the Lutherans of Germany. At one moment it seems that Henry VIII actually had thoughts of reconciliation with Rome, or at all events that he was in favour of the idea of reforming the Church by means of a General Council. However, the attitude of the Council of Trent made him abandon such notions. At the time of his death in 1547 he was thinking of concluding a "Christian League" with the German princes, and of replacing the Mass by a simple Communion service.

After him there was chaos. The minority of Edward VI (1547–1553) enabled the "Protectors"—the Duke of Somerset, followed by the Earl of Warwick—openly to favour Protestantism. The Mass was suppressed, images were removed from the churches, the celibacy of the priests was abolished, and a Prayer Book was adopted, together with new articles of religion, constituting the doctrine to which the Anglican Church has remained faithful to this day. All these things were imposed by violence, in the midst of a veritable religious anarchy. While the exasperated Catholics were inciting to revolt on every side, a new party had lately made its appearance, which demanded a radical reform of the faith and of the Church. Calvinism had entered upon the scene.

A generation separated the birth of Calvin (1509) from that of Luther. The religious crisis which no one could have foreseen at the moment when the German reformer began his career was the object of general concern when the French reformer entered the arena. Luther, like all his contemporaries, had been born into the world of scholastic theology. Calvin grew up in an environment which was passionately concerned with the questions of the authority of the Scriptures, grace, justification by faith, the validity of the Sacraments, the celibacy of the priesthood, and the primacy of the See of Rome. Luther was impelled by his conscience and by events to leave the Church in which he had vainly sought spiritual peace. Calvin, as a matter of fact, had never belonged to this Church. It cost him no effort to break with it; from the very first he had regarded it as a monument of error and imposture. He was spared the intimate tragedies of the conscience. He had no need to seek for God. He was positive that he had God's Word in the Bible, and that it was to be found only in the Bible. He was to devote his life to arriving at an understanding of the Bible, and imposing upon other men the teachings which he discovered in it. His heart and his emotions played no part in his religion. In him there was no trace of the Lutheran mysticism. Reflection, reasoning, logic—these were his means of conviction.

No doubt this was largely to be explained by his personality. Yet we should consider that what the Reformation needed, after its first outbreak, was a definite, rigid and coherent doctrine; a body of dogma, so to speak, to oppose to the old dogma, and a Church to contend against the old Church. And it had all the more need of this inasmuch as Catholicism was healing its wounds, was drawing new energies from the Council of Trent, and was preparing a powerful counter-attack, which the Reformation could certainly never have resisted without the aid of Calvinism.

There was no trace in Calvin of the pugnacious and impulsive character of Luther. It was by intellectual labour that he satisfied his religious cravings, and it is almost certain that without the events that determined his destiny he would have influenced the world only by his pen. He had arrived at adult years when the French monarchy was induced to assume a definite attitude in respect of the Reformation.

Just at first it had apparently felt the same sympathy for the Reformation as for the Renaissance; indeed, it seems to have confused the two. Francis I felt for Erasmus, to whom he offered a chair in the Collège de France, an esteem which disquieted and exasperated the theologians of the Sorbonne. Louis de Berquin, one of the disciples of Lefèvre of Étaples, preached at his court. His sister, Marguerite, professed a very liberal Christianity, marked by Platonic tendencies, and an evangelical mysticism which was closely akin to Protestantism. She openly protected the innovators, and it was in her little Kingdom of Navarre that Lefèvre peacefully spent the last years of his career. Diane de Poitiers herself was said to have a tenderness for the Lutheran doctrines. And it is certain that the king continued for some time to restrain the University and the Parlements from manifesting their zeal against heresy. But it is equally certain that he never dreamed and never could have dreamed of embroiling himself with the Papacy. The Concordat concluded with Leo X in 1516 assured him of an influence over the French Church (since it acknowledged his right to appoint bishops and abbots of monasteries, and imposed restrictions in respect of appeals to the court of Rome) which was so advantageous that he could not have been tempted to renounce it. Since the reign of Philip the Fair the Curia, in a spirit of prudence or of gratitude, had always abstained from restricting the exercise of the prerogatives which the Crown had arrogated to itself in respect of the clergy. The government had no reason to complain of the existing situation. None of the motives which impelled the German princes, or Henry VIII, to break with Rome, and replace the Roman Church by national Churches, had any application to France. The political interests which elsewhere did so much to favour the cause of the Reformation here impelled the government to resist it. It was therefore bound to happen, and it did happen, that the king was unable to prolong his toleration for a movement to which Rome was becoming more and more openly hostile, without incurring, in the eyes of the nation, the reproach of being its accomplice. From 1530 or there-abouts he ceased to resist the demands of those who wished to persecute the heretics, and although he did not go to the length of establishing a State Inquisition on the model of that of Spain, he allowed the religious and civil authorities to deal with heresy as they thought fit, the result being a ferocious persecution.

Calvin was twenty-five years of age when this persecution, in 1534, drove him into exile. The Low Countries, which had already been, and were so often to be in the future, a place of refuge for French exiles, were then inaccessible, owing to the laws of Charles V against heresy, so that he turned to Romansh Switzerland. For some years Geneva had been in a state of political and religious ferment. In order to resist their hereditary enemy, the Duke of Savoy, the burgesses had solicited and obtained the aid of Berne. In 1526 the Eiguenots (*Eidgenossen*) had driven the partisans of the Duke out of the city, but Berne was Protestant, and the alliance concluded with Berne quickly familiarized the Genevese with the Reformation. A French refugee, Guillaume Farel, conducted an impassioned propaganda in favour of the Reformation. As elsewhere, the bewildered Church offered little resistance, or none, and the new faith, favoured by the love of autonomy and the hatred of Savoy, whose partisans were blockading the city (1534–1535), was quickly triumphant. On August 10th, 1535, the Mass was discontinued by order of the Council; the people began to break the religious images, and the greater part of the clergy took to flight. The victory won over Savoy in the following year made Geneva an independent Republic. Thus a new political régime was introduced simultaneously with a new religious faith, and thenceforth the two were to remain indissolubly united.

It was while these things were happening that Calvin, on passing through Geneva, was detained by Farel. He was already a man who knew his mind; he had just published, in 1536, his *Institution Chrétienne*. Here was an opportunity to apply its principles in this young republic, still thrilled by its victory. Covered in the rear by the Swiss cantons, protected by the policy of France against the

repetition of the Savoyard offensive, Geneva had no reason
to fear for its independence, and could safely institute
within its walls the theocratic government which was to be
the most intensive, or perhaps one should say the only,
application of pure Calvinism, and which was to contribute
so powerfully to the diffusion of the latter in the outer
world. For Calvinism Geneva was the "Holy City" which
the Anabaptists ten years earlier, in their mystical dreams,
had hoped for a moment to establish in Münster.

Everyone knows that the cardinal dogma of Calvinism is
that of predestination. Salvation depends solely upon the
Divine will, and by that Divine will the elect are chosen
from all eternity. The Church consists in the union of these
elect. But as it is impossible to know if one has been elected
by grace, it is each man's duty, so to speak, to prove it to
himself by devoting himself with all his energies to the
service of God. The Calvinist predestination, instead of leading to quietism, accordingly incites to activity. It does this
all the more so inasmuch as God is not conceived as a
father but as a master, whose word, revealed by Scripture,
is the supreme law. One's whole life must be subject to this
law, and the State is legitimate only in so far as it respects
the law. While Luther confined religion to the domain of
the conscience, and left the temporal power to organize the
Church and follow its political interests after its own fashion, Calvin submitted all human actions to theology. He
was as universal, as absolute as the Catholic Church. I
would even say that he was more universal and absolute.
For, after all, the Church acknowledged that the "temporal
sword" had its own mission, above and beyond the mission
which had developed upon the "spiritual sword." The one
governed men's bodies, the other their souls, and the first
was subordinated to the second only in questions of faith.
For Calvin, on the contrary, the State, being willed by God,
had to be transformed into an instrument of the Divine will.
It was not subordinated to the clergy, in the sense that it
existed independently of the clergy, and did not derive its
power from them, but it acted in conformity with the end
for which it was created only by associating itself intimately
with the clergy, in order that the mandates of the Most

High should triumph here on earth, and in order to combat all that opposed these mandates or insulted His majesty: vice, heresy, idolatry, and more especially the Roman idolatry, the most abominable of all. Such a system of ideas, if it is fully applied, inevitably leads to theocracy, and under the inspiration of Calvin the government of Geneva did actually constitute a theocracy.

The Consistory, an assembly of pastors and laymen, exercised, so to speak, the moral superintendence of the Republic. It did not govern, but it supervised and controlled the councillors of the Commune, and kept them in the strait way. The "ecclesiastical ordinances" were applied by the civil authorities. The death-penalty, torture, banishment and imprisonment were imposed, according to the gravity of the offence, but always with exemplary severity, upon contraventions of the ecclesiastical or moral regulations. Attendance at the temple was obligatory; adultery was a capital crime; the singing of a profane song was punished by the imposition of public penitence. Each person's conduct was subjected to a permanent inquisition which pursued him even into his dwelling, and extended to the most trivial actions of his private life. Heresy was mercilessly repressed; it is enough to recall the martyrdom of Michael Servetus in 1553.

And while it became the pattern of the Christian State, Geneva also became an ardent centre of religious propaganda. The French refugees who flocked thither during the persecutions of the reign of Henri II provided Calvin with the first disciples who were truly inspired with his spirit. The most celebrated of them, Théodore de Bèze, was for him what Melanchthon was for Luther, the organizer of that education without which no Church was possible. In 1559 the Academy of Geneva was founded, whose essential purpose was the training of "ministers," or, one might almost say, of Calvinistic missionaries. For the training which they received there prepared them above all for the propagation of the doctrine. For Calvin the Apostolate, which Luther completely neglected, was the indispensable condition of the propagation of the faith. He would not have rejected the collaboration of the princes, but he came too late to be able to count on them. They had already taken up their positions. In Germany only the Elector Palatine adopted Calvinism, and therefore imposed it upon his subjects. Outside Germany the Continental monarchs had everywhere declared for Rome, and the King of England had recently imposed a national Church upon his subjects. Therefore, in order to ensure that the Word of God should triumph, it was necessary to prepare for battle. Everywhere the State was hostile to the new faith. More: the Roman Church, bewildered for a moment by the sudden attack, which had taken it by surprise, had recovered its wits, and was showing itself ready not only to defend itself but to reconquer the positions which it had lost. Paul III in 1542 revived the Inquisition, and in 1545 he convoked the Council of Trent. Already the young Society of Jesus was beginning to wage war upon heresy, to rouse men's souls from their lethargy, to stimulate Catholic piety, and to found the first Jesuit colleges. The situation was therefore infinitely more difficult for Calvin than it had been for Luther, who had been able to take the enemy by surprise; Calvin found him everywhere on the alert and fully armed. In order to undertake a successful offensive against such an enemy, he would have to employ all the resources of organization and to proceed with unfailing energy.

For that matter, although the Catholic defence was in a very much better position about the middle of the 16th century than it had been in 1517, the Protestant offensive was also more powerful. The religious problem now appeared everywhere with formidable clarity. The convulsions of the Peasant War and the Anabaptist risings, which had first tended to obscure it by their social demands, had ceased. On the other hand, it was no longer possible to hope for a reconciliation with the Church. It was therefore necessary to make the choice between the old faith and the new. Both were laying claim to men's souls, both were appealing to the conscience, and by that very fact were compelling men to undertake an examination of the conscience which in many persons led to what some called an apostasy and others a conversion. The religion of habit which had enabled so many to drowse through the 15th century was a thing of the past. Now it was necessary to take sides in a debate in which the question of eternal salvation was at stake, and every man, according to his decision, had to enter one of the two opposing camps and prepare for battle. Personal conviction, as we have seen, played a very secondary part in the authoritarian diffusion of Lutheranism; it played an enormous part in the diffusion of Calvinism, which could hope to conquer only through the loyalty of its adherents.

It was greatly helped by the social constitution of the 16th century. Capitalism, which was hampered by the restrictions imposed by the Church upon trafficking in money and speculation, must surely have benefited it by procuring the unconscious adhesion of great numbers of commercial adventurers and men of business. It must not be forgotten that Calvin acknowledged the lawfulness of lending money at interest, which Luther, faithful in this respect, as in so many others, to the traditional theology, had still condemned. The first resources placed at the disposal of the new Church to cover its costs of propaganda, if we may employ a very modern expression, which corresponds perfectly with the nature of the case, were advanced by the successful merchants. In Antwerp, about 1550, there were already a considerable number of new converts among the frequenters of the Bourse. The Catholics complained that they took advantage of their power over their workers to compel them, at least in appearance, to adhere to their faith. The nobles also, from the very first, provided a numerous contingent of adepts. This is readily understood if we reflect that they were now, for the most part, men of some education, and that under the influence of the humanists the foundations of the ancient faith had been undermined, while that influence had given rise to a taste for discussion and a love of innovations. Moreover, the French-speaking nobles had read the *Institution Chrétienne* as eagerly as the German nobles had read Luther's pamphlets. And we can imagine the impression which the impassioned logic of this little book must have produced upon minds which were only too ready, thanks to the perusal of Rabelais, whose work had appeared almost at the same time, to deride the Church, and to regard it as an obsolete institution. Lastly, the industrial proletariat, cherishing a rancorous memory of the persecution which had not wholly stifled the Anabaptist faith, furnished predestined recruits to the new faith, though in the beginning, at all events, these recruits were more remarkable for their turbulence than for their sincerity.

The democratic and authoritarian constitution which Calvin had given his Church was an astonishing aid to its progress. In effect, it summoned the faithful to collaborate directly in the organization of each religious community. While the minister was the spiritual head of the community, the consistory, which functioned at his side, was recruited among the laymen. The devotion of each believer was constantly kept on the alert in this little group of the elect, surrounded by enemies and able to rely only upon its own resources. The zeal, conviction and courage, and even the fanaticism of the ministers, assured them, wherever they went, of a contagious ascendancy. And their numbers, no less than their energy, attested to the vigour of the young Church. In the 1540's they were already to be met with in all parts of France, in the Low Countries, and in England. Trained at first at Geneva, but presently at Lausanne, Strasbourg and Heidelberg, they displayed all the characteristics of a regular clergy, but a clergy as active and as learned as the Catholic clergy was generally ignorant and apathetic. Educated, acting in concert, and keeping in touch with one another, they devoted themselves body and soul to their task. They made their way into the cities in disguise or under borrowed names, preaching the Gospel in the evenings behind closed doors in a hostelry, or a courtyard, or some remote corner of the suburb. Sometimes they exercised their mission at a meal or banquet in a friendly house, seeking to convert the guests by their edifying conversation, and distributing books and canticles to them. If they were surprised, they could expect no mercy, and they knew it. But their voices, which rose even amidst the flames and the smoke of the pyre, propagated to the last the faith for which they died. Before long the dismayed executioners gagged their victims before they led them out to die. We must go back to the origins of Christianity to find such constancy and such courage. And just as in those early days, the last moments of these martyrs were piously related in popular narratives, which, diffused through the printing-press, immediately became the most efficacious means of propaganda. On the other hand, by hunting down the faithful the Catholic persecution spread far and wide the flame which it was seeking to extinguish. In France, in the Low Countries, the refugees carried the faith from province to province. Others emigrated to England and Scotland. In the East of Europe, Poland and Hungary were visited by the ministers, and before long reformed communities were established in nearly all the cities.

Thus Calvinism was distinguished by the international character of its diffusion. The diversity of languages, manners, and political régimes was no obstacle to its progress. The ecclesiastical organization at its disposal gave it a penetrative force and an independence of conduct which were far to seek in Lutheranism. Instead of submitting, like the latter, to the tutelage of princes, it relied only upon itself. It did not ask for protection, nor did it avoid conflict. Wherever it appeared it loudly affirmed its dogmas and boldly took the offensive, and its radicalism tolerated no compromise. Between it and the sectators of the "Roman idolatry," the followers of the "Whore of Babylon," no reconciliation was possible. It was necessary to be for the new faith or against it. To the Catholic intolerance it responded by an equal intolerance. To persecution it presently replied by rebellion, and the violence of its conduct, the audacity of its provocations, and the extreme and bitter quality of its polemics angered and wounded even those who in their religious lukewarmness would not have opposed it. The quarrel which it provoked assumed a personal character for every protagonist; it fomented hatred in men's hearts, and was finally to end in civil war.

CHAPTER III

The European States from the Middle of the Fifteenth to the Middle of the Sixteenth Century

1. *International Politics*

The great social transformations, the great crises of thought, do not of necessity coincide with the modifications of international politics. The Renaissance, the Reformation, and Capitalism undoubtedly exerted a profound influence over the life of the various States; but they did not in any way influence the wholly novel condition which, since the middle of the 15th century, had determined the mutual situation of these States. It was in consequence of the hazard and interaction of events that Europe, just when it was passing through so many intellectual, religious and economic changes, was also disturbed by a radical transformation of the system of forces which had been in mutual opposition since the beginning of the 13th century. The fifty years which had elapsed since the end of the Hundred Years' War had sufficed to revolutionize the traditional order of politics. The conclusion of the great struggle between France and England merely confronted the European community with unexpected problems. While in the West new powers had made their appearance—the Burgundian State on the shores of the North Sea, and to the south of the Pyrenees the Spanish State, henceforth including Castile and Aragon in a single monarchical bloc—in the

East the Turkish Empire was threatening the Christian world with a new Islamic invasion. Thus hazard, that mysterious force which continually delights in frustrating the calculations of men, ordained that just as a critical period of the internal history of the Continent was beginning Europe was compelled to stem the external danger.

The Turkish invasion was undoubtedly the greatest misfortune to afflict Europe since the end of the Roman Empire. Wherever the invaders advanced they brought with them economic ruin and moral decadence. All those peoples which were subjected to the Turkish yoke—Bulgars, Serbs, Rumanians, Albanians, and Greeks—relapsed into a state verging upon barbarism, from which they never emerged until the beginning of the 19th century. The Germans, who had invaded the West in the 5th century, were no less brutal than the Turks. But they became assimilated to the superior civilization of the West; converted to Christianity, they were presently absorbed by the conquered population. Between the Islamism of the Turks, on the contrary, and the Christianity of their subjects no reconciliation was possible. The difference between the two religions rendered them mutually impenetrable and perpetuated the abominable system of a State founded only on force, supporting itself only by exploitation and existing only at the price of maintaining, in the hearts of the conquerors, contempt for the vanquished, and in the hearts of the vanquished hatred of the conqueror. With the exception of a portion of the Albanian people, not one of the nations subjected to the Sultan was converted to Islam, and for that matter the Turks made no effort to convert them. From the religious standpoint it glorified Allah sufficiently that His faithful should reign over the *giaours;* from the political standpoint all that was necessary in order to maintain the State, which never rose above the primitive conception of a pure military régime, was to reduce the Christians to the status of taxpayers. Thus their religion, by depriving them of all rights of whatever kind, helped to ensure their servitude. From the reign of Selim I (1512–1520) even their flesh and blood was subjected to taxation. Periodically the most beautiful children were torn from their parents, the girls to serve men's pleasure, and the boys to be enrolled in the corps of janissaries, having first been initiated into Islam.

Europe, which had been powerless to prevent the capture of Constantinople, was equally powerless to check the advance of the Turkish power across the Continent and along the shores of the Mediterranean. The Popes endeavoured in vain to revive the spirit of the Crusades. Their propaganda—of which the monk Campistan was the most remarkable agent—certainly succeeded in raising bands of volunteers, half enthusiasts, half adventurers, but what was needed was the co-operation of the various States in the common defence, and such co-operation was impossible. Historians who attribute this lack of co-operation to the alleged national egoism of the modern State forget that the States of the Middle Ages never put up a common defence against the Musulmans. The universal character of the Crusades was due to the participation of the peoples, not of the governments. Their failure, against adversaries far less formidable than the Turks, proves that nothing could really have been expected of them, even had not the moral and social conditions which favoured them disappeared for ever. The only means of successfully resisting the Turkish offensive would have been a general European league combining the financial and military resources of the Continent for a period of several years. The coalitions of the 17th century against Louis XIV, of the 19th century against Napoleon, and of 1914 against Germany, give one a notion of the kind of effort that might have succeeded. But the States of the 15th century were materially incapable of such an effort. Moreover, to the most powerful of these States the peril appeared merely as a menace too remote to call for their intervention. They left the burden of the conflict to those who were directly involved.

Unfortunately, the immediate neighbours of the Turks were in no condition to hold their own against them. Nothing could be more lamentable than the incapacity which they exhibited, and which rendered useless so many instances of heroic devotion. By uniting their forces, the Republic of Venice, the Habsburgs of Austria, and the

kings of Bohemia, Hungary, and Poland could have opposed an effective barrier to the enemy. But instead of doing this, each State allowed itself to be guided by its ambitions or its interests; they never acted with one common
accord. Venice resigned herself to making desultory attempts, prosecuted without vigour, which ended in the disastrous peace treaties of 1479 and 1502, which of all her
magnificent domain of the Levantine ports and islands left
her only Candia. As for the Habsburgs, who with a little
magnanimity might have become the saviours or at least
the champions of Europe, they never contrived to raise
themselves above the level of a greedy and hesitating
policy. Frederick III (1440–1493) and Maximilian (1493–
1519) prudently remained far from the line of battle, en-
visaging events whose importance they were capable of
understanding solely from the dynastic standpoint, watching for an opportunity of appropriating the crowns of Bohemia and Hungary, the supreme end of the equivocal intrigues of their ancestors.

After the death of Albert of Austria in 1439 his widow,
supported by Frederick III, had endeavoured to preserve
Bohemia and Hungary for her son Ladislas, a posthumous
child whose long minority promised to be as disastrous to
the peoples as it was advantageous to the plans of the
Habsburgs. The Hungarian nobles thwarted this machina-
tion by offering the crown to the King of Poland, Vladislav III, while the Czechs acknowledged George Podebrad
as their regent. Vladislav perished in 1444, sword in hand,
at the battle of Varna, fighting against the Turks. Ladislas
was then five years of age. The Hungarian magnates requested Frederick III to surrender him to them, but he
refused, whereupon they entrusted the government and the
defence of the country to the most valiant among them,
Hunyadi Janos. Hunyadi died in 1456 after saving Belgrade, and Ladislas himself died in the following year,
whereupon Frederick III hastened to claim the crowns of
Bohemia and Hungary for his house. However, being as
cowardly as he was greedy, he did not venture to take active steps, and the Czechs, ignoring his pretensions, elected
George Podebrad king, while the Hungarians chose Mat-

thias Corvinus, the son of Hunyadi (1458). This son of a
hero was a politician. Instead of taking up arms against the
Turks—who seized Serbia in 1458, overcame the resistance
of Albania (1479) after the death of George Castriotes
(Scanderbeg, 1468), took possession of Bosnia and Herze-
govina, and compelled the principalities of Moldavia and
Wallachia to pay them tribute—he preferred to work for
his own aggrandisement, to the detriment of his Christian
neighbours. When the Pope excommunicated George Podebrad, who was supported by the Czech Utraquists,
and pronounced his deposition, Matthias took this opportunity of attacking him and having himself proclaimed
King of Bohemia (1469) by the Catholics. He then turned
against Frederick III, who was cunningly seeking to undermine his power, marched against him, and expelled him
from Vienna in 1485. He died five years later; Hungary
owed to him a brief period of glory and some barren successes. He left no heir, and the Habsburgs, always on the
alert, immediately claimed the succession. It escaped them
again, but their patience was unwearied. The Hungarians
acknowledged as their king the Polish Prince Vladislas, to
whom the Czech Utraquists had already given the crown
during the lifetime of Matthias Corvinus. Maximilian of
Austria concluded with him one of those matrimonial
treaties which the House of Austria excelled in devising.
A double marriage united Louis, the son of Vladislas, to
Maria of Austria, the granddaughter of Maximilian, and
Ferdinand, his grandson, to Anne of Hungary. After the
death of his father (1516) young Louis II had to march
against Soliman II, who, having completed the conquest of
the Balkan peninsula, was now turning towards Hungary,
and had just entered Belgrade (1521). He was defeated
and killed at Mohacz in 1526. This battle was a magnificent triumph for Austria, for it gave her the long-coveted
crowns of Bohemia and Hungary, at last assured to her by
the victory of the Turks. For the rest, Ferdinand contented
himself with inheriting the rights of his brother-in-law.
This would have been the moment to summon Germany to
the defence of her menaced frontiers. But Germany, in the
throes of the crisis of the Reformation, was more incapable

than ever of any collective effort. The Protestant princes regarded the Turks as providential allies; and the Catholic princes had no intention, by fighting against them, of assuring the Habsburgs of an augmentation of their power, which already filled them with jealousy. Soliman therefore advanced without difficulty as far as Pest, and in 1529 he reached the walls of Vienna, which the inclement weather and sickness in his army prevented him from capturing. However, he retained all Hungary as far as the Enns, and Ferdinand, who was compelled to conclude a peace with him in 1547, undertook to pay him tribute. Hungary was divided into *sandjaks*, with the exception of a narrow strip of territory in the north and the west and some portions of Croatia and Slavonia which remained in the possession of the Habsburgs. Transylvania and the eastern portion of the country formed separate principalities under vassalage to the Porte. Soliman himself transformed the principal church of Pest into a mosque.

Under his reign (1520–1556) the Turkish Empire covered the largest area which it was ever to attain. The shores of the Black Sea had already been occupied under Selim I (1512–1520), and the Tartars of the Crimea were subjected to tribute. Rhodes, in the Aegean, was conquered in 1522, and the Knights of St. John, who had heroically defended it, removed to Malta, whither Charles V had summoned them, and which they were to retain until the French Revolution.[1] Mesopotamia, Syria, and Egypt were annexed (1512–1520). Algiers and Tunis, conquered by the renegade corsair Barbarossa, became the outposts of the Grand Seigneur in the eastern Mediterranean. Thus, in the middle of the 16th century the situation of Islam in Europe was far more formidable than it had ever been in the period of its great expansion. But this second advance was to share the fate of the first. The moment of its apogee was also the moment of its decline. But the Turks did not, like the Musulmans in the 10th and 11th centuries, atone by their civilization for their subsequent loss of martial vigour. Bar-

[1] Malta was captured by Napoleon in 1798, when he was on his way to Egypt.

barians they were and Barbarians they remained. In my opinion, however, their barbarism had nothing to do with their race. Whether in Asia or in Europe, the Turks came into contact only with the decadent civilizations of the Caliphate of Baghdad and the Byzantine Empire, which were too feeble to impose themselves upon their conquerors. On the other hand, the purely military organization of the State prevented any social progress. But as such a State is unproductive, it can maintain itself only by conquest. It becomes exhausted as soon as war ceases to provide it with the resources which it is incapable of producing for itself. It must be for ever enlarging itself, for ever subduing fresh tributaries in order to provide for its upkeep. Financial disorder and fiscal oppression, with all their political, economic, and moral consequences, made their appearance in Turkey directly her expansion was checked. It is true that she still exhibited momentary outbursts of energy. But regarded as a whole, the history of Turkey after the death of Soliman II was that of an incurable decline. She would have disappeared long ago as a State if the European powers had not safeguarded her existence, because they could not agree upon the partition of the spoils. The admirable situation which she occupied on the Straits gave her an international importance which saved her from the fate of Poland. Europe tolerated the crime committed against a Christian people; she has not yet succeeded in expelling the Musulman invaders, whose presence upon European soil is a misfortune and a disgrace to civilization. It is astonishing to think that the industrious and inoffensive Moors of the Kingdom of Granada were driven back into Africa at the end of the 15th century and that the Turks are still in Constantinople in 1918. Being unable to expel them, we have gradually become accustomed to their presence, and without ceasing to regard them as intruders we have ended by giving them a place in the European community. More, we have even sought to involve them in our quarrels. Did not Francis I seek the help of Soliman II against Charles V?

This alliance, so monstrous at first sight, was only one of

the consequences of the political disorder of Christianity since the middle of the 15th century.

The conclusion of the Hundred Years' War had left France and England in very different situations. In England the war between the Houses of York and Lancaster broke out almost immediately. While the nobles were slaughtering one another on the battlefield, and while, by means of abominable crimes and treacheries and murders, Edward IV, Henry VI, Edward V, and Richard III ascended the throne or were hurled from it, the country had to renounce all active intervention in the affairs of the Continent, until peace was restored with the advent of the first Tudor, Henry VII, in 1485. France, on the contrary, enjoyed a restorative period of tranquillity under Charles VII. One might have concluded that she was exhausted by the terrible crisis from which she had emerged. But in a few years all traces of the crisis had disappeared. For the first time the nation gave proof of the resilience and the nervous energy which it has always displayed after the great catastrophes of its history. When Louis XII succeeded to his father in 1461 France was incontestably once more the greatest power in the West. But the international position in which she found herself was entirely novel, and it was radically to modify the direction of her foreign policy.

One may say that since the end of the 12th century her foreign policy had always been determined by the vital necessity of expelling England from the soil of France. Her interventions in the Low Countries, like her relations with the Empire, or with the Iberian peninsula, were referable, almost without exception, to this great struggle. England was not only the essential enemy: she was the only enemy of France. She had no enemies on the Continent, or only such as were incited against her by England: Otto IV in Germany, and the Counts of Flanders in the 13th and 14th centuries. Apart from this, she had no enemies in the rear, and could devote all her energies to confronting the enemy in the West. Now, directly the Hundred Years' War came to an end this state of affairs ceased for good. There was an end of the ancient Continental security of the kingdom. Henceforth she would have to fight upon her land frontiers, and by a complete reversal of tradition England would never attack her in future except by entering into a coalition with the European enemies of France.

The formation of the Burgundian State marked the beginning of this new orientation of political history. We have seen already how Philip the Fair took advantage of his participation in the Hundred Years' War in order to group under his power, in addition to Flanders and Artois, the greater number of those territorial principalities which were nominally dependencies of the Empire, and which extended from the Ardennes to the Zuyder Zee: the Duchies of Luxemburg and Brabant, with the Counties of Hainaut, Namur, Holland, and Zeeland.

To this amalgam of possessions Charles VII, on concluding the Peace of Arras with the Duke (1435), annexed the cities of the Somme. The Duchy and the Franche Comté of Burgundy were added to this magnificent domain, from which they were divided only by Lorraine and Alsace, which they were threatening to absorb. Thus, in a few years there was constituted on the north and the east of the kingdom a new power which occupied approximately the place formerly occupied, in the 9th and 10th centuries, by the ephemeral Kingdom of Lotharingia. The Low Countries emerged from their feudal subdivision to unite themselves, under a single dynasty, in a single State, the common ancestor of Belgium and modern Holland. A fertile soil; an incomparable geographical situation on the shores of the North Sea; deep rivers and excellent harbours; a laborious population, denser than in any other part of Europe to the north of the Alps; flourishing cities, famed throughout the world for their cloth industry or their commerce, one of which, Bruges, had been for three centuries the great international port of the Occident, while another, Antwerp, was entering upon an even more astonishing period of prosperity, since the enterprising navigation of Holland and Zeeland was beginning to replace that of the declining Hansa; and lastly, in the agricultural regions of the Walloon country a robust and warlike people—all these things seemed to be united as by a miracle to make the young State a "promised land," and to confer upon its sovereigns the extraordinary prestige which surrounded Philip the Good and his son Charles the Bold. But the wealthier and more powerful this new neighbour became, the more dangerous it could become to France. Whether it would or not, it was a permanent menace. From Amiens its troops, in two days' march, could appear under the walls of Paris; and above all, owing to its situation it imposed itself upon England as a natural ally. There was reason to fear that in the first war it would play once more the part which the Counts of Flanders had so often played in the Middle Ages, but this time with tenfold effect. In short, it seemed as though France had expelled the English from her soil only to find herself exposed on her northern frontier, which was everywhere open and without natural defences, to the aggression of Burgundy.

The conflict, already latent between Charles VII and Philip the Good, was destined to break out under their successors, Louis XI and Charles the Bold. The crisis was violent but brief. The civil disorders in England prevented her from intervening at the opportune moment. In the beginning Charles was able to count only on the Duc de Berry, the king's brother, the Duke of Brittany, the last great vassal of the Crown, and a few seigneurs who were leagued with him on behalf of the "public welfare" of the kingdom. But the allies did not agree among themselves. After his defeat at Montléry the king at once entered into negotiations, and had no trouble in detaching them from one another. He now faced the Burgundian only, and was able to devote himself entirely to his destruction. He excited the Liégeois against him, to disown them in the moment of danger, and intrigued in Germany, England, Switzerland, Savoy, Milan, and Venice subtly and imperceptibly, gradually entangling his impetuous adversary in the meshes of the most cunning diplomacy. Charles and Louis XI have often been described as the last representative of the feudal system grappling with the first modern sovereign. Nothing could be more inaccurate. Apart from the difference of their personal genius, the king being as prudent and as skilful as the Duke was rash and adventurous, the difference of their policies arose from the very

difference of their States. The State of the French sovereign
held him fast to a secular tradition, so that he followed the
same ends of national unity and defence which had been
followed, since the 12th century, with more or less success
and ability by all the predecessors whose crown he inherited. The Burgundian power, on the contrary, was too
recent, had been constructed too rapidly, was still too imperfectly consolidated, too loosely knit, to be able to impose
precise and constant views upon its ruler. Created by conquest, it urged him to proceed to further conquests, inasmuch as the resources with which it furnished him were
very considerable, and easily deceived him as to his actual
strength. The conduct of Charles justifies the saying of
Machiavelli, that a State is maintained by the same forces
that have created it. It must be realized, moreover, that
many of his undertakings presented themselves to him as
the completion of the work of Philip the Good. The annexation of Guelders and Liége completed in the north the
bloc of the Low Countries, and his attempts to appropriate
Alsace and Lorraine are explained by the necessity of
uniting the Franche Comté and the Duchy of Burgundy.
But it is difficult for a conqueror to stop. Dazzled by success and the love of glory, Charles soon lost all sense of the
possible and actual, and forgot the interests of his peoples.
He dreamt of having himself crowned King of the Romans,
and of forcing old René of Anjou to cede his claims to the
Kingdom of Naples. His expedition against Neuss (1474–
1475), in which he persisted out of a morbid longing to
humiliate the Emperor and the Empire, caused him to miss
the moment for joining forces with Edward IV of England,
who had just disembarked at Calais in order to march
against Louis XI, and who, on seeing himself abandoned
by his ally, hastened to conclude peace with the king. In
the following year the occupation of Lorraine involved the
Duke in a war with the Swiss. Defeated first at Granson,
then at Morat (1476), his prestige as a soldier, which had
still imposed upon Europe, was destroyed. Louis XI made
ready to take the offensive. René of Lorraine re-entered
Nancy. Charles's final overthrow was certain. It was more
rapid, more tragic, and more complete than his enemies

could have hoped. Attacked by the Swiss while he was be-
sieging Nancy, with an army reduced to a few thousand
by the treachery of his Italian mercenaries, he flung himself
desperately into the mêlée. Two days later (January 7th,
1477) his body was found on the surface of a frozen pond,
half devoured by wolves and pierced with three mortal
wounds.

If it had only depended on Louis XI, the Burgundian
State would have disappeared with Charles. While he was
seizing the cities of the Somme and invading Artois and
Burgundy, the king devised a plan for partitioning the Low
Countries which, by reserving a part for himself and giving
the rest to French seigneurs or German princes, would have
reduced them again to a condition of subdivision and impotence. The particularist reaction provoked by the death
of the Duke in all the provinces exasperated by this despotism admirably seconded his project. He was too subtle
a diplomatist to fail to impose his will on the ingenuous
bourgeois ambassadors, deputies elected by the States-
General hurriedly assembled at Gand, and blinded by their
desire for peace and the restoration of urban privileges and
franchises. But a genealogical hazard, one of those mysterious factors on which the destinies of States depended
above all in the days of monarchical politics, was about to
confront him with a danger much more serious for France
than the Burgundian peril which he flattered himself he
had destroyed. Charles the Bold had left only a daughter,
Marie of Burgundy, whose marriage would decide the fate
of his domains. Naturally, the Habsburgs had not failed be-
times to cast their eyes upon so wealthy an heiress. Seven
times betrothed in accordance with the enterprises and alliances of her father, she had finally been promised to
Maximilian of Austria. Doubtless this promise would have
been worth no more than the others if the Duke had lived.
For Marie of Burgundy it became the sole hope of salvation
in her distress. In order to escape from the attempts of
Louis XI, she offered her hand to the Austrian. The opportunity was too good to miss. Maximilian hastened to her
side, and the marriage was concluded at Bruges on August
28th, 1477. This was an expedient hastily devised under

the pressure of necessity; yet never has a political marriage exercised such an influence over the future of Europe. By bringing the young Burgundian State into the hybrid complex of the Habsburg domain, not only did it condemn it to suffer henceforth the repercussions of the various schemes of the most ambitious and greedy of dynasties, but at the same time it opened between France and the House of Habsburg the long conflict which came to an end only in the 19th century. Austria, a power which everything had seemed to orientate upon the Danubian countries, suddenly obtained a footing on the shores of the North Sea between the two great monarchies of the West. Nothing but territorial greed had called her thither. She had no mission to fulfil there, no interest to defend, save that of her princes. From the very first her purely dynastic policy was in conflict with the needs and the aspirations of the peoples. If it had been her aim to re-establish over the Low Countries the obsolete suzerainty of the Empire! But on the contrary, her only purpose was to keep them for herself, and it was always her endeavour to separate them from Germany. Her position in the Low Countries, regarded from the standpoint of the European community, seems therefore as absurd as it was artificial. And it was this anomaly that was responsible for the catastrophes which she was to bring upon the country. For the interests of the princes and those of the peoples to be completely divergent has always, in any period of history, been disastrous. Of this the history of the House of Habsburg is the most striking proof. By its acquisition of the Low Countries it found itself drawn into that career of universal domination, that policy of aggrandisement for the sake of aggrandisement, in which nations were reckoned only as heritages and countries as domains, and which was to make the Habsburgs, down to our own days, the sworn enemies of all national aspirations and all public liberties.

We must not be astonished that the Low Countries allowed an action so fatal to themselves to be accomplished in silence. Their fusion into a single State was still too recent to have provoked the sentiment of national independence. Moreover, in the heat of the particularist revolution each province was thinking only of itself, and the burgesses of Gand, the leaders of the movement, were concerned only to re-establish the old municipal privileges and did not look beyond the narrow circle of their local policy. When they found themselves confronted with the accomplished fact it was too late for action. The marriage of their "natural princess" had made them the subjects of the House of Austria while they were debating upon their franchises.

Under Louis XI, as under Charles VIII, there was no lack of French intrigues to excite and to nourish the general discontent in the Low Countries; to rouse the men of Liége and encourage Guelders to revolt, and thus to paralyse the forces of Maximilian. After the death of Marie of Burgundy (1482) the majority of the cities and of the nobles regarded him merely as an intruder, and attempted to claim the tutelage of his son, Philip the Handsome. The people of Liége, subjected by Charles the Bold, recovered their independence, and Guelders did the same. Maximilian, treated with complete indifference by the Empire, struggled impotently in the midst of this chaos. In 1488 he even had to suffer the humiliation of being detained for several weeks as the prisoner of the people of Bruges. Despite his alliance with the King of England and the Duke of Brittany, his intermittent war with France could not lead to any definite conclusion. It was provisionally interrupted in 1493 by the Peace of Senlis.

The changes introduced into international policy by the birth of the Burgundian State were presently followed by complete confusion, in consequence of the unification of Spain, which resulted from the marriage of Isabella of Castile and Ferdinand of Aragon (1469). Until then the Spanish kingdoms had been too weak to intervene actively in the destinies of Europe. The war against the Moors had absorbed all their energies until the middle of the 13th century. Then, just as the task was on the point of accomplishment, dynastic rivalries, the quarrels between the kings and the nobles, and between the nobles and the cities, had interrupted the war, safeguarding the precarious existence of the Musulman Kingdom of Granada. Favoured by its maritime situation, Aragon had been busy beyond its frontiers, expelling Anjou from Sicily on behalf of a collateral line of its dynasty, conquering the Balearics and obtaining a foothold in Corsica and Sardinia. But this vigorous expansion was checked in the middle of the 14th century, as the result of conflicts with Castile, dissensions in the royal family, and revolts in Barcelona and Catalonia. Castile was even more disturbed and enfeebled by the insubordination and the claims of the nobles. Force had been powerless to subdue this vigorous but anarchical society; but the doubly national union of Ferdinand and Isabella, while it put an end to the long mutual conflict which was exhausting their kingdoms, enabled them also first to rally and then to subordinate the peoples to their power. So completely did they subject them to their guidance in every domain that assuredly, in no country and at no period of history, have sovereigns exercised so profound an influence. In the Spanish State, as established by them, Catholic and political sentiment were associated so completely that it was impossible to dissever them. The monarchy summoned to its aid the old religious fanaticism of its subjects, and in their eyes its cause was identified with that of the Faith. Its zeal for orthodoxy had rendered it profoundly national, and now, surrounded by the most intolerant of peoples, its intolerance was the instrument of its success. From 1480 onwards the Inquisition, entrusted with the task of watching over the converted Jews (*maranos*), became, without losing its ecclesiastical character, a State institution, since the State appointed the Grand Inquisitor and there was no appeal to Rome against the sentences which he pronounced. The figure of Torquemada is inseparable from the figures of Ferdinand and Isabella. All three were sincere in their hatred of heresy, and while the Crown confiscated for its own benefit the property of the victims who died at the stake, enriching itself by their agonies, it employed this wealth only in fresh enterprises, which were as profitable to itself as they were to the Church. The Holy War, long interrupted, was resumed against the Moors, so that the final constitution of the national territory seemed like the result of a Crusade. But it was not enough to fight the Musulmans; the Jews, no less than they, were the enemies of Christ. In 1492, the very year of the conquest of Granada, they were expelled from the State. This conquest and this expulsion swelled the treasury to overflowing, and provided the necessary resources for further political and religious expansion. While Christopher Columbus set forth to discover a new world to subject and convert, the expeditions against the coasts of Morocco, Algeria, and Tunis seemed to announce that all the forces of Spain were about to league themselves against Islam. Nothing appeared to be more consonant with her character, her historic rôle, and even her interests as a Mediterranean people. And in any case nothing could have won her greater glory and greater ascendancy than to constitute herself, in the face of the Turk, the champion of the Church and of Europe. And lastly, nothing could have more completely justified the title of "Catholic Kings" which Ferdinand and Isabella had just received from Alexander VI. But having arrived at this decisive moment of her history, Spain turned aside. She turned aside from the Holy War and allowed herself to be involved in the dynastic ambitions of her princes. Without understanding that she was renouncing her mission, she proceeded to concentrate all the energies which she had acquired in her secular conflicts with the Crescent in order to subject the Christian Continent to her princes, only in the end to collapse, ruined and exhausted by two hundred years of effort, almost as barren as the neighbouring shores of that Morocco whose certain and profitable conquest she had sacrificed to her sovereigns' dreams of universal dominion.

To find the point of departure of so remarkable a development, we must go back to the intervention of Aragon in the affairs of Sicily. Since then the Anjou dynasty, in possession of the Kingdom of Naples on the mainland, and the Aragonese princes reigning in the island, had been in continual conflict. The death of Queen Joanna of Naples (1435), who, after acknowledging Alphonso of Aragon as her successor, had afterwards bequeathed her crown to René of Anjou, would certainly have resulted in the outbreak of a war if the weak and indolent René had been capable of the effort. But on his death-bed (1480) he bequeathed his claims to the House of France. Charles VIII, the heir of Louis XI, was eager to assert them. Having provisionally safeguarded the northern frontier from the encroachments of the House of Habsburg by the Peace of Senlis (1493), he crossed the Alps (1494), and to the astonishment of Italy marched southwards to assume the crown of Naples. This was destined to be no more than the brief adventure of a young prince in love with glory. In the following year the Pope united Milan and Venice against the invader. Ferdinand and Isabella, supporting their Sicilian relatives, joined the coalition. Charles had only just time to beat a retreat and return to France, where he died in 1498. His successor, Louis XII, unfortunately followed in his footsteps. In addition to Naples, he claimed the crown of Milan as a descendant of Valentino Visconti, and in 1499 he took possession of the city without striking a blow. A treaty with Ferdinand of Aragon, which stipulated the partition of the Kingdom of Naples, enabled him without further difficulty to take possession of that part of the kingdom which the treaty granted him. But Ferdinand very soon broke the pact. War broke out, the French were defeated, and Louis XII in 1505 renounced all his claims to Naples, which was to remain, down to modern times, a mere Spanish possession. He did not retain Milan very much longer. Pope Julius II in 1511 united against him Venice, Ferdinand, and not long afterwards Maximilian and Henry VIII of England. Louis had to leave Italy and hasten northwards in order to confront the English, who, after defeating him at Guinegat, re-embarked, dissatisfied with Maximilian, and concluded peace.

Regarded against the entire background of French history, the Italian expeditions of Charles VIII and Louis XII had the appearance of mere excursions. They were not related to any national necessity. Inspired purely and simply by dynastic ambition, they were "wars of magnificence"; which is to say, useless wars. No doubt they helped to accelerate in France the diffusion of a passionate interest in the Renaissance. But the policy which they inaugurated, and which was not definitely abandoned until the reign of Henri II (Peace of Cateau Cambrésis), had no other consequence than a futile waste of men and money. Their only lasting result was that they orientated Spain toward Italy, and so, as an inevitable consequence, produced a *rapprochement* with the House of Habsburg.

It was evident, in fact, that between Maximilian, fighting against France in the Low Countries, and the Catholic kings, fighting against France in the Kingdom of Naples, a political alliance and its inevitable consequence, a dynastic alliance, was imminent. In 1496 the double marriage of Don Juan, the heir of Ferdinand and Isabella, with Margaret, the daughter of Maximilian, and of Philip, the son of Maximilian, with the Infanta Juana bound the two families closely together. At the moment there was nothing that could enable it to be foreseen that their several heritages would ever be united. But once more Nature favoured the Habsburgs. Death cleared the way for them. The successive deaths of Don Juan (1497), of his elder sister Isabella (1498), and of Isabella's son, Don Miguel (1500), resulted in the inheritance by Philip and Juana of the succession to the Spanish kingdoms. Six years later Philip was unexpectedly carried off by inflammation of the lungs, bequeathing his rights to his son Charles, then barely seven years of age. Ferdinand lived long enough to save his weakly brother from the danger of succeeding to him before he had emerged from childhood. When the old king died in 1516 his grandson had just been declared of age.

Charles V was one of those very rare characters of modern history whose name was to become universally known. He became very nearly as famous as Charlemagne or Napoleon. Yet it was not to his genius but to his heritage that he owed his eminence. With no more than mediocre abilities, he was raised by circumstances to such a position that only Charlemagne before him, and Napoleon after him, exercised such an influence over Europe. He was the meeting-point of three dynasties and three histories: those of Austria, Burgundy, and Spain. The grandson of Maximilian of Habsburg and Marie of Burgundy, and also of Ferdinand of Aragon and Isabella of Castile, he found himself in possession of so many portions of Europe that it seemed as though his power would finally extend over the whole Continent. In Germany he possessed the Austrian

Duchies; on the shores of the North Sea, the Low Countries; on the Atlantic coast, Spain; and in the Mediterranean, the kingdom of Sicily. And with these heritages went the claims attaching to them: the claims of Austria to the Empire, to Bohemia and Hungary; the claims of the Low Countries to Burgundy; and the claims of Spain to Italy and the coasts of Barbary. And to all this must be added the New World which the conquistadors had laid at his feet. Fernando Cortez made himself master of Mexico between 1519 and 1527, and Pizarro of Peru between 1531 and 1541. The astonishing conquest of South America was completed before Charles died. During his reign, however, it was still too recent to augment his power or influence his policies. Its consequences became manifest only under his son. For him all his projects, like his resources, were still determined by Europe. His title of "Ruler of the Isles of the Ocean" and his motto, *Plus oultre*, were merely prophecies of the future which he could do no more than foresee.

At the moment when Spain fell into his hands through the death of Ferdinand (January 23rd, 1516), and Austria through the death of Maximilian (January 12th, 1519), he knew no more of the one country than of the other. Educated in the Low Countries by Belgian seigneurs, who, regarding him merely as "their natural prince," did not even think to have him taught German—and he never did learn it—nor Spanish, he so shocked the Castilians when he appeared among them in 1517, speaking only French and surrounded by Flemish and Walloon favourites, that they welcomed him by the revolt of the Comuneros. But it did not take him long to adopt the distant, cold, and impersonal attitude which seemed necessary in a prince destined to reign over such a variety of countries and peoples. If he retained all his life some preference for the Belgians, among whom his youth was passed, he did not really belong to any of the peoples whose crowns he inherited, and he found it easy to treat them all with an impartiality which arose from his indifference. Insensible to all national feeling, he thought of nothing but the greatness of his house. He reigned over the countries which chance had brought under his sceptre without taking an interest in any of them; or perhaps one should say he was interested in them only in so far as they facilitated his designs. There was a striking contrast between him and his contemporaries, Francis I and Henry VIII, who seemed the very incarnation of France and England. Compared with them he was merely a sovereign, without a character of his own because he was without a country, and a sovereign who was nowhere popular.

Ferdinand and Isabella, by their Italian policy, had already begun to divert Spain from the war against Islam, and to involve her in the quarrels of Europe. Charles V definitely and finally embroiled her in these quarrels. It is true that he did not absolutely abandon the attempt to conquer the coasts of Barbary. His expeditions against Tunis in 1535, and Algiers in 1541, were still in accordance with tradition. But these were only brief interludes, ventures without a sequel. Charles had to make his choice between war in Africa and war in Europe, and how could he have abandoned war in Europe without at the same time renouncing his inheritance? His policy was not and could not be that of a King of Spain; it was and it had to be the policy of a Habsburg, and Spain, under his guidance, devoted her energies to the realization of schemes that were not only alien but opposed to her true interests.

As for these schemes, France was bound of necessity to resist them with all her might. The long duel between Charles V and Francis I is not explained by the opposition of their characters or their ambitions. Its fundamental cause was the incompatibility of the dynastic policy of Charles with the national policy of Francis. One might describe this duel by saying that it was a conflict of a dynasty, a House of Habsburg, with a nation, the French nation. Hemmed in on every side by the domains of Charles, in the south by Spain and Italy, on the west by Burgundy, in the north by the Low Countries, France found herself in danger of being stifled by an adversary who, once he had triumphed over her, would exercise universal dominion over Europe. It was not only the prestige of France but her security that was threatened by a veritable encirclement.

And to this must be added the danger involved by her expansion into Italy, where Francis I had reconquered the State of Milan on the field of Marignan (September 1515).

The death of Maximilian in 1519 rendered the situation still more formidable. Charles could not fail to put himself forward as a candidate for the Empire, which, since the reign of Albert of Austria, had always been held by the House of Habsburg. Francis did his very utmost to turn the Electors against this too powerful rival, and to induce them to give their votes either to himself, or at the worst to Frederick of Saxony. But the Medici could not provide him with as much money as the Fuggers advanced to Charles. The Electors, being in the market, sold themselves to the highest bidder. On June 28th, 1519, the German bank having purchased all their suffrages, they concluded the bargain, and delivered the crown of Germany to the King of Spain.

Henceforth war was certain. It broke out in 1521, on the frontiers of the Low Countries at first, where the forces of Henry VIII joined those of Charles, and was then transferred to Italy, being interrupted only by the signal defeat of the King of France at Pavia (February 25th, 1525). Having fallen into the hands of his enemy, Francis finally consented to the Peace of Madrid (January 14th, 1526). But he had fully made up his mind to disregard the peace and to take up arms again. His defeat had improved his position. Charles's victory had startled the whole world, and France now appeared as the champion of European liberty. Pope Clement VII, in order to free Italy from the Spanish yoke, made approaches to France, and after the sack of Rome by the German troops of the Emperor he formally entered into an alliance with that country. Henry VIII did the same, perceiving when it was too late that in the recent campaign he had been merely an instrument of the Habsburg hegemony. Finally, the outbreak of Protestantism in Germany, and the invasion of Hungary by the Turks, ensured the neutrality of the Empire. Equilibrium was re-established. In 1529 the Peace of Cambrai restored Burgundy to France, who on her side renounced her lapsed suzerainty over Flanders and Artois, as well as her claims in Italy. However, the two adversaries were merely awaiting a fresh opportunity for resuming the struggle. The attitude of the Lutheran princes encouraged the King of France to do so, and he even went so far as to conclude a treaty of peace, in 1546, with Soliman II. Thus, in order to wage war upon the Catholic king who had recently sacked Rome, the Most Christian king allied himself with heretics and Musulmans! The Peace of Crespy, concluded after indecisive campaigns (1544), left matters in status quo. The peace at all events enabled the Emperor at last to turn against the Protestant princes of Europe. His victory over them at Muhlberg had the effect of flinging them, terrified, into the arms of France. In order to obtain the assistance of the successor to Francis I—Henri II, who in his own country was cruelly persecuting the heretics—they offered him the three bishoprics, Metz, Toul, and Verdun (1552). This finally directed French policy to one of the aims which it had envisaged in the patient campaign which it had been conducting ever since the 13th century with a view to restoring the frontier traced in 843 by the Treaty of Verdun. Charles was immediately compelled to face towards the west and turn his back upon the Protestants. All his efforts failed before Metz, which was obstinately defended by the Duke of Guise. Before abdicating he concluded with his adversary the Truce of Vaucelles (1556).

He left Europe in a condition that was full of menace and pregnant with inevitable wars. The succession which he transmitted to his son Philip II comprised, in addition to Spain, the Kingdom of Naples, the Milanese State, the Franche Comté of Burgundy, and the Low Countries, without speaking of his immense possessions in the New World. Italy, subjugated in the north and the south, bade farewell to the dreams of liberation which had inspired men of such diverse genius as Guicciardini, Machiavelli, Julius II, and Clement VII. Italy, until the modern era, was to be no more than a geographical expression, and the heavy-handed dominion of Spain was finally to crush what still survived of the civilization of the Renaissance. The States of the

Pope, and those of the Venetian Republic, alone preserved their independence, that of the first being guaranteed by Catholic tradition, while that of the second was due to their maritime situation. As for the Low Countries, enlarged by the final annexation of the Duchy of Guelders and the Frisian provinces, they were henceforth to constitute in the north of Europe the "citadel of steel" of the Spanish kings. By the Pragmatic Sanction (1549) Charles had been careful to regulate the right of succession in such a manner that they could not escape his descendants, and by including them, by the Convention of Augsburg (1548), in the sphere of Burgundy he had so conditioned their relations with the Empire that the latter really had no other right over them than that of defending them. The Imperial dignity had served him only to assure the future of his house. He had not only taken the Low Countries from Germany; he had even obtained for his brother Ferdinand, in 1521, the crown of the King of the Romans, and had ceded to him the patrimonial duchies of Austria, which, together with the crowns of Bohemia and Hungary that fell to Ferdinand in 1526, finally safeguarded the Habsburg power in Central Europe. Divided into two branches, the family none the less remained united by its dynastic interests. Through Italy, Spain communicated with Austria; through the Low Countries, Austria was more readily able to dominate Germany; and thanks to the services which she was able to render her, she was assured beforehand of that nation's docility.

Thus the Continent was crushed by the Habsburg colossus, established in Austria and Spain. Beside it France and England appeared weak indeed, and seriously menaced. But this was a case of David and Goliath. They had something that was lacking to the monstrous dynastic power which confronted them. Instead of being, like that power, a juxtaposition of peoples and countries agglomerated by the hazard of inheritance, with no mutual bond save the rights of their sovereign proprietor, they possessed that collective conscience that resulted from the community of their destinies, the constancy of their efforts, and the harmony between the policies of their kings and their national tendencies. It was from this that their strength was derived, and it was this that enabled them not only to escape the danger but to triumph over it, after vicissitudes to which the religious problem posed by the Reformation was to give the poignant interest of the wars of religion.

2. *Internal Politics*

What strikes us first of all, if we take a general survey of the constitution of the European States between 1450 and 1550, is the increase of monarchical power. With Louis XI in France, with Henry VII in England, and with Ferdinand and Isabella in Spain, it attained a strength and a prestige which it had never before possessed, and which were to attain still further development under their successors. In Hungary, under Matthias Corvinus, and in Sweden, under Gustavus Vasa, it made such progress that the whole political organization was transformed by it. It imposed itself upon the young Burgundian State under Philip the Good and Charles the Bold. Germany was the only country that did not feel the increase. For there, while the Kings of the Romans and the Emperors continued to exert only a nominal authority, the individual princes, in their territories, assumed more and more the character of local sovereigns; while on Austria, Bavaria, Saxony, and Brandenburg institutions were imposed which were in fact monarchical.

A phenomenon so general presupposes causes as general as itself. Naturally the personality of the princes, tradition, and circumstances gave the monarchy an individual character in each country. But however great the local differences, the similarity of certain essential features shows that this development corresponded everywhere with irresistible social tendencies. Here we have a movement analogous to that which in the 10th century produced the feudal system, and in the 12th century the urban régime. And as in the case of these latter, it is permissible, without paying attention to the details and the subtler differences, to sketch the main outlines of a movement which manifested itself throughout the whole of Western Europe.[2]

The monarchical power was too closely related to the social constitution to escape the influence of the great economic and intellectual transformation to which the latter was subjected from the middle of the 15th century. Capitalism, the Renaissance, and Lutheranism could not fail to affect it, and it is easy to see that they all played their part in endowing it with new vigour. Each of these great forces, in conflict with the past, had of necessity to seek and obtain the alliance of the monarchical authority. Their hostility to the ancient privileges and institutions and ideas which restricted this authority assured them of its co-operation. It assumed the same attitude toward them which it had assumed in France and Spain in respect of the bourgeoisies when the latter had solicited its aid against the feudal nobles. Now, as then, its own development depended on the general development of society. By acting for the benefit of society it was acting for itself. It was most obviously to its advantage that it should be modern, that it should combat the conservative tendencies which opposed its own progress as well as that of society. Was it not acting in its own interests when it helped capitalism to defeat the particularism of the cities, when it favoured the propaganda of the humanists against moral and political prejudices, and when it protected the Lutherans who offered it the direction and the properties of the Church? All the privileges that were opposed to the power of the Crown were based on tradition. It was only necessary that it should approve in good faith of all the criticisms of this tradition, and that it should conceive it to be its mission to enfranchise from this same tradition both its subjects and itself.

The facts illustrate the issue with perfect clarity. In all

[2] In Russia also the expansion of the principality of Moscow began at the end of the 15th century, and the power of its princes began to increase at the same time. But these movements were due to the collapse of the Tartar domination, and had nothing in common with European developments. Poland also remained outside the European movement.

those countries in which capitalism was developing we see that the princes lavished upon it the proofs of their benevolence. In the Low Countries they constantly pronounced in its favour and against the reactionary policy of the urban guilds; and they did their utmost to encourage the development of Antwerp, the stronghold of commercial liberty. In England, from the reign of Henry VII onwards, the Crown supported the enterprises of the merchant adventurers and interested itself in all schemes of maritime expansion. In Spain it was the intervention of the Crown that rendered possible the discovery of the New World; in France Louis XI acclimatized the silk-worm in the Midi, caused the mines to be exploited, and encouraged economic initiative in every possible way; while Francis I tried to introduce some of the Italian industries. Protected by the sovereigns, capital in return placed its resources and its credit at their disposal. Thanks to it, they were able to avoid resorting to the Estates in order to procure the sinews of war. The bankers liberated them from the embarrassing control of their subjects. The long duel between Charles V and Francis I would have been unthinkable without the co-operation of the financiers. During the whole of the Emperor's reign the Fuggers, and a number of other business houses in Antwerp, continued to advance him the colossal sums which he required.

The princes favoured intellectual liberty no less definitely than economic liberty. With the exception of the kings of Spain, all manifested their sympathy for the ideas which were propagated by the men of the Renaissance, without regarding the protests of the theologians. Erasmus was protected by Charles V and Francis I. Thomas More was made Chancellor of England by Henry VIII. Gattinara and Granvelle, the two chief ministers of the Emperor, were convinced adherents of the new orientation of the intellect. It was only too evident, as a matter of fact, that this new orientation was entirely to the advantage of the State, for since the humanists could obtain the reform which they desired only from the princes, the government of the princes appeared to them, for this very reason, the essential instrument of progress. Their disdain of the past made them expect everything of the monarchy, and they brought it the support of that intellectual aristocracy which in every nation was henceforth to enjoy the monopoly of representing public opinion.

The Reformation, in fact, at all events in its beginnings, shared no less than the Renaissance in this conspiracy of all the great social forces on behalf of the sovereign power. Whether the princes protected it or fought against it, they none the less profited by it.

INDEX

ANCHOR BOOKS